Buzz Lightyear

Captain Buzz Lightyear has the most important qualities that a Space Ranger should have: courage, independence, and, above all, determination. When he and his crew become stranded on a hostile alien planet, Buzz becomes more determined than ever to finish his mission—*his* way. But as the obstacles to his success mount, Buzz's friends begin to show him a different way of working . . . as a team.

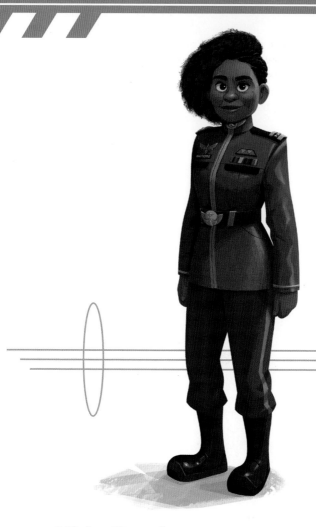

Alisha Hawthorne

Commander Alisha Hawthorne is one of the most respected Space Rangers in the corps. She loves going on adventures, traveling amongst the stars, and teasing her best friend, Buzz, whenever she gets the chance. After she and Buzz get stranded on the planet T'Kani Prime, Alisha leads her crew on the ground in starting a new life there.

Sox

Sox is Buzz's adorable robot cat companion. Created to support Buzz after his time away, Sox makes it his own mission to be as helpful to Buzz as possible, using advanced analytics, computer programming, and an array of gadgets. But more important, this cute kitty quickly becomes a friend and sidekick Buzz can always rely on.

Izzy Hawthorne

As the granddaughter of Space Ranger Alisha Hawthorne, Izzy has always dreamed of a life of adventure and exploring the universe. Unfortunately, she is absolutely terrified of space. But to the always upbeat and determined Izzy, that is just a minor setback. She joins the Junior Patrol in hopes of getting the training she needs—maybe even from the most famous Space Ranger of all: Buzz Lightyear.

Darby Steel

Darby is the oldest member of the Junior Patrol, but don't be fooled by her age. She is tougher than most, with her no-nonsense attitude and ability to put any three things together and make them explode. As part of her prison parole program, Darby begrudgingly joins the Junior Patrol, but with her fearlessness and grit, she becomes an indispensable part of the team.

Maurice "Mo" Morrison

Mo isn't sure what he wants to do with his life, but he knows for
an absolute fact that he doesn't want to die. Avoiding conflict and
risk as much as possible, Mo isn't thrilled when the Junior Patrol
gets involved in a high-stakes mission to save the planet from
alien forces. But all Mo needs is a bit of confidence, which his team
is happy to help him with.

Cal Burnside

As the new leader of Star Command, Commander Burnside is content to stay on T'Kani Prime. His pride and joy is the advanced laser shield, built to protect Star Command and all the citizens from vines, bugs, and alien invasions. Buzz Lightyear sees it differently—the laser shield is keeping everyone in!

Zurg

Zurg is the terrifying and powerful robot that has invaded T'Kani Prime. With its bloodred eyes, huge stature, and even bigger ship and robot army, Zurg is the most fearsome foe that Star Command has ever faced. This mechanical menace will stop at nothing to find Buzz Lightyear—even if it means searching the entire galaxy!

ISBN 979-11-91343-45-8 14740

Longtail Books

Disney · PIXAR
LIGHTYEAR

Adapted by *Meredith Rusu*

Chapter 1

A hazy green **mist** hung low over the **alien swamp**land, thick and still, **obscuring** the **vegetation** beneath. There was no telling what strange plants—or life—might be **lurk**ing there. Waiting. Watching. And perhaps they were, at that very moment, **slither**ing closer to the Space **Ranger**'s boot, which had just made its first **footprint** in the **extraterrestrial goop**.

The owner of the boot spoke into his **wrist** communicator. "Buzz Lightyear mission **log**: Star Date three-nine-oh-one." It was Captain Buzz Lightyear, Inter**galactic** Space Ranger. He stood tall, **survey**ing the **expanse** before him, his **keen gaze** observing every **nuance** that younger, less experienced Space

Rangers might **overlook.**

"Sensors have **detect**ed valuable resources on an **uncharted** planet," Buzz continued, "so we're making a **detour** to **investigate**. Space Rangers will make **initial evaluation**s, then **assess** whether it's worth waking the science **crew** from their hypersleep. . .[1] or simply continuing our long journey home."

Buzz allowed just the **ghost** of a smile to pass across his lips. He had journeyed to dozens of star systems[2] and **venture**d across **countless** extraterrestrial **terrain**s in the past, but something about this planet—known as T'Kani Prime— sent a thrill through him that was rare for a **seasoned** Space Ranger. According to their ship's computers, the unexplored swamplands of this world were **teem**ing **with potential** resources that could **further** the crew's scientific exploration by years—or it could present danger the likes of which they had never seen. To Buzz Lightyear, everything about T'Kani Prime was new and exciting and strange.

Perhaps the planet viewed him in the same way.

---

1 **hypersleep** 공상 과학 영화나 소설 등에서 사용하는 표현으로, 인간의 신체 기능이 거의 완전히 정지된 가사 상태에 빠져 마치 죽은 것처럼 보이는 것을 의미한다.
2 **star system** 항성들이 우주 공간에 모여 이루는 집합 체계.

Buzz **pressed** the toe of his boot into the **bog**, and the thick mud **squelched** with **unsettling resist**ance. "Terrain seems a bit un**stable**. No **readout** yet, if the air is breathable. And there seems to be no sign of **intelligent** life anywhere."

"Who are you talking to?"

A woman's voice **interrupt**ed his report. Buzz **whirl**ed around and came face-to-face with his fellow officer **Command**er Alisha Hawthorne.

"No one," Buzz said, quickly lowering his wrist communicator.

"You were **narrating** again," Alisha said. Her tone was **disapproving**, but Buzz knew better. She was just **teasing** him.

To anyone else, Commander Alisha Hawthorne was a **strict, by-the-book** Space Ranger. But to Buzz Lightyear, she was the kind of friend only time could bring. The two of them had entered the academy and trained together as **cadet**s. They had studied side by side, running **drill**s and **memorizing** Star Command **code**s until they became **second nature. Eventually**, Buzz and Alisha achieved the **ultimate accomplish**ment: joining the Space Ranger **Corps**. Together, they had entered the great unknown of space.

Buzz **shrug**ged. "Just doing the mission log." He **activate**d his laser[3] **blade** to **slice** through a **gnarl**ed **patch** of swamp **vine**s that suddenly seemed to be blocking his way. "Narrating helps me focus. Stay sharp. If it bothers you, Commander Hawthorne, I'm happy to wait back on the Turnip.[4]"

Alisha activated her own laser blade and **forge**d a path into the jungle alongside Buzz. "Please don't call it the Turnip."

"But the ship looks like a root vegetable," Buzz pointed out.

They both **glance**d back at the SC-01 **transport** ship, its **outline blur**ry through the haze. There was no denying that its **bulbous** shape did indeed give it the appearance of a turnip.

"Yes, you made that very clear at the design review," Alisha noted.

"How long have you known that I narrate?" Buzz asked as he **hoist**ed himself up and over a **cluster** of vines so thick, they almost seemed like a fallen tree trunk.

---

3 **laser** 레이저. 증폭기 안에서 유도 방출을 반복하여 증폭된 빛 또는 그러한 빛을 내는 장치.
4 **turnip** 순무. 무의 일종으로, 팽이를 닮은 둥근 뿌리가 특징이다.

"Forever," Alisha admitted with a half smile. "Since you and I were cadets. Speaking of which, you forgot to take the **rookie** with you."

"Ugh. Commander Hawthorne, you know how I feel about rookies," Buzz said, **hack**ing through more vines. "They don't help. They just over**complicate** things. I'm **better off** doing the job myself."

"Which is why *I* brought the rookie," Alisha replied.

Only then did Buzz **notice** the extra **figure inch**ing **cautious**ly behind Alisha in the **muck**. The rookie. In Buzz's opinion, he was an **awkward**, **gangly** cadet playing **dress-up** in a Space Ranger suit.

"Uh. Hello." The rookie gave a **meek** wave.

"No." Buzz turned away.

"Buzz," Alisha said. "**Protocol** requires we bring him along. Look at the rookie."

"No," Buzz repeated.

"Buzz, look at the rookie," ordered Alisha.

"No!" Buzz **insist**ed. "He's gonna have sad eyes. You know I can't deal with the sad eyes."

"Look, look, look," said Alisha.

Against his better **judgment**, Buzz glanced at the rookie. Sure enough, there he was, **staring** at Buzz with his super-wide, eager-to-please eyes, looking **pitiful**, like a small child. Or a puppy.

"All right!" Buzz **groan**ed. "You win. Look, Feather . . . Featherings . . . Feather . . ." Buzz **squint**ed as he tried to **make heads or tails of** the long and complicated last name **stamp**ed on the rookie's dog tags.[5]

"It's Featheringhamstan, sir," the rookie said eagerly.

"Look, rookie." Buzz's voice was tight. "First, you will not speak unless spoken to."

"Yes, sir!" said the rookie.

"Still talking," Buzz reminded him. "Second, respect the suit. This suit means something. It's not just protecting your body; it's protecting the universe. This suit is a promise to the world that you, and you alone, will do one thing above all: finish the mission. No matter the cost, you will never quit. Whatever the **galaxy** may throw your way— Will you please turn that off!"

Buzz **huff**ed as he turned to Alisha, who had begun

---

5 **dog tag** 군인들이 목에 거는 인식표를 지칭하는 속어로 성명이나 일련번호 등이 새겨져 있다.

playing **triumphant** fanfare[6] music from her Space Ranger suit **chest panel**. Alisha dialed down the volume, slowly, until the music **fade**d and the only sound remaining was the **sway** and slither of the alien vines.

"It's just too easy," Alisha laughed.

"You're **mock**ing me, aren't you?" said Buzz, un**amused**.

"Yes, but in a **supportive** way," Alisha replied.

"Look, what I'm trying to say, commander," Buzz continued, "is that you and I have this job down—"

"Uh, sir?" the rookie said behind him.

"Still talking," Buzz **rebuke**d him, still looking at Alisha. "At any moment, I know what you're thinking. I know where you're going to be. But this guy, I don't know—"

Buzz finally turned.

The rookie was gone.

And in his place was a slithering pool of vine tentacles,[7] reaching **ominous**ly toward the two Space Rangers who didn't belong on this planet.

---

6 **fanfare** 팡파르. 축제나 의식 등에서 트럼펫이나 호른 같은 금관 악기로 연주하는 소곡(小曲).

7 **tentacle** 촉수. 동물의 몸 앞부분이나 입 주변에 있는 가늘고 긴 돌기처럼 생긴 기관으로, 감각 기관의 역할을 하며 공격을 하거나 자신을 방어하는 데 사용하기도 한다.

Chapter 2

"**V**ines!" Alisha cried. The **swamp**land around them had **sprung** to life, with hundreds of **squelch**y **extraterrestrial** vines all attacking at once.

A low **hum** began **vibrating** in the **hazy** green **mist**.

"Bugs!" Alisha shouted as a **swarm** of giant insects **descend**ed upon them.

Buzz **whip**ped around and **realize**d with a **flash** of **alarm** that their ship was being **suck**ed into the ground.

"The ship!" he warned. "It's sinking!"

"Everyone back to the Turnip!" Alisha **command**ed.

"Oh, so we're calling it the Turnip now?" Buzz said as

they **sprint**ed toward the ship.

But they were quickly **overtake**n by bugs.

"**Engage stealth** mode!" Alisha **exclaim**ed. "It should buy us just enough time."

Alisha and Buzz **press**ed a button on their suits and disappeared under stealth mode. But the protection soon **ran out of** power. As the duo reappeared for all the bugs to see, they realized they had only one option. In perfect **unison**, they **ignite**d their laser **blade**s and **slice**d their way through the attacking **predator**s. Each **had the other's back**. As a bug would **swoop**, Buzz would **blast** it away with his **wrist** laser, turning just in time for Alisha to **sever** a vine that was **grasp**ing for his **outstretch**ed arm. They were performing a **precise** Space **Ranger** ballet of jumps and **duck**s and blasts, each knowing the other's move before they had even performed it. Vine by vine, bug by bug, they battled their way back to the Turnip and **slam**med **shoulder to shoulder** into their ship's landing elevator. It began filling with swamp mud and then short-**circuit**ed.

"Blast![1]" Buzz cried as he tried to **operate** the mud-**splatter**ed control **panel**.

"Here, I can reroute it," Alisha said. She ripped open the panel and began expertly rewiring the controls.

In times like these, Buzz was grateful to have such a cool-and-collected partner at his side. A rookie could never have—

Buzz paused. "Where is the—"

"Help!" the rookie suddenly screamed. The poor kid was being simultaneously carried off into the sky by a bug *and* dragged down to the ground by a vine in a terrible tug-of-war in which the rookie was the rope.

Buzz sprinted forward and sliced through the vine trapping the rookie's leg. Without missing a beat, he grabbed the kid's outstretched hand to keep him from being carried off by the bug. But the bug wasn't giving up that easily. It flicked its iridescent wing at Buzz, knocking the laser blade from the Space Ranger's hand. Then a vine snaked a tentacle around Buzz's waist and hoisted him into the air.

"No!" Alisha shouted. She fired her laser blaster[2] at the bug—a direct hit! The creature shrieked and dropped Buzz

---

1 blast 여기서는 '폭발'이라는 뜻이 아니라, '젠장' 또는 '제기랄'이라는 의미로 실망이나 짜증 등을 나타내는 감탄사로 쓰였다.

2 blaster 공상 과학 영화나 소설 등에서 사용하는 무기의 일종. 주로 총 모양이며 폭발을 통해 공격을 가한다.

and the rookie down into the **oozing bog**. But they weren't safe yet. Three more vines **stretch**ed up from the ground, **encircling** Buzz and the rookie to drag them to a squelchy **demise**.

"Buzz!" cried Alisha.

Buzz looked at his commander, and they both knew what to do. But they had only one shot.

Buzz reached out his hand just as Alisha drew back hers, prepared to throw her laser blade.

"Now!" cried Buzz.

With perfect aim, Alisha **hurl**ed the blade to Buzz. He caught it just as the vines dragged him and the rookie beneath the surface.

Alisha sucked in her breath. A moment passed that felt way too long. And then . . .

Buzz **burst** out of the **pile** of vines, holding the **glow**ing laser blade high in **triumph**. **Heroic**ally, he **swung** the **exhaust**ed rookie over his shoulder and **charge**d back to the ship, slamming inside the closing elevator doors just in time.

"I'll go to the engine room," Alisha announced as the muddy elevator took them to the bridge.

"I'll take the helm,[3]" Buzz said.

"And I will—" the rookie started.

"Do nothing!" Buzz commanded him sharply. "I've got this!"

Buzz **leap**ed into one of the two captain's chairs, and the auto**pilot instant**ly **chime**d to life.

"How may I assist you?" it asked **cheerily**.

"Ugh, autopilots," Buzz **groan**ed. If there was one thing Buzz trusted even less than rookies, it was autopilots. He confidently took hold of the control wheel on the **console**.

Normally, two pilots worked together to command the ship. But at the moment, it was **crucial** for Alisha to **monitor** the engine room. It was possible for Buzz to **rely on** the autopilot to pick up the **slack** . . . but if anyone could fly the Turnip off this **hostile** planet solo, it was him. Buzz Lightyear.

"Is there anything I can do, sir?" the rookie asked, **timid**ly reaching toward the copilot controls.

"No!" Buzz **smack**ed his hand away. "This is not a **simulation**!" Then Buzz spoke into his radio. "Commander,

---

3 helm 우주선이나 선박에 있는 조타 장치로, 나아갈 방향과 속력을 조종하는 역할을 한다.

status?"

Alisha's **static**ky voice came over the radio. "Fuel engaged. All systems go!"

Buzz **punch**ed the **launch** button, and the Turnip's engines blasted to life. But an **unsettling** groan **shudder**ed through the ship. The **resist**ance from the mud was strong. The Turnip lifted off **awkward**ly, battling to rise as if escaping quicksand.[4]

"Warning. Launch **trajectory unsound**," the computer announced.

Something was wrong. The Turnip's forward trajectory had **kick**ed **in**, but they weren't gaining **altitude**.

Buzz felt an angry **bead** of sweat **drip** down the side of his **temple** as he pulled hard on the wheel. The Turnip was flying almost **parallel** to the ground, and there wasn't a lot of time. Straight ahead, a **massive** mountain rose from the swampland. Buzz needed to get this ship higher—now!

"**Collision imminent**," said the computer. "**Abort**. Abort. Abort."

Buzz turned off the autopilot.

---

4 **quicksand** 바람이나 물에 의해 흘러내리는 모래로, 언뜻 보기에는 딱딱해 보이지만 일단 빠지면 헤어나오지 못하고 점점 가라앉아 결국 사라져 버리기 때문에 위험하다.

"Captain Lightyear, do you need my help?" the rookie asked, **cling**ing to the back of Alisha's empty copilot chair as the ship **lurch**ed to one side.

"Negative![5]"

"Are you sure?"

"I'm Buzz Lightyear," Buzz said through **grit**ted teeth. "I'm always sure."

Finally, the ship began to climb! The mountain was getting closer, but the ship was rising higher. They were almost up and over the mountain. They were going to make it!

CRASH!

At the last second, the under**belly** of the ship **snag**ged the **peak** of the mountain. Buzz heard the horrible **screech**ing sound of metal being ripped apart—and then a big **boom**. A **pit** formed in his stomach. He knew what that second sound meant.

Chaos erupted.

The bridge was **engulf**ed in a **cacophony** of warning sirens and flashing lights. They were losing altitude fast.

---

5 **negative** 무선 통신에서 부정의 대답을 할 때 'No' 대신 사용하는 표현. 직업 의식이 투철한 버즈는 평상시에도 이와 같은 말투로 대화한다.

Buzz **strive**d to **regain** control, but everything was wrong. The Turnip **hurtle**d back toward the swampland, the ground **racing** up to meet them as the ship crashed belly-first in a massive **rupture** of mud and **muck**.

"It's bad, Buzz." Alisha **emerge**d from the **wreckage** of the engine room, covered in **soot**, holding a **shatter**ed fuel cell.[6] Buzz **stare**d at it, **numb**, while the rest of the **crew** engaged in **emergency evacuation protocol** around him. Thankfully, the crew's hypersleep **pod**s had protected them during the crash. Everyone had survived. But the ship had not.

"Our hyperspeed crystal[7] was totally destroyed," Alisha said. "Long story short . . . we're **maroon**ed."

Buzz let those words **sink in**. It was like a bad dream. Just an hour ago, they had been finishing up their last **assign**ment of a five-year mission before heading home. Now everything

---

6 **fuel cell** 연료 전지. 수소와 산소 등의 화학 반응을 이용하여 발생하는 에너지를 직접 전기 에너
지로 변환하여 사용하는 전지.
7 **crystal** 크리스털. 결정이 나타나는 모양이 분명한 석영(石英) 또는 그것으로 만든 제품을 말한다.
원래는 색이 없고 투명하지만 불순물이 혼합된 정도에 따라 다양한 빛깔이 나타난다.

had changed. Would they ever get home? *Could* they ever get home? This was all terribly wrong.

And it was Buzz's fault.

Dejectedly, Buzz removed the nameplate from his suit and handed it to Alisha.

"What are you doing?" Alisha asked, **confused**.

"I'm court-martialing[8] myself," Buzz said. "Commander Hawthorne, I hereby **relieve** myself of all Space Ranger duties. This was my fault, and these people deserve better. You can throw me in the brig.[9]"

"Finish the mission, Buzz." Alisha put her hand on his shoulder. "*That's* what we do. We're not done until everyone gets home."

"But we have no fuel crystal," Buzz **protest**ed.

"So we **mine** the resources of this planet—create a new crystal," Alisha told him.

Buzz **frown**ed and shook his head. "Crystallic **fusion** is

---

8 **court-martial** 군사 재판을 관할하기 위해 설치된 특별 법원인 군사 법원을 뜻하는 말로, 여기서는 '군사 법원에 회부하다'라는 뜻의 동사로 쓰였다.

9 **brig** 보통 전함 안에 있는 구금실을 가리키는 말이지만, 여기서는 버즈가 속한 부대 내의 군사 감옥을 가리키는 말로 쓰였다.

highly un**stable**."

"Then we test it," Alisha **counter**ed.

Buzz felt like his head was swimming. "It's too dangerous. **Manufacturing** a crystal capable of hyperspeed is like . . . like trying to **lasso** the sun. Then someone has to attach that sun to a ship. And then that ship needs someone to fly it without blowing themselves into **oblivion**. Who in their right mind would—Ohhh . . ."

Alisha **smirk**ed at Buzz as he finally **caught on**. She **slap**ped the nameplate back on his suit while he **furrow**ed his **brow** in **determination**.

Chapter 3

"**B**uzz Lightyear mission **log**: Star Date three-nine-oh-two. After a full year of being **maroon**ed, our **specialize**d crew and robotic **assistant**s have put this planet's **vast** resources to **incredible** use. Finally, our first hyperspeed test flight is a go."

Buzz threw open the door from the locker room, letting the sunshine **blast** upon him.

The crowd cheered as Buzz **hop**ped aboard a truck that was waiting to take him to the **launch**pad. He **gaze**d at the fruits of his crew's yearlong efforts: **perimeter** fences surrounded their **encampment** to keep **vine**s out. A **patrol** had been established to protect them from daily attacks. It hadn't been easy, but they had managed to make T'Kani Prime **livable**. **Hospitable**, even. Except for the days when the vines were feeling extra **grab**by. Buzz had to admit, the resources on T'Kani Prime were im**measurable**. They had even managed to **mine ore** from the dark side of the planet to build a **rudimentary** space station. Crew members had individual living **quarter**s. Some had started referring to this planet as "home."

But not Buzz. That day, he would finally finish the mission.

His truck pulled up to the launchpad, where the biggest achievement of the year **await**ed: the XL-1, a ship that was capable of reaching hyperspeed. The **initial** test flight was scheduled for today, and, according to their **calculation**s, it should take only about four minutes. But those would be the four most important minutes of Buzz's life.

"Ready, Captain Lightyear?"

Alisha stood at the edge of the launchpad, her gaze fixed on Buzz, rather than the spaceship. Buzz could see she was worried. The **stake**s were high—and so was the risk. But if anyone could **lasso** the sun, it was Buzz Lightyear.

"Ready as I'll ever be, Commander Hawthorne."

Alisha held out an **index finger**. "To **infinity** . . ."

". . . and beyond," finished Buzz.

Buzz **tap**ped his finger to hers, and together they "**boom**ed" their hands apart like a mini **explosion**. Neither of them could remember when they had started this small **ritual**, but it must have been during their **cadet** years. It was **second nature** now, like a handshake or a hug.

A young crew member named Díaz came running up. "Captain Lightyear! We're all ready when you are, sir."

"A year of work for a four-minute flight," Buzz **marvel**ed. "Isn't that something?"

"Ha! Sure is!" Díaz agreed.

Buzz **square**d his shoulders. "Well, let's go find out if this new hyperspeed fuel is stable, so I can get us off this rock."

"Oh! Almost forgot!" Díaz handed Buzz a small computer. "Here's your IVAN, sir. Fully loaded."

Buzz **roll**ed **his eyes**. IVAN—an **Internal** Voice-**Activat**ed **Navigator**—was an auto**pilot**. The last thing he needed for the most important mission of his life was an autopilot.

Next, Díaz led Buzz to a **sophisticated** fuel station where Everyday Robotic Industrial **Colleague**s—otherwise known as

ERICs—were carefully **combining chemical**s to **concoct** the perfect **formula**. Buzz **bent** down low, the blue **glow** of the fuel **reflect**ing off his white space suit.

"So, this is the fuel that's gonna reach hyperspeed?" he asked.

"It has an eighty-seven-point-six percent chance," an ERIC replied.

Buzz **nod**ded. "I'll take those **odds**."

Buzz and Alisha watched the ERICs load the fuel cell into the XL-1's fuel **compartment**. Then Alisha went to Mission Control while Buzz climbed aboard the ship and **strap**ped in.

"XL-1 to Mission Control. Do you copy?[1]" he said into his radio.

"Copy, XL-1," Alisha replied. "I'm going to **grant** you four minutes to be off-planet, but then you come right back to us. That's an order."

Buzz smiled. "Roger that.[2]" He took a deep breath and gazed out the clear **dome** wind**shield** to the waiting sky above.

---

1   **do you copy?** 무전기로 통신할 때 자신의 말이 들리는지, 자신의 말을 잘 이해했는지 묻는 표현이다. 이에 대해 긍정으로 대답할 때는 'Copy'라고 한다.

2   **roger that** 'Copy'와 같이 무전기로 통신할 때 상대방의 말을 수신했으며, 이해했다고 응답하는 표현.

"Hyperspeed, here I come."

Buzz **brace**d himself as the launch **sequence initiate**d.

A **steady** computer voice counted down. "T-minus ten
. . . nine . . . eight . . ." The ship began **vibrating** with bone-
shaking **intensity**. "Three . . . two . . . one. Launch."

Buzz was **thrust** back against his seat with intense **force**,
his teeth **clatter**ing together hard enough to **numb** his entire
face. The **pressure** was **massive**. It was both **exhilarating**
and **terrify**ing at the same time.

His crew's **makeshift** space station grew smaller beneath
him as the XL-1 rocketed into the sky and reached the upper
atmosphere. Then, in a **breathtaking** heartbeat, the vibrating
ceased, and the blackness of space **envelop**ed the ship. Buzz
exhaled. He was back where a Space Ranger belonged—
among the stars. Now for the real test.

"IVAN, pull up the flight plan, please," Buzz commanded.

"Hello—*BZZZZT*—I am your—*BZZZZT*—" IVAN **fritz**ed.

"Ugh, autopilots!" Buzz removed IVAN from the **console**
and blew into the cartridge.[3] Then he **replace**d it.

---

3 cartridge 카트리지. 기계류에서 필요한 부품의 내용물을 바꿔 끼울 수 있도록 설계된 용기.

"Hello, I am your Internal Voice-Activated Navigator," the computer said, smoothly now. "Call me IVAN."

"Ready the flight plan, please, IVAN," Buzz **instruct**ed.

"Certainly. Your mission is to **accelerate** through deep space, **slingshot** around Alpha T'Kani, then through the **deceleration** rings and back here to T'Kani Prime. Target flight time: four minutes, twenty-eight seconds."

Buzz nodded. "Initiating hyperlaunch." He pressed a glowing green button and the ship **lurch**ed forward, a **streak** of shining silver **slicing** through the blackness of space.

"Approaching fifty-percent hyperspeed," IVAN announced.

Buzz checked the fuel-stability **readout**. "Fuel stable. Increasing speed to point-six-c."

Buzz pushed the **throttle**. It **hum**med as the ship gained **momentum**.

"Sixty-percent hyperspeed," IVAN announced.

The **brilliant** glow of Alpha T'Kani grew brighter and brighter as his ship flew impossibly fast toward the star. Buzz's heart **pound**ed. The XL-1 **whip**ped around the star, using its **gravitational** force to perfectly slingshot around and turn back toward home.

He was halfway there. This was going to work.

"Approaching point-eight-c," he **confirm**ed. "Pushing to hyperspeed."

Buzz **grip**ped the throttle and forced it forward.

BOOM!

An explosion **rip**ped through the **hull**! Alarms **wail**ed.

"Failure in engine one," said IVAN. "Fuel cell unstable."

"IVAN, **status**!" Buzz **yell**ed.

"**Trajectory** error: plus four degrees."

Buzz looked at the **project**ed path on the **dashboard** screen. The explosion had pushed them off-course. The ship was **veer**ing away from T'Kani Prime.

"Failure to course-correct will result in missing the rings. We'll fly off into deep space, resulting in certain death," IVAN explained.

"Yes, thank you," Buzz said.

"**Eject**ion is your only option," IVAN **state**d, **pop**ping open the cover to a glowing red eject button.

"No, no," Buzz shot back, **slam**ming the cover closed. "I can do it."

He grabbed a circular slide rule[4] and a **grease** pencil to work out flight calculations on the canopy[5] of the ship. He could fix this—he was sure he could. It was just like a **crisis simulation** from his cadet days. He could solve the course-correction calculation by hand and get them back home. He didn't need an autopilot to tell him it was impossible. Nothing was impossible—not for Buzz Lightyear.

"Warning: You have twenty-six seconds to course-correct," IVAN said. "You now have twenty-five seconds to course-correct."

"Stop counting, please," Buzz **snap**ped. His calculations were close—he needed to focus.

"Mission failure **imminent**," IVAN stated. "Please record your last words."

"Not today, IVAN!" shouted Buzz.

"Not today, IVAN!" IVAN repeated. "If you are **satisfied** with this recording, speak or select one."

Buzz circled his answer and slammed the grease pencil down. "IVAN, push the engines all the way! **Maximum** power!"

"That action is in**advisable**," IVAN said. "Fuel-cell

---

4 **slide rule** 계산자. 아날로그식 공학용 계산기로 복잡한 함수 계산을 할 때 사용한다.
5 **canopy** 캐노피. 항공기 등의 조종석 윗부분에 있는 투명한 재질로 된 덮개.

detonation—"

"Is exactly what I'm **count**ing **on**," Buzz **interrupt**ed.

IVAN did as it was told. The vibration from the ship was nearly un**controllable**—it was going to **tear** apart.

"Open the fuel door!" Buzz yelled **urgent**ly.

IVAN **complied**. The fuel door **sprang** open, and through the windshield, Buzz could see the dangerous blue glow of the **volatile** fuel crystal **illuminating** the ship. He **flip**ped up the safety cap and **hover**ed his hand over the button **label**ed EJECT FUEL CELL.

"Detonation in five . . . four . . . three . . . two . . . one . . ."

"NOW!" Buzz commanded as he **smash**ed his finger on the button.

The fuel cell ejected, and a millisecond[6] later . . .

KA-BOOM!

The detonation ripped through space, its explosive force **knock**ing Buzz's ship to the right . . . exactly four degrees.

Buzz was **pin**ned back against his seat as the ship **hurtle**d toward T'Kani Prime. **Miraculous**ly, the deceleration rings

---

6   millisecond 시간의 단위 밀리세컨드. 1밀리세컨드는 1초의 1,000분의 1이다.

caught the **vessel** and slowed its momentum. But without a fuel cell to power the ship, Buzz was **helpless** to control the XL-1 as it **plummet**ed back toward the planet.

"Course corrected. You failed to reach hyperspeed," IVAN announced.

"I didn't need to hear that, IVAN."

"You didn't hear that? I'm sorry. I'll repeat."

"No, I meant—I didn't need to—"

"You failed to reach hyperspeed."

"Thank you, IVAN."

"I said—"

Buzz shut off IVAN and braced for **impact** as the ship **barrel**ed to the ground, the burning **scent** of **scorch**ed metal **overwhelm**ing his senses.

Finally, he landed. Buzz opened the **visor** on his helmet and **slouch**ed back in his seat. He was alive. He jumped out of the **cockpit** and saw a **figure** running up to him.

"Captain!" the figure cried. It was Díaz. "Are you okay?"

Buzz had just begun to nod when he **notice**d something strange. Díaz was different. His hair was long, and he had a goatee.[7]

"Whoa, Díaz," Buzz said, **confused**. "You grew a **beard**. How did you grow a beard?"

"Oh, right." Díaz **stroke**d the goatee on his **chin**. "Uh, first off, welcome back. Secondly—"

"Wait," Buzz interrupted, looking over Díaz's shoulder. The command base was different, too—larger, with an entirely new building constructed to one side.

"What is this?" Buzz asked, an **unsettling** feeling growing in his **chest**. "How long was I gone?"

Díaz **pause**d before answering. "Four years, two months, and three days."

---

7 **goatee** 염소수염. 염소처럼 양 방향으로 난 턱수염의 일종으로 별로 길지 않고 숱이 적다.

Chapter 4

"**W**e thought we'd lost you, Buzz." Alisha hugged her old friend with a **ferocity** that **startle**d even the **seasoned** Space Ranger.

"Alisha," Buzz said, shaken. "What happened?"

Alisha looked Buzz in the eye. "Time **dilation**."

She took Buzz to the hangar[1] where an ERIC had **map**ped **out** mathematical equations[2] on a chalkboard.

"Time dilation is quite simple," ERIC explained. "As you approached hyperspeed, your time slowed **relative** to our own.

---

1 **hangar** 격납고. 우주선이나 항공기 등을 넣어 두고 점검하기 위해 마련된 창고 공간.
2 **equation** 등식. 등호(=)를 사용하여 양쪽에 있는 수나 문자, 식이 같음을 나타내는 식.

So, during your mission, you aged only minutes while the rest of us have aged years."

Buzz studied the math, deep in thought.

"Simply put," ERIC continued, "the faster you fly—"

"The faster I fly, the further into the future I travel," Buzz **interject**ed. "I get it."

Buzz walked out of the hangar with Alisha close behind. "So, what are we going to do now?"

"I don't know," Alisha admitted. "But I think we should **hold off** on any more test flights until we **figure out** something else."

"Commander," Buzz **protest**ed. "We said 'finish the mission.' That's what Space Rangers do."

"At what cost, Buzz?" Alisha asked. "Are you **willing** to lose another four years?"

For once, Buzz didn't have an answer. He took in her expression—the **crease**s that **etch**ed her **brow** and the way the corners of her mouth **sag**ged ever so **slight**ly in a **weary frown** that he wasn't used to seeing on her face. These weren't the **consequence**s of age, Buzz **realize**d with a **pang**. They were from **grief**. He may have felt like he'd been gone for only four minutes, but Alisha had been carrying the weight of losing her best friend for four *years*.

Alisha offered to drive Buzz home. He was unusually quiet during the ride to the crew **compound**. Accepting failure wasn't in the **code** of being a Space Ranger. This new **hurdle**—this new problem—felt like one he alone needed to solve. He just needed time. And that was the one thing working against him.

"So everyone is just stuck here. Because of me," he said bitterly as they reached their **quarter**s.

"Hey . . . you all right?" Alisha asked him, clearly worried about her friend.

"Yeah," Buzz said, trying to brush away his dark mood. **Sulk**ing wasn't in the code of a Space Ranger, either.

That was when he noticed the light **glint** off a **sparkly** ring on Alisha's hand.

"Wait—what's that?" he asked, pointing to it.

"Oh, I got **engage**d!" Alisha **reveal**ed.

"Wow! That's—that's great!" Buzz said, feeling a mixture of happiness and surprise. "What's her name?"

"Kiko," Alisha told him proudly. "She's one of the science

crew. It's funny. I never would have met her if we hadn't been **strand**ed."

"You got engaged to someone you just met?" Buzz asked, confused.

"Buzz, I met her three years ago," Alisha said gently.

"Oh, right . . . right." He pointed at Alisha's door. "Well, **congratulation**s. I'd love to meet her."

Alisha smiled. "There's plenty of time for that. Get some rest. That's an order."

She **swipe**d her ID card[3] to enter her apartment. And then Buzz was alone.

He **sigh**ed and swiped his own card, **plod**ding heavily into his quarters. He **glance**d down and noticed an unopened Star Command box on the floor. On top was a note: *You're welcome! Alisha.*

He **knelt** to open it, removing the cardboard[4] packaging to reveal a small **mechanical** mouse and an **adorable** robotic cat.

"Uhhh . . . ," Buzz said, confused.

---

3 ID card 'ID'는 'identity' 또는 'identification'의 줄임말로 'ID card'는 기관이나 회사, 학교 등에 소속된 사람임을 확인해 주는 증명서를 말한다.

4 cardboard 판지(板紙). 두껍고 질긴 종이의 일종으로 주로 물품 포장 등에 쓰인다.

"Hello, Buzz." The cat suddenly opened its eyes.

"Ack!" Buzz jumped, startled. The cat **hop**ped out of his arms and sat in front of him.

"I am Sox, your personal **companion** robot," the cat **inform**ed him.

"My what?" Buzz asked.

"I was **issue**d by Star Command to ease your **emotional transition** after your time away," Sox explained, **swish**ing his tail **rhythmic**ally.

"Oh . . . uh . . . well," Buzz **stammer**ed. "That's very **considerate** of you, robot **feline**. But . . . no. No, thank you."

"I'm afraid it's **protocol**," Sox said. "Sensors **indicate** you've missed four birthdays. Would you like a **frost**ed snack cake to **celebrate**?"

Buzz shook his head as he opened his kitchen's **cabinet**s and selected a **freeze**-dried meal. "Negative. That would **compromise** my **nutrition**al regimen.[5]" He shook the box until the food heated and expanded.

"We can talk about your feelings," Sox suggested. "I am

---

5 regimen 식이 요법. 질병 치료나 예방 또는 건강 유지를 목적으로 개인에게 필요한 영양이 잘 공급될 수 있도록 음식이나 식사를 조절하는 방법.

an excellent listener."

"No, no." Buzz shook his head between **bite**s. "Look, I've had a really long—" Buzz paused. "Day? And it did not go as planned."

Sox's round eyes grew rounder. "The mission was unsuccessful?"

Buzz nodded. "Affirmative.[6]"

"Oh, no," Sox said with **genuine sympathy**. "I am so sorry to hear that."

Buzz looked at the little cat. Somehow, its shiny robotic eyes seemed to **glisten** with real emotion. It was strangely **comfort**ing.

"Thank you, Sox."

"You're welcome, Buzz. Shall we play a game?"

"No, thank you."

Sox wasn't ready to **give up**. "I can create a game **specific**ally for you based on your exact **personality profile**."

Buzz walked toward the bed. "Hey listen, Sox, **buddy**. I'm pretty tired. So I'm gonna go ahead and **hit the rack**."

---

6 **affirmative** 무선 통신에서 긍정의 대답을 할 때 'Yes' 대신 사용하는 표현.

"Of course," said Sox. "I can provide sleep sounds if you like. I have several options. Summer night. Ocean paradise. **Whale** calls!"

"No, no," Buzz said, **collapsing** onto the bed. "White noise[7] is fine."

"Very well," Sox replied. He hopped up onto Buzz's **nightstand**.

Buzz wearily closed his eyes. "Good night, Sox."

"Good night, Buzz," Sox replied. Then he began to **emit** a **steady** hum of white noise that blocked all **extraneous** sound.

The Turnip was flying almost **parallel** to the ground, and there wasn't a lot of time. Straight ahead was a massive mountain.

"Uh, Captain Lightyear, do you need any help?" the rookie asked from behind Buzz.

"No! I can do it!" Buzz **grip**ped the control wheel and pulled with all his **might**. He needed to get this ship higher now or they were going to **crash**.

---

7   **white noise** 백색 소음. 자연에서 들을 수 있는 빗소리나 파도 소리와 같이 비교적 넓은 음폭을 가지고 있어 귀에 쉽게 익숙해지는 소리로 심리적으로 안정감을 준다.

Desperately, he reached over to the second wheel. If he could just pull both together, they'd gain **altitude**. But the more he **strain**ed, the farther away the second wheel seemed to be.

He heard a woman's voice. "Buzz?"

Buzz turned around. Instead of the rookie, it was Alisha who stood behind him.

"Are you sure?" she asked.

"I can do it!" Buzz shot up in bed, his heart **racing**. He was **drench**ed in cold sweat.

Confused, he looked around the darkened room. There was his **dresser**. His window. The **sleek** white **décor** of Star Command living quarters. And **gradual**ly, his breathing slowed.

Sox stopped his white noise from the nightstand and **tilt**ed his head. "Sensors indicate you had a nightmare. Would you like to talk about it?"

"Negative," Buzz sighed.

"Okay," replied Sox. "But remember, my mission is to help you. And I'm not giving up on my mission."

Buzz looked at the little robotic cat. "Yeah," he **mumble**d.

He **wipe**d the **clammy moisture** from his **forehead** and **clench**ed his **fist**. He didn't like feeling like this. Uncertain. **Frighten**ed.**Helpless**. This wasn't *him*. Buzz Lightyear, Space Ranger, found hope where there was none. **Illuminate**d **pathway**s out of danger when all else seemed lost. Buzz Lightyear, Space Ranger, was the captain everyone else looked to when they needed a leader to make the tough choices that would get them home.

Buzz Lightyear, Space Ranger, *always* finished the mission.

"Yeah. You know what, Sox?" Buzz gazed out the window where Alpha T'Kani was just rising over the **horizon**. "I'm not giving up on my mission, either!"

"Great!" Sox followed Buzz to the kitchen. "So what can I do?"

"Why don't you engage with your mouse buddy?" Buzz said between bites of a freeze-dried breakfast **supplement**.

Sox looked **doubtful**ly at the little mouse **putter**ing around on the kitchen floor. "Is there anything more . . . **challenging**?"

"You want a challenge?" Buzz asked, still **chew**ing his

breakfast. "Okay . . . I guess you could work on this fuel-stability thing."

He presented Sox with a small computer tablet that held all the latest research on the hyperspeed fuel crystal.

"Crystallic **fusion**. Of course," Sox said in wonder. He began typing on the computer's keyboard.

Meanwhile, Buzz grabbed his **gear** and headed for the door.

"When should I expect you back?" Sox asked.

Buzz glanced over his shoulder and smiled. "About four years."

"Hold on! You don't have to do this!" The **urgency** in Alisha's voice was **drown**ed **out** by the mechanical **whir**ring of an ERIC preparing another fuel mixture. Buzz stood at **attention**, already geared up in his test flight suit.

"Commander, this is my mistake," Buzz said. "I need to make it right."

Buzz's **determination elicit**ed a **spark** of hope inside Alisha that she hadn't felt in . . . a long time. She'd almost forgotten what it had been like to be a Space Ranger. Four years of **adapt**ing to life on a **hostile alien** planet had **dull**ed her sense of adventure. And risk. But Buzz had **awaken**ed something in her, like a memory from a life left behind. Maybe Buzz could help them get that life back.

"Okay," she said, **resign**ed. "But maybe we should think about this." She watched as Buzz loaded the fuel cell into the XL-2 and climbed into the **cockpit**.

"Think about what?" Buzz asked. "Come on, we're Space Rangers."

"Would be nice to wear the suit again," Alisha **muse**d. "People are starting to forget Space Rangers ever mattered."

Buzz shut the **visor** on his helmet with a **solid** click. "Well, I'm about to fix that." He held out his finger. "To **infinity** . . ."

Alisha studied her friend's face for a long beat. She wouldn't see this face for four years.

She touched her finger to his. ". . . and beyond."

Chapter 5

Buzz had no way of knowing what the future held. Even a Space **Ranger** couldn't **predict** that. But his **determination** was strong. He never **let go of** the **undying faith** that if he tried hard enough, he could **eventually** succeed.

Maybe that was why after the XL-2 mission failed the same way the first one had, he pushed for an XL-3. And then an XL-4. And then another. Four heart-**pound**ing minutes each time for him. Four years of life for the **crew** back on T'Kani Prime.

Alisha had been right: the memory of Space Rangers and what they **represent**ed had all but **fade**d throughout the base.

The crew went about their business, hardly giving thought to the **lone** Space Ranger out there—somewhere—on a mission to get them back home.

But Alisha never forgot. She was always there to **greet** Buzz in her office, offering him a warm hug and a hero's welcome. After the XL-2, Buzz returned to discover that Alisha was **expect**ing a baby with Kiko. Four years after that, Buzz met her son, Avery. Four years, and four years, and another four more. Avery graduated from high school. Alisha and Kiko **celebrate**d a **milestone anniversary**.

Everything changed around Buzz, but there was always Alisha, at her desk, waiting to greet him. Each time Buzz entered her office, he stood a little taller when he saw the Space Ranger suit still proudly **display**ed next to her chair. It, at least, looked the same, even as its owner grew older beside it.

One day after another failed mission, Buzz **trudge**d down the **hallway** toward Alisha's office. Another failure. Another fuel crystal that got so close to working before **shatter**ing in a **terrific explosion**.

But when Buzz opened Alisha's office door, the room was

empty. No photos. No Space Ranger suit. No Alisha.

Just a desk with a small **electronic** device **label**ed BUZZ resting on top.

With a cold fear **creep**ing over him, Buzz **insert**ed a chip attached to the note into the device. A hologram[1] of Alisha appeared. Buzz **gasp**ed. The image of his friend was one he hardly recognized. In it, she was old and weak, **prop**ped up on pillows in a hospital bed.

Alisha smiled **feebly** at him in the recording.

"Hi, Buzz," she said. "You'll be back here in a year or two. And, well . . . I won't." Alisha smiled sadly. "I don't know when it happened, but I seem to have gone and gotten very old."

Tears **mist**ed Buzz's **vision** as he continued to watch.

"I always thought we'd get to be Space Rangers again," Alisha admitted. "I missed being out among the stars. All the adventures. But more than any of that . . . I missed you."

Then a young girl **bound**ed into the frame of the hologram **project**ion. She was wearing a homemade Space Ranger suit.

---

1 hologram 홀로그램. 평면상에 장면이나 사물 등을 영상과 같은 3차원으로 기록한 것으로, 보는 사람에게 실제와 같은 입체감을 제공한다.

"Hi, Grandma!" she **exclaim**ed.

Alisha hugged the child. "Hey, **sweetheart**. I'm leaving a message for my friend Buzz."

The little girl gasped. "The Space Ranger?"

"That's right. He's in space right now."

"Wow!" Izzy exclaimed in wonder.

Alisha looked back at the camera. "This is my granddaughter, Izzy."

"I'm gonna be a Space Ranger, too!" Izzy announced to Buzz, **puff**ing out her chest.

"Just like him?" Alisha asked.

Izzy shook her head. "Just like you."

Alisha **squeeze**d her granddaughter tight. Then she **sigh**ed and smiled. She turned to look at Buzz one final time.

"Goodbye, Buzz," she said. "I'm sorry I won't be there to see you finish the mission."

She **extend**ed her **pointer finger** toward the camera. "To infinity . . ."

Buzz touched the hologram. His finger passed through it **slight**ly so that their hands **meld**ed into one. ". . . and beyond."

The recording ended, and the hologram disappeared. Buzz

was alone. He looked down and noticed a white piece of paper stuck under the desk. He **flip**ped it over to see a photo of himself and Alisha in their Space Ranger suits. Two young cadets, **grin**ning with un**bridle**d **optimism**, their heads filled with dreams of adventure and glory among the stars.

A single tear fell onto the photo.

Suddenly, a knock and a **carefree** voice rang out behind Buzz, **echo**ing off the empty office walls. Shaken, Buzz turned.

A tall man dressed in a **command**er uniform pushed a rolling chair **pile**d high with moving boxes into the office.

"Sorry to interrupt!" the man said. "I'm just moving into my new—" He gasped. "Look at that! The actual Buzz Lightyear in the **flesh**!" He **salute**d.

Buzz returned the **gesture absentminded**ly. "Affirmative," he **mumble**d.

"Commander Cal Burnside. I was a big fan of yours when I was a kid."

Buzz tried to shake himself out of his **daze**. He wanted to **grieve**. But a Space Ranger didn't do that in the **presence** of a commander. There would be time to **process** his emotions later, in **private**. He needed to focus on the mission.

"Then I look forward to working with you to finally get us out of here," he said, **squaring** his shoulders.

"Oh . . . uh, did no one tell you?" Commander Burnside **fidget**ed nervously. "We're **shut**ting **down** the program."

The words **suck**ed Buzz's breath away. "What?"

"We've decided we're gonna go ahead and stay right here," Commander Burnside **inform**ed him.

"Wait, *here*?" Buzz said **incredulous**ly.

Commander Burnside brightened, like he had the solution to a big problem. He showed Buzz a hologram of the base surrounded by a laser **shield**.

"It'll keep all the **critter**s out!" Commander Burnside said **enthusiastic**ally. "And we'll just **tuck** right in here and **make do with** what we've got."

Burnside started to lead Buzz to the door. "No, wait, you don't understand, commander," said Buzz. "I can still do it! I can get us out of here."

"Man, it's great you still believe that!" Burnside said, as if **compliment**ing a young child's artwork. "But we're good, Buzz. Got the laser shield!"

Then he closed the door on a **stun**ned Buzz.

Later, Buzz gazed out the window of his quarters. In his hand was the old photo of him and Alisha.

In the **distance**, he watched workers **haul** long metal bars to construct the **framework** for the new laser shield. A **steel grid** to lock the bugs out . . . and lock the crew in. A prison they were building with **gusto**, one bar at a time.

Buzz **hung his head**. How had this all gone so horribly wrong?

"Buzz?"

Sox softly came up beside his Space Ranger **companion**. "I've got some good news, Buzz. I **figure**d **out** the fuel problem."

"What?" said Buzz, breaking out of his **reverie**.

"It was an interesting combination," Sox explained. "Just the slightest **variance**. But it made all the difference."

Buzz watched as Sox brought up a hologram of the crystallic **fusion formula**, **highlight**ing a green element that when activated, caused the crystal to glow with a rainbow of colors.

"Sox . . . ," Buzz breathed in **disbelief**. "How did you do this?"

"It took me sixty-two years, seven months, and five days," Sox replied.

"And it's **stable**?" Buzz asked, a fractal[2] of hope **crystalizing** inside him.

Sox nodded. "**Theoretically**. I look forward to finding out. On your next mission."

Buzz couldn't believe it. All those years, the result had always been the same. Nothing had ever moved the needle. And now, finally—this was it. The missing piece of the puzzle.

A heavy knock on Buzz's door **startle**d both the Space Ranger and Sox from their discussion.

Buzz opened it to find two Star Command **security** guards.

"Evening, captain. We're here to pick up your companion robot."

Buzz **blink**ed. "What do you mean?"

"Security purposes," one of the guards **state**d. "You understand."

---

2 **fractal** 프랙털. 작은 구조가 전체 구조와 비슷한 형태로 끝없이 되풀이되는 형상. 여기서는 연료 문제를 해결한 것에 대한 버즈의 희망을 비유적으로 묘사하기 위해 사용되었다.

Buzz frowned. "No, actually, I don't."

The other guard held up a cat carrier. "We're shutting down the program, so . . . we have to **decommission** your cat."

The guards moved toward the door, but Buzz blocked their way.

"Now, hold on!" Buzz exclaimed. "Just—"

The guards **grunt**ed, and Buzz looked them up and down. They were physically **intimidating** and **equip**ped with security **gear**. Buzz may have been a skilled **combat**ant, but he wasn't going to win a fight in his sweatpants.[3] Still, he couldn't let them decommission Sox like an old piece of **hardware**. And not when they were so close to finally having a solution!

"At least let me do it," Buzz sighed.

He took the cat carrier and closed the door. The guards waited outside. Suddenly, the guards heard a loud crash. They **burst** through the door and were greeted by the **sight** of the empty cat carrier on the floor, a window shattered, and Buzz and Sox gone.

---

3 sweatpants 땀을 잘 흡수하는 소재로 만들어진 운동복 바지.

Chapter 6

"**U**h, Buzz, where are we going?" Sox asked, his usually even voice **indicating** robotic **concern** as they sped off in Buzz's truck toward the Star Command base.

"We're going to space!" Buzz announced.

"What?" exclaimed Sox.

Buzz **skid**ded up to the **launch**pad, **grab**bed Sox, and raced into the locker room. He suited up and **activate**d his **wrist** recorder. "Buzz Lightyear mission **log**: Star Date . . . I have no idea. In **possess**ion of stable fuel **formula**. I plan to reach hyperspeed, and this time finally finish the mission."

"Who ya talking to, Buzz?" Sox asked.

"Doesn't matter," Buzz said.

Together, they **snuck** toward the launchpad elevator.

"Buzz," Sox said seriously, "my programming **compel**s me to **notify** Star Command that you have gone—"

"Star Command was going to **decommission** you," Buzz **interrupt**ed.

Sox **froze**. "What?"

"That's right." Buzz **nod**ded. "Lights out. No more Sox."

Just then, the elevator door opened—right in front of a **security** guard!

"Hey!" the shocked guard exclaimed. "You're not **authorize**d to be in this area—"

Sox opened his mouth and shot a **tranquilize**r **dart** at the guard. She **collapse**d on the floor, immediately asleep.

"Whoa," Buzz said, **impress**ed. "I didn't know you could do that." He **pause**d. "Wait a minute. Was that for me? In case I **got out of line**?"

Sox looked at Buzz. "I bought you five minutes."

Together, they **hastily** made their way to the fuel **depot**. Normally, ERICs would be rolling about, mixing the formulas. But the depot was empty. Not one **mechanical** helper was in **sight**.

Sox pulled up the stable fuel formula. Carefully, Buzz filled the fuel cell according to Sox's exact **instruct**ions.

"Okay, here goes," Buzz said, lifting the handle of the fuel cell. The **liquid** inside turned into a multi-colored crystal that **refract**ed rainbows of light. Buzz could already see that this fuel crystal was different from the others.

Suddenly, a door **slam**med nearby, and a guard began **sweep**ing the area with a **flashlight**. Buzz **lean**ed back, **knock**ing over the tablet with the formula.

"The formula!" Sox **gasp**ed.

The tablet lay broken on the ground. But Buzz couldn't worry about that. He grabbed the fuel cell and Sox and ran to the nearest ship.

The XL-15 was covered with a **tarp**. Buzz **insert**ed the precious fuel crystal into the fuel port, then he and Sox climbed into the cockpit.

"Tango to base! Tango to base! Security **breach** in the launch **bay**!" another guard shouted into his radio.

"**Blast**!" Buzz **whisper**ed.

"We have a guard down! Repeat, we have a guard down!" the **alarm**ed guard continued.

Buzz was **run**ning **out of** time. He quickly **scan**ned the controls while Sox found a **cozy perch** behind Buzz's **headrest**. If they were quiet, they could power up the ship before anyone realized they were on it. Then it would be too late for Star Command to stop the **liftoff**.

Buzz plugged in IVAN.

"Hello!" IVAN announced loudly. "I am your **Internal** Voice-Activated **Navigator**."

"No! IVAN, no! Shhh!" Buzz said as he tried to **muffle** IVAN with his hands.

"Call me IVAN," the computer continued.

Suddenly, heavy footsteps **thud**ded their way. IVAN's **commotion** had attracted **attention**!

A **technician**'s voice came over the ship's radio. "XL-15, this is Control. Is there someone in there?"

Buzz froze and **stare**d at the radio.

"Say something," Sox encouraged.

"XL-15? Please respond," said the technician.

"Uh, copy, Control," Buzz said, thinking fast. "Just the, uh, cleaning crew. Cleaning crew! We're cleaning the cockpit. Cleaning . . . items . . . in here?"

"Commander, did we authorize a cockpit cleaning for the XL-15?" Buzz heard the **confuse**d technician talking to her **superior** on the radio.

"What?" Commander Burnside's voice said in the background. "No!"

Buzz **initiate**d the launch **sequence**, sending the XL-15 rolling toward the launch site. The guards arrived and began **bang**ing on the cockpit window.

"Stop right now and put your hands over your head!" one of the guards ordered.

Buzz **press**ed another button that **elevate**d the ship to the **vertical** launch position. The guards tried to hold on, but they **slid** off the ship and landed on the ground in a **heap**.

When he thought he was in the **home stretch**, Buzz pressed the button for the silo[1] doors.

"Unauthorized," IVAN said.

Buzz pressed the button again.

"Unauthorized," IVAN repeated.

Buzz **notice**d elite security guards from the Zap **Patrol**

---

1 **silo** 사일로. 미사일이나 발사 장치를 보관하는 지하 격납고.

entering the hangar. He was most certainly **outnumber**ed.

"C'mon! We're sitting ducks[2] here!" he shouted helplessly at IVAN.

"Allow me," Sox said. He climbed onto the **console** and the tip of his tail opened to **reveal** a flash drive.[3] He plugged his tail into the port.

"Beep boop beep boop beep boop," Sox said as he **overrode** the override.

Finally, the silo doors closed, and Buzz pressed the launch button. The XL-15 rocketed into the **atmosphere**, leaving the **flash**ing lights and **wail**ing alarms far beneath them.

"Lightyear!" Burnside's voice was **furious** over the radio. "I know you can hear me! Return the ship to base right now, or so help me—"

Buzz turned off the radio with a **resound**ing *click.*

"Sox," he said, "let's break this hyperspeed **barrier** and get everyone home."

---

2 **sitting duck** 수면 위에 떠 있는 오리처럼 속수무책으로 공격에 노출되어 있는 상태를 가리키는 관용적인 표현.

3 **flash drive** 플래시 드라이브. 플래시 메모리를 이용한 컴퓨터의 휴대용 저장 장치로 전원이 끊겨도 저장된 정보가 지워지지 않는다.

Chapter 7

"**A**pproaching seventy-percent hyperspeed," IVAN announced as Buzz and Sox rocketed around Alpha T'Kani.

Buzz **brace**d himself, watching the **gauge steadily** climb.

"Approaching eighty-percent hyperspeed," IVAN said.

Every **inch** of the ship **rattle**d as the **velocity** increased. Normally, at this point, a huge explosion would **rip** through the engines, shattering Buzz's hopes of success. But things were different this time. The gauge kept climbing.

"Fuel is stable," Buzz breathed. He had never made it this far before.

"Ninety-percent hyperspeed," IVAN announced.

Buzz watched as the needle pushed further, as though it was the simplest thing in the world, until—

ZHOOOOOM!

Everything around Buzz and Sox suddenly went quiet. The ship powered forward, and Buzz's head was **pin**ned against his seat.

"One-hundred-percent hyperspeed," IVAN announced.

Buzz **strain**ed against the **force**. From the corner of his eye, he could see colorful lights **streak**ing past the ship's window, an **array** of **glow**ing white, pink, and gold. The familiar lights of hyperspeed travel that Buzz hadn't seen in . . . what felt like a lifetime. Tears escaped his eyes and rolled straight back onto the **headrest**. Those **serene, shimmer**ing lights were the most beautiful sight Buzz had ever **witness**ed.

Then without warning, Buzz and Sox were **thrust** forward violently. The XL-15 had just passed through the first **deceleration** ring **orbit**ing above T'Kani Prime. The velocity decreased with stomach-**churn**ing **intensity**.

FWOOM. Another **impact**. They had passed through the second deceleration ring, then the third. Buzz looked out the window as a **hazy** gray sky rolled by. **Unexpected**ly, a

celebratory burst of confetti[1] shot out from the control **panel**.

"**Congratulation**s, Captain Lightyear," IVAN said. "You have achieved hyperspeed."

"We did it," Buzz **whisper**ed, his voice breaking in **relief**. "Sox, we did it!"

Sox, now **grip**ping onto Buzz's leg after having been pushed there by the force of their **acceleration**, looked up with his large, round eyes. "Congratulations, Buzz," he said. "That was **utter**ly **terrify**ing, and I **regret** having joined you."

Buzz couldn't believe it. He had *finally* finished the mission. He could fix what he had broken. He could get his crew home!

Buzz checked to see how close they were to landing at the Star Command base. There it was, approaching with . . . way too much speed.

"No, no, no!" Buzz said, **snap**ping back to Space Ranger mode.

"What is it, Buzz?" Sox asked.

Buzz pulled hard on the control wheel. "Our velocity is

---

1 confetti 결혼식이나 축제 등의 특별한 행사에서 뿌리는 색종이 조각.

still extremely high."

Despite his best efforts, the ship **whiz**zed right past the **runway** in a **blur**.

"Are we going to **crash**?" Sox asked.

"No!" Buzz said. "Well, **technically**, yes. Just hang on!"

The tiny crew braced for impact as the XL-15 **careen**ed toward the **wilderness** beyond the base. Buzz gripped the wheel, just barely keeping the ship under control. In a **plume** of dirt, the wheels of the XL-15 touched down and **skid**ded hard to the left. For a **nerve-wrack**ing few seconds, Buzz was certain they were going to crash into the un**tame**d **swamp** far beyond the **perimeter**. But **miraculous**ly, the XL-15 slowed to a **halt** just before the tree line.[2] Buzz sank back in his seat. They had made it.

The **cockpit** canopy opened, and in the **distance**, Buzz could **swear** he heard a bird singing. It was more likely an **alien** bug **chirp**ing. But that day, it sounded sweet all the same.

"After all these years!" he exclaimed. Somewhere, he hoped that Alisha was watching. He hoped she knew that

---

2 **tree line** 수목 한계선. 위도나 고도가 높은 지역이나 습도가 낮은 지역 등에서 환경 조건의 변화로 인해 나무가 자랄 수 있는 경계선을 말한다.

he'd kept his promise. But he hadn't done it alone. Buzz looked down at Sox with **immense gratitude**. "Thank you, Sox!"

With **renew**ed energy, Buzz jumped down from the cockpit and fired his flare**³** gun into the air. The Mission Control **rescue** team would be there any minute. Hopefully, having successfully achieved hyperspeed would **absolve** him of any ship-stealing **wrongdoing**.

Then he went to the fuel port on the ship and **extract**ed the fuel cell. The crystal glowed with its rainbow of color, full of power. Buzz smiled.

"Mission log **supplemental**," he spoke into his wrist recorder. "After 'borrowing' a ship from Star Command, I've achieved hyperspeed and I'm finally ready to leave this planet once and for all."

Buzz **glance**d out over the swampland, expecting to see a **convoy** already en **route**. But there were no signs of **emergency** vehicles. Everything was unnaturally still. Buzz **frown**ed. The crew must have seen his flare gun. Where was everyone?

---

3 flare 조명탄. 터뜨리면 강한 빛을 내는 탄알로, 적을 관측하거나 밤에 주변을 밝혀 위치를 표시하는 데 사용한다. 'flare gun'은 이러한 조명탄을 탄약으로 사용하는 총을 말한다.

"Buzz Lightyear to Star Command," he said into his wrist communicator. "Come in, Star Command."

Buzz **peer**ed across the **expanse** just as **thud**ding footsteps pounded up behind him. Someone **tackle**d him and Sox to the ground!

"Hey!" Buzz exclaimed.

"Shhh!" his **assail**ant warned. It was a woman in a full helmet and uniform. "The robots!"

"The what?" Buzz **sputter**ed, his face **splatter**ed with mud.

"The *robots*!" the woman **hiss**ed through **clench**ed teeth.

She pulled them behind a **boulder** just as a giant yellow robot **emerge**d from the trees. Buzz had never seen anything like it. The mechanical monster was three times the size of a human, with heavy metal **armor** and a single red laser eye in the center of its **dome**d head. It approached the XL-15, **scan**ning it.

"Wait," Buzz whispered **urgent**ly. "What's it doing?"

"Shhh!" the woman said.

Buzz, Sox, and the woman watched as the robot completed its scan. Then it attached a **metallic disc** to the **hull** of the

XL-15 and pressed a red button in the center. In a flash, both the robot and ship disappeared, **teleport**ed away.

"My ship!" Buzz cried, jumping up in a panic.

"Be quiet!" the woman warned.

"Where'd it go?" Buzz **demand**ed.

The woman pointed to the sky, and Buzz looked up. He gasped. **Hover**ing overhead was a **massive** alien **spacecraft**.

"What *is* that?" Buzz exclaimed. "What is going on?"

"Get down!" the woman ordered.

They **duck**ed back behind the boulder as an alien space **pod** launched from the ship, on course for their location.

"Shoot!⁴" the woman **spat**. "Come on!"

Swiftly, she led them into the **dense** swamp and up a hill. Her head **swivel**ed this way and that. She knew exactly where to go.

But Buzz didn't know where they were going, or even what was going on. And he didn't like it. "Why are there robots?" he demanded. "Where did the robots come from?"

"Where did *you* come from?" the woman **counter**ed.

---

4 shoot '빌어먹을' 또는 '제기랄'이라는 의미로 놀라움이나 불쾌함 등을 나타내는 감탄사.

"I came from here!" Buzz exclaimed.

"Here?" she **scoff**ed. Then suddenly, she stopped, as though a thought or a memory had struck her cold. She turned to him, took a step closer, and **wipe**d the mud from his face.

"Buzz?" she whispered.

Buzz noticed her nameplate, which had the name: HAWTHORNE. The woman removed her helmet. Buzz couldn't believe his eyes. It was a face he hadn't seen a long time. One he hadn't thought he would ever see again.

"Alisha?" he asked, his voice catching.

"Oh, no," said the woman. "That's my grandmother. I'm Izzy."

"Izzy?" Buzz asked. "But—but you were just a little . . ."

He indicated the height of a small child with his hand, thinking back to the recording he'd watched just hours before in Alisha's office. Hours in his time, anyway.

A **sicken**ing **realization** caused his stomach to sink. "Sox, how long were we gone?"

Sox's ears turned as he **gather**ed the data. "Twenty-two years, nineteen weeks, and four days."

Buzz's head was **spin**ning as Izzy pulled him into a rock

cove high up on the **hillside**. Twenty-two years. An entire new **generation** had grown up on T'Kani Prime while he had been away.

He watched Izzy scan the perimeter using **binoculars**, her **keen gaze** scanning for any sign of robots. And for the **brief**est moment, he couldn't help feeling like he was watching Alisha, the way she had been back in their **cadet** days, always leading training exercises with **precise** confidence.

"You know, your grandma and I could **practically** finish each other's sentences," Buzz told her. "If you're anything like her, we're going to make—"

"—some robots cry," Izzy said.

"—a great team," said Buzz at the same time.

Buzz **furrow**ed his **brow**. "Okay. So . . . get me up to speed on this."

"Right." Izzy nodded. "The Zurg ship showed up about a week ago."

"What's a Zurg?" Buzz asked.

"Oh, that's the only thing the robots say," Izzy explained. "So that's what we call the big ship. The Zurg ship arrived, the robots surrounded the base, and then, well—"

Izzy activated a hologram on her watch. Buzz saw an older version of Commander Burnside.

"Citizens of T'Kani Prime: robot aliens have attacked!" Burnside shouted. Behind him in the hologram, blasts **engulf**ed the base as **troop**s and robots exchanged laser fire. "Everyone, inside the perimeter! Look out!"

Burnside turned to shoot a robot coming up behind him. "We are activating the laser shield immediately!" he said. Then the message cut out.

"And that's the last we heard," Izzy said. She handed Buzz her binoculars, and he looked across the **valley** to the **distant** Star Command base. The **glimmer**ing laser shield **envelop**ed the entire **colony** in a protective bubble while hundreds of robots **unleash**ed **relentless** laser **assault**s.

"All those people . . . ," Buzz said, "they were **count**ing **on** me. And now they're trapped."

"We've tried to reach them, but there's no communication in or out," said Izzy.

"Sox?" Buzz asked.

"Meow, meow, meow, meow." Sox's ears **pivot**ed as he scanned the area for communication signals. "She's correct."

Izzy raised an eyebrow. "Did you just check me against your cat?"

"Well, he's not your **standard**-issue **feline**," Buzz admitted. "Actually, Sox was a gift from your grandmother."

"Hello, Izzy," Sox said.

Izzy smiled and **pet**ted Sox. "Hello, Sox."

Sox **purr**ed.

"Hey, what's that noise?" Buzz asked. "C'mon, don't break my cat."

"He's purring," Izzy said. "He likes it."

Buzz looked at his robot **companion**. "Sox, do you like that?"

"I do," Sox admitted.

Buzz **tilt**ed his head. "Huh." He'd had no idea.

"Well, I hope you're ready for action," Izzy said, standing. "Because all we needed was a pilot."

"For what?" Buzz asked.

Izzy smiled confidently. "I have a plan. And a team. Come on!"

Chapter 8

A short while later, Buzz and Izzy stood inside a large outpost.[1] Waiting for them were two soldiers in full uniform with helmets, guarding a spaceship that Buzz recognized as an Armadillo.

"All right, team. **Fall in!**" Izzy **command**ed.

"Hup, hup!" The two soldiers **march**ed forward at attention. One was very tall and the other rather short.

"Whoa," Buzz said, **impress**ed.

"I found a pilot." Izzy **grin**ned at her **cohorts**. "**Operation**

---

1 **outpost** 전초(前哨) 기지. 적의 이동을 감시하기 위해 부대의 맨 앞에 위치해 있는 전투 기지.

Surprise Party is a go!"

"I like this." Buzz nodded **approving**ly. "An elite **squad**. Best of the best." Buzz **motion**ed to Izzy. "You know, her grandmother was the greatest Space **Ranger** in the history of the **corps**. It'll be an honor to work with you."

Izzy activated a hologram showing the robots surrounding the base and the alien ship hovering above it. "Let's review our **objective**s."

"Kill the robots!" the shorter soldier **exclaim**ed.

"And don't die," added the taller soldier.

The shorter soldier **huff**ed. "'Don't die' is just something you want to do *every* day."

"It's still an objective," the taller soldier **insist**ed.

Buzz **clear**ed **his throat**. "If I may . . . We have *one* objective." He held up the glowing fuel cell with the crystal. "We need to put this crystal in the Turnip and get out of here. That's been my mission ever since I—" He paused, realizing his new team probably had no idea what he was talking about. "Well, since before you were born. So, to do that, we need to get onto the base."

"To do that, we have to kill all the robots," the shorter

soldier **declare**d, pointing at the robots in the hologram.

"To do that, we have to destroy the Zurg ship." Izzy pointed to the alien ship hovering **ominous**ly in the hologram.

"And to do any of that, we have to *not* die," the taller soldier **conclude**d.

"So, Operation Surprise Party," Izzy said to Buzz. "It's a **variation** on Operation Thunderspear. Didn't you get a medal for that one?"

"Two, actually," Buzz said proudly. "But—wait, how do you know about Operation Thunderspear?"

Izzy grinned. "I've read all my grandma's Space Ranger books from cover to cover. Twice." She pointed at her Hawthorne nameplate.

Buzz nodded, impressed yet again. He hadn't realized how much he'd missed having a confident partner. It was almost as if he were **debrief**ing for a high-**stake**s Space Ranger mission, just like the old days, with Alisha Hawthorne by his side.

"We've **figure**d **out** the Zurg ship powers the robots on the ground," Izzy said. "So we fly up there, we **blow up** the ship, and 'Surprise, robots!'"

She **manipulate**d the hologram to show the Zurg ship

blowing up and all the robots falling to the ground.

"Then we put your crystal in the Turnip," she said to Buzz.

"And finish the mission," Buzz added. He felt a **rush** of hope. Izzy's confidence was a mirror of her grandmother's. "It's a good plan."

Instinctively, Buzz held out his finger. "To **infinity** . . ."

But instead of **tap**ping his finger back, Izzy looked at it, **bewilder**ed.

"Are you trying to get me to pull your finger?" she asked, **suspicious**.

"Don't fall for it," the taller soldier warned.

Buzz shook his head. "No, not like that. It was—sorry. It's just a thing your grandma and I used to do."

Izzy **pull**ed **a face**.

"Ew," the shorter soldier said.

"I . . . we would never . . . she didn't mean to—" Buzz said, **fluster**ed. "Anyway, forget it. Moving on."

Buzz **regain**ed his **composure** and **strode** over to the Armadillo ship. "Let's load these **munition**s into the Armadillo and **steel** ourselves for **combat**."

Izzy pumped her **fist** in the air. "Operation Surprise Party is on!"

Just then, Sox's little robotic ears began to **spin**. "Buzz, do you hear that?"

Everyone stopped and held their breath, listening.

"I hear something," Buzz whispered. "You think it's a robot?"

"No," replied the taller soldier, "we've never seen a robot this far from the base."

Izzy **cock**ed her head. "I don't hear anything."

Suddenly, a robot arm **burst** through the outpost wall.

"Oh, *now* I do!" Izzy cried.

Before Buzz could **defend** himself, the robot grabbed hold of Buzz's **waist** and pulled him through the wall, **fling**ing him to the ground. Buzz's blaster went flying, just out of reach. He **scramble**d for it, but the robot's heavy, mechanical footsteps were upon him before he had a chance. The bot picked Buzz up by a leg as though he **weigh**ed nothing, holding him upside down. Then it reached for a **disc** on its **chest** plate that had the same round red button as the one that had **teleport**ed the XL-15 away.

Buzz **lash**ed out at his **captor** with his free leg, and the toe of his boot connected with the disc on the robot's chest plate, knocking it loose and sending it **skitter**ing several feet away. Realizing what had happened, the robot turned and began marching toward the fallen **transport** disc while Buzz hung **helpless** in its **grasp**.

"Don't worry, we got you!" Izzy cried to Buzz.

"Meow!" Sox added.

The team climbed through the hole in the **fort** wall.

POP!

Something struck the robot! Buzz looked up, his **vision** swimming from all the blood rushing to his head. The bot was covered in what looked like green paint.

Several yards away, Izzy held a bazooka[2]-like weapon. Next to her was a **crate** with the words TRAINING AMMO[3] clearly stenciled[4] on the side.

"What? Ugh," Izzy **groan**ed. Then she called back to Buzz, "Fear not! The Junior Patrol **has your back!**"

---

2 **bazooka** 바주카포. 적의 전차를 공격하기 위한 둥그런 형태의 로켓 무기로, 가벼워서 어깨에 맬 수 있다.

3 **ammo** 'ammunition'의 줄임말로, 폭발을 사용하여 적에게 공격을 가하는 탄약 등의 총칭.

4 **stencil** 스텐실. 글자, 도형, 또는 그림 등의 모양을 오려낸 뒤, 여기에 물감이나 잉크를 넣어 무늬를 찍어내는 화법.

"The Junior . . . *what?*" Buzz exclaimed.

Izzy fired another paintball[5] round at the bot while she scrambled back to the box of live ammo. The shot knocked the robot's shoulder plate off, revealing some wiring. The robot **extend**ed its arm toward Izzy and fired a laser blast directly at her. Izzy **duck**ed out of harm's way just in time—but the blast hit the Armadillo instead. The ship **explode**d!

"No! The ship!" Buzz cried.

The robot turned back toward the disc on the ground. Suddenly, out of nowhere, Sox **pounce**d on the robot's head.

"Meow, meow, meow!" the little cat **yowl**ed, **gouging** deep scratches into the bot's single laser eye. **Disorient**ed, it **stumble**d back, just as a harpoon[6] came **whiz**zing past and sank deep into a tree trunk behind it.

Buzz **wince**d. The harpoon hadn't hit the bot, but it had come within millimeters[7] of hitting *him*!

"Did I get it?" the taller soldier called, removing his

---

5 **paintball** 페인트볼. 표적을 맞혔을 때 물감이 터져 나오는 가짜 탄환으로, 모의 전투 훈련이나 게임에서 사용된다.

6 **harpoon** 작살. 끝이 뾰족한 작대기 끝에 쇠를 박은 도구로, 보통 짐승이나 물고기를 잡는 데 사용되지만 전투 무기로도 쓰인다.

7 **millimeter** 길이의 단위 밀리미터. 1밀리미터는 1미터의 1,000분의 1이다.

helmet.

"Pretty close!" Izzy called out **encouraging**ly.

"Sorry, I've not trained with this weapon," said the soldier. "Let me reload it!"

"Not trained?" Buzz exclaimed, his deepest fear coming true. There was no mistaking the **frighten**ed and **slight**ly bewildered face of the **lanky** soldier who had removed his helmet. A **rookie**, if Buzz had ever seen one. "What do you mean you're not trained?"

Meanwhile, the bot grabbed Sox by the tail and flung the cat off its face. In doing so, the robot **tore** some of its **exposed** shoulder wiring. The **spark**s didn't escape Buzz's notice. If he could shoot off the bot's arm, he could **wriggle** free.

Buzz's blaster was still out of reach on the ground. But the shorter soldier was near enough to get it.

"You, there! Grab it!" Buzz cried **frantic**ally. "Grab it!"

"Grab what?" the soldier asked, **bend**ing to see what Buzz was pointing to. She took off her helmet, revealing an old woman with **weather**ed skin and **dishevel**ed gray hair. "Oh, no. I'm not allowed to handle weapons." She held up her hands when she realized Buzz was pointing to his blaster. "That would be a **violation** of my parole.[8]"

"Parole?" Buzz cried **incredulous**ly.

As if on cue, Izzy came skidding up and **snatch**ed the weapon from the ground. Buzz **suck**ed in a breath. They had one chance.

"Izzy, now!" Buzz cried.

She **swift**ly threw the blaster. Izzy aimed for Buzz's left hand . . . while Buzz was reaching out **expectant**ly with his right. The blaster went **sail**ing by, landing somewhere in the **thicket**.

"Huh? No!" Buzz **wail**ed.

"Okay, new plan!" Izzy shouted.

"New plan?" Buzz exclaimed. "What was the old plan?" He couldn't believe what was happening. He was locked in battle against a **hostile** alien robot, with three *rookies* as his team. Rookies, the one thing a Space Ranger couldn't **count on** to do anything except be **reckless** and un**predictable**.

Buzz was going to have to take care of it himself. With a burst of effort, he **crunch**ed from his upside-down position

---

8 **parole** 가석방. 징역이나 금고형으로 수감된 죄수를 형이 집행되는 기간이 만료되기 전에 조건부로 석방하는 제도.

to grab the bot's exposed wiring, and managed to rip a bolt[9] loose before the bot shook him back down. But he'd done it—the bot's arm **slump**ed a bit more.

Another harpoon came whizzing by, missing Buzz's head by a hair. The harpoon hit the transport disc, and in a flash of light, both it and harpoon **vanish**ed.

"Did I get it?" the taller soldier shouted.

"A little to the left!" Izzy instructed.

Buzz **grunt**ed. **Muster**ing superhuman strength, he crunched up again and tore the remaining bolt from the bot's shoulder plate. The wiring **sizzle**d and popped as the arm came loose, firing its laser **ray** wildly, now that it was disconnected from its main controls. Buzz **tumble**d down once he was free from the robot's grasp.

The robot **thunder**ed toward the Space Ranger as Buzz scrambled to grab the **sever**ed robotic arm.

"Ha-ha!" Buzz laughed **triumphant**ly, **swing**ing the arm around to fire the robot's own laser at itself. But just as Buzz took aim, the laser **fizzle**d and died, out of power.

---

9 **bolt** 볼트. 건축이나 기계 재료를 고정하기 위해 쓰는 부품으로, 길고 둥근 막대기에 홈이 파여 있고 보통 육각형 모양의 머리가 달려 있다.

"What?" Buzz **stammer**ed. The robot **clench**ed Buzz's **ankle** with its good hand, lifting him from the ground.

THUNK!

The robot **fritz**ed, **sputter**ing out a **garble**d *"Bzzzrrrrg. Bzzzrrrrg. Bzzzrrrrg."* Then it collapsed to the ground in a **listless heap**. Buzz **wrest**ed his ankle free and stared at the deactivated bot in surprise. Sticking out from its neck was a harpoon.

The taller soldier **cup**ped a hand to his mouth like a **makeshift** megaphone. *"Now did I get it?"*

Chapter 9

"**W**hat—exactly—" a **disheveled** Buzz stammered as he **paced** in front of the **smoldering** **wreckage** of the Armadillo. "How did that . . . who *are* you?"

Izzy stood and **saluted**. "We're the Junior **Patrol**. At your service."

"I'm gonna need more information," Buzz said.

"We're a **volunteer** team of self-**motivated** cadets," explained Izzy. "We train one weekend a month here at the outpost. Mo and Darby"—she pointed at the taller, **lanky** soldier and the shorter, old woman soldier—"and I were the first to arrive last weekend, when the robots showed up. So . . . we **cooked** **up**

Operation Surprise Party."

Buzz **sigh**ed. "So you're rookies?"

"Oh, boy,[1]" said Izzy. "We'd love to be rookies. Still building up to that."

Buzz couldn't believe this was happening. Just when he thought he had some luck working with an elite **squad**, they turned out to be a **bunch** of rookies—*volunteer* rookies at that!

"Do you have **munition**s training?" Buzz asked.

"**Partial**," Izzy replied.

"**Tactical engage**ment?"

"**Pending**."

"**Combat** experience?"

"Yes!" Izzy pointed **enthusiastic**ally at Buzz. "If you count the robot situation we just went through."

Buzz took a deep breath. These rookies seemed nice enough, and Izzy was clearly eager to **live up to** her grandma's **legacy**. But they were no **replace**ment for trained and battle-tested Space Rangers.

He headed over to the ammo **crate**s and began loading

---

1 **boy** 여기서는 '소년'이라는 뜻이 아니라, '맙소사' 또는 '어머나'라는 의미로 놀람이나 실망, 기쁨 등을 나타내는 감탄사로 쓰였다.

gear into a rover[2] that hadn't been damaged in the attack.

"What are you doing?" Izzy asked.

"Look, you seem like nice people." Buzz **heave**d a harpoon gun into the rover. "I'm very **supportive** of your training **initiative**s. But I'm gonna go ahead and take it from here."

"We just saved you from that robot!" Izzy insisted.

"Excuse me?" Buzz said.

"Mo made the kill shot!"

"Mo got lucky."

Mo **nod**ded. "Very."

Buzz closed the rover door. "So . . . if you could just point me in the direction of another ship . . ."

"Oh, they have some old ships at the **abandon**ed **storage depot**," Mo said.

"Great," Buzz replied. He **pause**d. "Where's that?"

"Oh, you can't miss it. It's over near the resource-**reconstituting** center," Izzy said.

Buzz shook his head. "And where's that?"

"You know, right by where the old **fabrication plant** used

2　rover 탐사차. 행성이나 위성 등의 표면 위를 이동하며 탐사하는 차량.

to be," Darby explained.

Buzz **stare**d at the three of them **blank**ly.

"What *do* you know?" Izzy asked.

"I know the base," Buzz said.

A smile crossed Izzy's face that reminded Buzz of the times when Alisha had him cornered into doing something her way. "We'll just show you," she said.

A little while later, the team's rover **rumble**d up to the abandoned storage depot. Buzz had never been to this part of T'Kani Prime before. He hadn't really been anywhere on T'Kani Prime outside the base and his living **quarter**s.

He'd learned more about this team of rookies on the way. Darby had spent time in a **correctional facility** until she had been **release**d on parole. She was **mum** about what had gotten her into **jail** in the first place, but she had let **slip** that she could take any three things and make them explode.

Mo was more of an **enigma**, even to himself. He'd held lots of **odd** jobs and couldn't seem to decide what to do with his life, so he'd **sign**ed **up for** the Junior Patrol on a **lark**. In his own words, he'd **instant**ly **regret**ted it.

And as for Izzy, she was obviously Alisha's granddaughter. Maybe with time she could cut it as a Space Ranger. But now wasn't that time—not when so much was at **stake**.

"We can help you," Izzy insisted as Buzz unloaded the ammo and fuel crystal from the rover onto a **rust**ed rolling cart he'd found tipped over just outside the depot.

"I **appreciate** that," Buzz told her. "Just go back to your training facility. Stay **alert**. Stay safe." He pointed to the Armadillo inside the depot. "I'm going to **commandeer** this P-thirty-two Armadillo and go **blow up** the Zurg ship."

"So, this is just goodbye?" Izzy asked, the disappointment in her voice clear.

"Affirmative." Buzz nodded. "Goodbye." Then he pushed the **squeak**ing cart carrying the supplies and Sox into the building, leaving the Junior Patrol behind.

The storage depot had obviously been out of use for some time. Inside, it was dark and **creepy**, with only an **occasional shaft** of light **filter**ing in through the **filmy** skylights above. Buzz looked up and **recoil**ed in **disgust**. The building's rafters³ were filled with **row**s and rows of enormous **chrysalis**es. Sox scanned them, **reveal**ing **thermal** signals.

"Life forms **detect**ed," he told Buzz.

"What are they?" Buzz asked.

"Giant insectoid[4] **organisms**," Sox **confirm**ed. "This building appears to be some sort of **hive**."

Buzz took in the thousands of chrysalises **droop**ing from the rafters and felt his skin **crawl**. "Are they a threat?"

"Sensors **indicate** they are **hibernating**," Sox replied.

"Very good." Buzz nodded. Just then, he caught a **glint** of light **reflect**ing off something white in a fenced-in locker area of the depot. His eyes grew wide. "Whoa. . . ."

"What is it?" Sox asked.

"I'll show you," Buzz said. He **hurried**ly **wheel**ed the squeaking **dolly** over to the locker area. On **display** was Buzz's old Space Ranger suit, alongside three others. There was no mistaking the name badge on the suit: LIGHTYEAR. It was his! The thrill of seeing that suit again was like jumping

---

3   **rafter** 서까래. 목조 건축물의 경사진 지붕판을 구성하는 가늘고 긴 나무 조각들.
4   **insectoid** '곤충'을 뜻하는 'insect'와 '~모양의'를 뜻하는 접미사 '-oid'가 합쳐진 말로, '곤충 같은'이라는 의미이다.

into a time **portal**. Buzz didn't waste a second in putting it on.

He struck a few **pose**s, **revel**ing in its **comfort** and familiarity.

He turned and saw Izzy, Mo, and Darby standing there.

"Sorry to interrupt," Izzy said. "Looks like you were having a real nice moment."

"What are you doing here?" Buzz **hiss**ed, eyeing the sleeping insects up above. "It's not safe!"

"You took the keys to our truck," Darby said.

"Oh, there they are!" Mo **spot**ted them on the dolly. He went to **grab** the keys, but **accidentally knock**ed them off the cart, causing them to hit the floor and **trigger** the truck's alarm outside. **Flash**ing lights and the **honk**ing **horn reverberate**d around the depot.

"Shhh, quiet!" Buzz warned as Mo **fumble**d with the key **fob**.

Mo finally turned off the alarm, but it was too late. The bugs were already **stir**ring from their sleep. Two chrysalises **crack**ed down the center. Insect **appendage**s reached out **grotesque**ly, ripping the **cocoon**s in half. Two of the most **hideous**, stomach-turning insects Buzz had ever seen emerged from the chrysalises. They spotted the team and **shriek**ed, **awaken**ing their hibernating **sibling**s.

CRACK. CRACK. CRACK.

One by one, all the chrysalises began to **split** open, revealing thousands of alien insects.

Chapter 10

In a **horrific swarm**, the insects **descend**ed on the team!

"Somebody get the door!" Buzz and Izzy shouted in **unison**.

Scrambling, the team **rush**ed forward and **slam**med the locker-area gate closed just in time. The bugs angrily **claw**ed at the fence, their **appendage**s reaching through the bars.

"Well, I'm going to be **blunt** here," Mo said. "I wish that hadn't happened."

"So do the rest of us!" Darby **snap**ped.

"Everyone grab a weapon!" Buzz ordered, **toss**ing the team blasters from the ammo cart.

"Boy, I'd love to," Darby said. "But my parole—"

"As a Star Command officer, I **grant** you **authority**," Buzz directed. "We're going to **blast** our way out of here."

Darby smiled and grabbed a weapon. "Now we're talking."

"Buzz," Sox said seriously, "the **probability** of surviving a **frontal** attack is only thirty-eight point two percent."

"Seems a bit low," said Mo.

"Oh! What about **stealth** mode?" said Izzy, pointing to a button on Buzz's chest plate.

"How do you know about stealth mode?" Buzz asked, surprised.

"Grandma and I used to play stealth mode all the time," Izzy explained. "It was like **hide-and-seek**, but with a **twist**."

"Okay, well, it's actually good thinking," Buzz said. "I'll use stealth mode to **disorient** them."

Izzy pointed at the other three Space Ranger suits. "Or . . . and stick with me here. We could *all* use stealth mode and just walk right out."

Buzz hesitated. Not just anyone could wear a Space Ranger suit.

Izzy showed him a nameplate on one of the suits. "This

one even has my name on it!"

Despite himself, Buzz was **impress**ed. It was a good plan. Everyone would use stealth mode. Buzz and Sox would head to the Armadillo, and the rest of the group would go in the **opposite** direction, toward the truck.

A few minutes later, the team of four stood suited up and at the ready.

"Check it out! I'm Feathers . . . Featherin . . . Featherinsham . . . ," said Mo, trying to read the long name. He **notice**d a small pen **tuck**ed into the chest plate of the suit. "Oh, look! A pen! Cool! Does yours have a pen?"

"Okay, pay **attention**," Buzz **instruct**ed. "Stealth mode is fairly simple. There are just two parts. You **press** the button—"

"Is it this button?" Mo **interrupt**ed, pointing to a bright red button on his suit.

"I will tell you which button," Buzz said.

"What does this button do?" Mo pointed to a shiny blue button instead.

Buzz **wave**d Mo's question **away**. "I'm sorry, we're not going to have time to go over all the buttons."

"Okay, what about this thing?" Mo reached for a red pull

tab on the side of his suit.

"No!" Buzz grabbed his hand. "*That's* the **surrender string**. You never pull that."

"There is no more **shameful maneuver** for a Space Ranger," Izzy said seriously.

"Excuse me, did I miss *which* button is the stealth mode button?" Darby asked, **annoy**ed.

"You push *this* button!" **Frustrate**d, Buzz **jab**bed his finger at a bright green button on the chest plate. "But *not* yet!" He grabbed Mo's hand again just as the **cadet**'s finger **hover**ed over the button. "You push *this* button, then *you* go out the front door, and *I'll* go blow up the Zurg ship. Ready?"

"Ready," the Junior Patrol replied in unison.

"Okay. Goodbye—again." Buzz **motion**ed for them to all press their buttons. Together, they **fade**d from view.

While the Junior Patrol **crept** toward the **entrance**, Buzz **wheel**ed the ammo cart to the Armadillo, avoiding **crawl**ing insects along the way. Sox was **cram**med into Buzz's helmet.

"Sox, you're **inhibit**ing my **visual**," Buzz said, **spit**ting **fur** out of his mouth.

Sox **shift**ed slightly. "Is this better?"

"Negative," Buzz replied.

Buzz placed Sox on his shoulder, making Sox appear to **float** in **midair** along with the cart that seemed to be rolling on its own. None of the bugs paid them any attention.

"Very good," Buzz **whisper**ed to himself. "Stealth mode is working as planned."

He loaded the ammo and **insert**ed the **glow**ing fuel crystal into the Armadillo with a **satisfying** click. Then he checked the stealth mode **countdown** on his **wrist display**. He still had ten seconds left before stealth mode ran out and he was **visible** again. He **hop**ped into the Armadillo just as the countdown ended and his stealth-mode bubble **fizzle**d out.

Then he **gasp**ed. "Wait—the timer! They don't know about the timer!"

Panicked, Buzz looked out the **hatch** door to where Izzy, Mo, and Darby were only halfway toward the **depot** exit—in full view!

The Junior Patrol **realize**d they were visible at the same time the bugs did. With blood-**curdling shriek**s, the insects crawled toward them!

"I surrender!" Mo cried, **yank**ing the red surrender string on his suit. It **inflat**ed like a giant raspberry.[1]

Izzy and Darby tried to roll Mo toward the exit, but it was blocked by a **legion** of bugs. With a **yelp**, they turned around and started pushing him toward the Armadillo. The army of bugs followed.

"No, no!" Buzz **yell**ed. "Do *not* approach the vehicle!"

Before Buzz could stop them, Izzy and Darby rolled Mo right up to the ship—except his suit was too wide to fit through the Armadillo door! Thinking fast, Buzz reached in and pulled the **release** on Mo's suit, **deflating** it to its normal size. The Junior Patrol **topple**d in just as Buzz slammed the door closed. The insects screamed angrily, **scraping** at the **hull**.

"All right!" Izzy **pant**ed. "Way to **adapt**, team!"

"Why are you **congratulating** yourselves?" Buzz asked incredulously.

"Because I Hawthorned us right out of that situation!" Izzy exclaimed.

Buzz couldn't hide his frustration. "But you could have made it if—"

---

1 **raspberry** 라즈베리. 우리나라의 산딸기와 비슷한 열매로 대부분 붉은 색을 띠며 둥그런 모양이다.

"If you had *told* us stealth mode **wears off**," Mo said, still shaken.

Buzz wanted to snap back, but in a rare moment, he realized he didn't have a **retort**. The cadet was right. How could they know about the stealth mode timer if Buzz hadn't told them?

Suddenly, the ship **lurch**ed. The insects had swarmed it, covering the hull and wind**shield**, rocking it **back and forth**. There wasn't any time left.

"Okay, everyone just **strap** in!" Buzz commanded. It looked like they were going to **bust out** of here the **old-fashioned** way.

Buzz powered up the ship.

The **navigation** system **chime**d to life. "Hello. I am—"

Buzz slammed IVAN off and engaged the thrusters.[2] With a **belabor**ed **metallic** groan, the ship lifted off the floor and rose toward the ceiling, **shatter**ing through the skylights.

"Hold on!" Buzz ordered, pushing the **throttle**. Several **alien** bugs still **clung** to the hull trying to **tear** their way in,

---

2   thruster 반동 추진 엔진. 우주선의 자세를 변경하는 데 사용되는 로켓 엔진.

even as the ship blasted higher into the **atmosphere**.

"Are . . . are we going into space?" Izzy **stammer**ed from the seat behind him. Her voice sounded strange.

"No, I'm going to drop you somewhere," Buzz told her. But as he **barrel**-rolled³ the ship to shake the remaining bugs loose, they crossed the **threshold** of the atmosphere just enough to see stars.

"I can see stars!" Izzy yelped in **terror**. "That *is* space!"

Buzz looked over his shoulder at her. "What is happening right now?"

"She's afraid of space," Darby said bluntly.

"What!" Buzz exclaimed.

"Look out! A ship!" Izzy cried.

Buzz turned back just in time to see a fighter ship directly in front of them. It was on an intercept⁴ course—and it was **open**ing **fire**!

---

3 **barrel-roll** 곡예비행의 한 종류로 수평으로 나선형을 그리며 연속으로 횡전하는 것을 의미한다.
4 **intercept** 요격(邀擊). 공격해 오는 대상을 기다리고 있다가 도중에서 맞받아치는 전술을 지칭하는 군사 용어.

Chapter 11

"What is that?" Buzz cried, **swerving** to avoid the **enemy** ship's blasters.

He rolled the Armadillo, narrowly escaping the first three blasts. But the fourth shot **clip**ped the right wing of their ship, and they **plummet**ed back toward the ground.

"I can't see anything!" Buzz cried as they passed from gray skies into sudden darkness.

"Oh, no!" **exclaim**ed Izzy. "We're on the dark side of the planet!"

Sox **spun** his head around, **scan**ning the area. He stopped, eyes wide. "Oh! Over there! Ten o'clock!"

Buzz saw the **faint** glow of lights and fires from a **mining operation** in the **distance**.

"Hold on!" he shouted, **grip**ping the control wheel. "This isn't going to be pretty!"

Mustering all the control he had, Buzz **steadily** held the wheel and guided the **flail**ing ship down to the ground, even though he knew it was going to be a rough landing.

FWA-BOOM!

The ship slammed into the **terrain**, and in a **plume** of dust, it came to a rest.

"Is everyone okay?" Buzz **wince**d as he started to move his body.

"I think so." Izzy sat up, **wind**ed.

The others nodded, **daze**d but unharmed.

Buzz snapped his attention back to the windshield, looking for signs of the enemy ship that had shot them down. He couldn't see anything—it was **pitch black** out there.

He **clamor**ed to the door and opened it with a *whoosh*. Thankfully, there was no sign of the fighter ship anywhere. But their ship didn't look to be in very good shape.

"Sox, get me a damage report," he said.

"One moment, please," Sox said. *"Beep boop beep boop beep boop . . ."*

Meanwhile, Izzy **knelt** on the ground, taking deep breaths. "Okay," she **pant**ed. "This is better."

Buzz stared at her, all his **frustration** bubbling over. *"This is better?"*

"No, obviously this is worse overall," Izzy **conceded**. "I just meant—you know." She pointed up toward the stars.

Buzz **clutch**ed his head. "Wait, *how* are you afraid of space?"

"Oh, it's pretty easy," Izzy explained. "Did you know if you let go out there, you just keep going in the same direction? Forever. Just . . ." She made a whooshing sound and **pantomime**d **float**ing off into space.

"Then how were you going to blow up the Zurg ship?" Buzz pressed.

"Oh, I would have been ground support." Izzy **shrug**ged, embarrassed. "I know Grandma wasn't afraid of space."

"No, because she was a *Space* **Ranger**. Astrophobia[1] is

---

1 astrophobia 별이나 천체 공간을 보고 두려움과 공포를 느끼는 증상.

an **automatic disqualification!**"

Izzy looked down at the ground, and Buzz softened a little. He didn't want to hurt the kid's feelings. But there was a difference between pretending to be a Space Ranger and actually *being* a Space Ranger. Facing your fears **head-on** and having the courage to **conquer** them was a **crucial component** of joining the Space Ranger **Corps**. It was one of the first things Alisha had taught him—something she had understood even better than Buzz.

"What was that thing?" Darby asked, breaking the **tension**. She **squint**ed up into the dark sky.

Buzz shook his head. "I don't know." Then he **plod**ded over to the ship and removed the fuel crystal. It was unharmed, glowing with its ever-steady **shimmer**y colors. But now they were all **strand**ed. Again. With a broken ship and **hostile forces** surrounding them. No matter what he did, Buzz couldn't catch a break. No matter how hard he tried, he couldn't seem to make things right. At every turn there was a **roadblock**, and then another, and another.

"I was done," he said, allowing himself to **wallow** in self-**pity** for just a moment, which was something Alisha had always

discouraged. "I finally had the crystal. This was supposed to be over." He **groan**ed. "But who am I kidding? I don't need a crystal. I need a time machine to get out of this **mess**."

Just then, Sox snapped back to reality. "*Bing!* **Assess**ment complete."

"How bad is it?" Buzz asked, **figuring** he already knew the answer.

"The blast was **absorb**ed by the heat shield," Sox explained. "It only caused a **minor** electrical short.[2]"

"Okay . . . ," Buzz said, unsure if this was a good thing or a bad thing.

"So in order to be flight operational," Sox continued, "the Armadillo will require **material** of **specialize**d capacitance.[3]"

"Oh! Like an electrical **thingy**," Mo replied.

"How do you know that?" Darby asked.

"We learned this," Mo said. "Specialized capacitance? Remember? We built those field radios[4] last month."

---

2 **electrical short** 누전. 전기의 일부가 전선 밖으로 새어 나와 회로 외의 곳으로 전류가 흐르는 현상.

3 **capacitance** 전기 용량. 물체가 전하를 축적할 수 있는 능력을 나타내는 물리량.

4 **field radio** 야전용 무전기. 산이나 들과 같이 야외에서 전투를 벌일 때 전파를 이용하여 서로 통신할 수 있도록 하는 기기.

"Oh, yeah," said Izzy. "That was fun."

"Yeah, Darby messed hers up," Mo **chuckle**d.

"I'm gonna mess *you* up," Darby **grumble**d.

Meanwhile, Buzz was analyzing the ship's engine. He turned to the group, **annoy**ed. "Please, I'm trying to think here."

But the Junior Patrol continued **bicker**ing about their radios.

"Hey!" Buzz **interject**ed. "Honestly . . . there is a lot of room out here. If you want to **reminisce**, you can go . . . over there!" Buzz pointed to the distance. "Or, look! There's no one trying to think over there." He **gesture**d again to another area.

Izzy pointed to the mining **facility**, which was glowing in the distance. "We can go up there!"

"Fine. Perfect," Buzz said, **waving** them **away**.

"Okay, new plan!" Izzy nodded.

"Wait, what?" Buzz said.

"That mining facility will have a **console**, right?" said Izzy. "That console will have a little **coil** thing, right? And that little coil thing will have the . . ." She pointed at Mo.

"Specialized capacitance," Mo finished.

"Huh," Buzz said. Despite his earlier frustration, he couldn't help feeling a tiny bit proud of Izzy for figuring a way out of their **predicament**. "Now that's thinking like a Hawthorne," he told her. "Let's go get that part and get out of here . . . before that thing finds us again."

Together, the team **trek**ked over the rocky terrain that led to the mining operation. When they reached the top of a **ravine overlook**ing the entire **enterprise**, Buzz **whistle**d. The mine was **massive**—a **gigantic crater** dug deep into the planet's surface, where, far below, mining robots had **excavate**d resources from T'Kani Prime's **crust**. A **command**-center building stood several yards[5] away, **extend**ing **precarious**ly over the ravine **ledge** and held in place by giant metal **stilt**s. Darby was the first to reach the door, but it was **seal**ed tight. She **fumble**d with something in her pocket while Buzz spoke into his wrist recorder.

"Buzz Lightyear, mission **log**," he **narrate**d out of habit. "In order to repair our ship, we have to find some way to get inside this command center, and—"

---

5 **yard** 길이의 단위 야드. 1야드는 91.44센티미터이다.

Just then, the door **slid** open. Darby stood, satisfied, holding a lockpick[6] she'd used to **hot-wire** the control system.

"Oh," Buzz said, surprised. "Nice job, elderly **convict**."

Quickly, they **slip**ped inside the command center and slid the door shut behind them. It was dark inside the control room, which was lit only by **emergency** lights. Normally, operators from Star Command would be on duty there, but they were all trapped back at the base.

"Okay, the **activation** coil should be in here," Izzy said, pointing to a large control console nearby.

Sox **shimmied** underneath it.

Mo pulled out the pen from his suit. "Oh! Need a pen?"

Sox didn't respond. All everyone heard was the sound of an electric screwdriver.[7]

"And . . . got it!" Sox shouted **triumphant**ly as he **emerge**d holding the activation coil in his mouth.

"Okay, yeah. Another time," said Mo.

As Mo pocketed the pen, his elbow hit a large red button on a wall.

---

6 **lockpick** 열쇠 없이 자물쇠를 따는 기구를 총칭하는 말.
7 **screwdriver** 스크루드라이버. 각종 나사를 죄고 푸는 데 사용되는 공구.

"**Security measures** activated," a robotic voice announced.

Warning lights flashed, and before the group could react, the door to the control room sealed shut. Force fields[8] shot down from the ceiling, surrounding each of them in individual energy **cone**s.

"No! Not again!" Darby exclaimed.

"Not *what*? What is this?" Buzz cried.

He pushed against his force field and it moved along with him. He was trapped inside!

"It holds you until *they* come and get you," said Darby.

"Well, no one is coming to get us," Mo argued. "They're all trapped in the base. So we should just leave, right?"

"We can't just leave!" Darby exclaimed.

"Sure, we can," Mo said. "Take it from me. You can always just leave."

Mo slammed his cone into the door button, and **instant**ly, the door **whiz**zed open again. But the energy field prevented him from passing through it.

Darby warned Mo to be careful, but Mo **crash**ed into the

---

8 **force field** 공상 과학 소설이나 영화에 주로 나오는 눈에 보이지 않는 힘이 작용하는 장애 구역.

closing door and **collide**d with Darby, **merging** their force fields into one. They were **squish**ed uncomfortably close together inside.

"All right, sorry," said Mo. "But maybe if we both try it?"

"That's not gonna work!" Darby exclaimed.

"You haven't even tried!" Mo said.

Mo threw his body at the door button once more, but without Darby's help, they **stumble**d back and knocked into Izzy and Sox. Now their force fields all merged into one uncomfortably tight cone.

Squished, they turned toward Buzz.

"Stay away from me!" Buzz warned. "I'm no help to anyone if I'm stuck in there with you." He looked at the activation coil in his hand and sighed, **tuck**ing it into his pocket. One more roadblock. "Sox, can you turn these off?"

Sox **claw**ed at the group's force field. "I can't reach the controls."

With the team squished together, even the **slight**est movement caused them to **stagger**. They **accidental**ly **bump**ed into a gray power source box, causing the lights and cones to **flicker**.

That gave Buzz an idea. "I'll open the door, you slam into the power source . . . these things will disappear, and we'll walk right out."

Everyone nodded.

"Ready?" Buzz asked. "Go!"

Buzz slammed the door button while the other four **charge**d at the power source. The door opened upon contact, but the team's force field just **bounce**d off the gray box. Nothing happened.

Izzy gasped. "We're just not heavy enough. Buzz, we need you!"

"Wait, in there? But if it doesn't work, I won't be able to save you," Buzz **protest**ed.

"You don't need to save us," Izzy said. "You need to *join* us."

Buzz considered her words. It did seem like the best possible option. After all, there was little he could do in his force field alone. But together, maybe there was a chance.

Squaring his shoulders, Buzz slammed into the door control button, causing the door to **spring** back open. He used the **recoil** to power his **momentum** toward the team's force field. As soon as they **combine**d, they crashed into the gray box. They slammed into it again and again until it finally **explode**d.

The blast knocked everyone to the floor while **simultaneous**ly cutting the power. Their energy cones disappeared, and the door, which had been automatically closing, slid to a stop halfway.

Buzz shook his head—he'd hit it hard in the **aftermath**. In his **stupor**, he felt the floor of the control room **shift** and drop. Then he realized that the support structures holding the building over the ravine were **giving way**.

"Go, go!" he **croak**ed, **motion**ing the team toward the half-open door. Everyone **scramble**d to their feet and began heading for the exit, when Buzz heard a metal *clang*. He felt his pocket and turned when he discovered that it was empty. The activation coil had slipped out and was rolling along the **pitch** of the floor . . . toward the **collapsing** walls over the ravine!

Buzz **sprint**ed toward it.

"Buzz, no!" Izzy cried when she saw what was happening.

But Buzz didn't listen. He **leap**ed for the activation coil, his fingers closing around it just before it could fall through a hole that had **crumble**d away in the floor. In one smooth motion, he **pivot**ed on his knees and sprang back up, clamoring up the **tilt**ed floor back to where his **horrified crew** watched. He was almost there. Fresh **crack**s formed under his boots as he **dodge**d falling **debris** and grabbed hold of an edge of the control console to **propel** himself forward. The floor was **practically vertical** at this point. With a **sicken**ing groan, the entire room pulled away from the ledge where his friends stood, forming a **chasm** between him and the open door. There were only milliseconds to make a choice. Buzz leaped across the **split**, flying through the air. With the coil clutched firmly in one hand, he **stretch**ed his other hand out to grab hold on to the ledge. He just barely made it as the rest of the control center collapsed away. He was safe!

And then, without warning, the piece of ledge Buzz clung to broke away, too. Suddenly he was falling, dropping down toward the darkness with nothing left to grab hold of, nothing left to cling to, nothing to save him from the choice he had made—

Then Izzy's hand **clasp**ed around Buzz's wrist, **abrupt**ly

halting his descent. He looked up in **disbelief**. The team had formed a chain, one hand to another, giving Izzy just enough length to reach down and catch him.

"We got you," she said.

Chapter 12

A short while later, the team sat together in a break room, which somehow hadn't **collapse**d in the **destruction**. They were all still **stun**ned, Buzz most of all. He sat quietly, **staring** across the darkened room.

"Here, let's all **recharge** a little." Mo offered Buzz a sandwich he'd **scrounge**d from the **vending machine**. Sox un**cap**ped the flash drive on his tail and plugged it into a wall **outlet**. His eyes **lit up** with **charging** symbols.

Buzz **distracted**ly **peel**ed off the sandwich's wrapper. But when he felt the **slimy texture**, he looked down. The sandwich appeared to be several pieces of **juicy** meat wrapped around a piece of bread.

"What, uh—what's happening here?" he asked.

"Something wrong with your sandwich?" Izzy took a **bite** of her own.

"Why is the meat on the outside?" Buzz asked, completely **confuse**d.

"'Cause it's a sandwich," Mo **mutter**ed with his mouth full.

"No," Buzz said. "The bread is supposed to be on the outside."

"What, like bread-meat-bread?" Mo asked.

"That's too much bread," Darby added.

"Yeah, but this is all . . . wet." Buzz held his sandwich up at an **angle**, allowing some of the juice to **drip** onto the floor.

"Yeah, juicy fingers," Mo **nod**ded. "That's the best part."

"When's the last time you had a sandwich?" Izzy asked.

"I don't know," Buzz **shrug**ged. "A hundred years ago? **Give or take**?"

Mo chuckled to himself. "This guy . . . bread-meat-bread."

"It's too much bread," Darby repeated. "That would just **suck** all the **moisture** out of your mouth."

Mo laughed and accidentally kicked Sox loose from the outlet. Sox's eyes faded away to darkness.

"Oh, no, Sox!" Mo cried.

The team **rush**ed over to the robotic cat. After a moment, his eyes turned on once more. He looked at the group, **disorient**ed.

"Excuse me," Sox said. "I require a **reboot**." His eyes closed and a chime began to play.

"I'm sorry," Mo said, his voice tight with emotion. "I almost killed Sox. I almost got us all killed back there."

"Hey. Listen to me," Izzy said. "It was just a mistake."

But Mo didn't seem **comfort**ed. Izzy looked to Buzz for support. "Right, Buzz?"

Buzz **blink**ed, shaken from his thoughts. "Oh, uh." He **clear**ed **his throat**. "Just . . . try to be a little better," he told Mo.

Buzz's words only made Mo's shoulders **slump** further. Izzy shot Buzz a look.

"Listen," Buzz continued. "When I first went to the academy, I was not . . . you know . . . good. I **screw**ed **up**. Every day. I got **tangle**d in the **obstacle** course. My hands shook so much, I couldn't hit the target. Not the **bull's-eye**, the *whole* target. And I was going to quit after the first week. It was clear I was *not* Space Ranger **material**."

Mo looked up at Buzz. "Really?"

"Yeah," said Buzz, "but Commander Hawthorne saw something in me. So I started looking for it, too."

Just then, Sox opened his eyes. "Re**calibrating**. One **corrupt**ed file **restore**d."

He began to show a hologram of Alisha.

"Hey, he's lighting up!" Alisha exclaimed in the hologram. "It's working." She turned to Sox. "Hello, Sox. I need you to **look after** my best friend." She held up a photo of Buzz. "His name is Buzz. He's away right now, but he'll be back soon. He's going to save us."

The message ended, and the group was quiet. Buzz walked over to the edge of the room, looking at the **mine** below.

"What's wrong?" Izzy asked.

"What's wrong?" Buzz repeated. "Did you not hear that? She believed I could fix the mistake I made. And that belief cost her everything."

"Everything?" Izzy said **incredulous**ly. "No. She had

Grandma Kiko, my dad and me, all her friends. She didn't plan to be here, but she had a whole life on this planet, Buzz. All of us have." She **pause**d. "Except . . . for you."

Buzz shook his head. "Yeah, but we wanted to be Space Rangers again. We wanted to *matter.*"

Izzy looked Buzz in the eye, and her expression suddenly seemed much older. "Believe me . . . she mattered."

For a moment, Buzz could **swear** he heard Alisha's voice in Izzy's. Maybe he had been thinking about this all wrong.

He **absentminded**ly took a bite of his juicy sandwich and **tilt**ed his head. "You know, it is pretty good this way."

"Yeah," Izzy said. "Bread-meat-bread . . . how long did you do it like that?"

"Forever," Buzz admitted, making everyone smile. And this time, their smiles didn't fade.

Ba-ding!

The team looked over at Sox as he unplugged himself from the wall.

"Fully recharged," Sox **confirm**ed.

"Come on," Buzz said. "Let's go put this part in the ship and get out of here."

As the team walked out of the command center, Sox turned on his **flashlight** mode, leading them through the darkness.

"This is exciting," Izzy said. "Operation Surprise Party, here we come!"

Buzz looked at her, confused. "Negative. I can't put you in harm's way like that."

"What, are you going to do the whole mission alone?" Izzy **protest**ed.

"I can do it," Buzz said confidently.

"Because you have a Hawthorne right here!" Izzy pointed at herself.

Buzz couldn't help smiling. Izzy really had **inherit**ed her grandmother's **gumption**. Maybe that was why it was even more important to him now to keep her safe. He saw so much of his old friend in Izzy. And he didn't want to fail Alisha again by putting her granddaughter in danger.

"I **appreciate** that," he said. "And I'll let you know if I need you. Until then, let's just try to get back to the Armadillo without any more trouble."

Suddenly, a giant explosion **erupt**ed in the rock face behind them. The team was **knock**ed off their feet, **strewn** about the ground like **rag** dolls.

Buzz **cough**ed and **peer**ed through the dust. Standing **ominous**ly in the **aftermath** of the explosion was another robot. But this one was different. It was **humongous**, constructed out of **shimmer**ing purple metal, its bloodred eyes glowing **vicious**ly beneath a silver **horn**ed crown.

"Run!" Buzz cried to the team.

Everyone **clamber**ed to their feet in the **chaos**, trying to find an escape **route**. But Mo crashed into Darby and the two **topple**d to the ground, **snag**ging Sox in the **fray**. Izzy, who had been following closely behind Buzz, turned and gasped. She sprinted back to help her friends.

When Buzz realized the others weren't behind him, he **skid**ded to a **halt** and **spun** around. His heart dropped. All of them—Mo, Darby, Izzy, and Sox—were tangled in a **heap** several yards back. And the robot **loom**ed over them. There was no escape now.

"No!" Buzz cried in **despair** as the robot lifted a massive foot, ready to **crush** the **rookie**s like bugs.

Izzy and her friends **cower**ed, **bracing** for the end.

The robot's foot lowered . . . and passed right over them.

The bot **march**ed on, leaving the team untouched, heading straight for the Space Ranger.

"What?" Buzz whispered, backing away. He looked at his team, then back at the **advancing** robot. And his eyes grew wide with a cold rush of **clarity**.

"It's after me . . . ," Buzz said, realizing. He **urgent**ly waved his team toward the ship. "Go!" he yelled. "Go back to the ship!"

"But, Buzz!" he heard Izzy cry after him as he **leap**ed back down into the mining **canyon**. He had to lead that robot away—it was the only way to save his friends.

He slipped and skidded down a **steep embankment** and **dart**ed into a tunnel. Charging at full speed, he **curve**d around a **bend**, following a soft glow of light that guided the way toward another exit. But just as he got there, the robot's shadow loomed large. It blocked the exit with a metal rebar,[1] stopping Buzz **in his tracks**. The Space Ranger **pivot**ed and ran back in the other direction. To his left was a small **crevice** between two rock faces. Buzz slipped inside, hoping to hide.

---

1 **rebar** 철근. 콘크리트를 보강하기 위해 그 속에 넣어서 사용하는 쇠막대.

But the robot **smash**ed the entire wall to pieces, sending Buzz **flee**ing once more.

No matter where Buzz ran, the robot always seemed to be two steps ahead of him. It was like it knew his every move. Buzz sprinted down a large **storage passage**, past **rows** of deactivated plasma² drills . . . and came to a **dead end**. The robot's shadow crept over him. He was trapped.

Buzz **whirl**ed, bracing for a fight. The robot pointed its blaster at him.

"Buzz . . . ," the robot said in a deep **mechanical** voice.

"What?" Buzz **pant**ed hard. "How do you know my name?"

The robot's blaster **retract**ed inside its metallic arm, and was **replace**d by a robotic hand. "Come with me."

"What?" Buzz stared in total confusion.

BOOM!

Buzz jumped back, shocked. The plasma drill next to him had powered up and blasted the robot in the **chest**. It was knocked offline! Buzz stared in disbelief as three figures and

---

2 **plasma** 플라스마. 매우 높은 온도에서 전하를 띤 입자들이 기체처럼 섞여 있는 상태로, 디스플레이 화면이나 연료 등에 사용된다.

a little robotic cat **reveal**ed themselves from behind the plasma drill.

Darby chuckled. "This is *definitely* a **violation** of my parole." Then she aimed the plasma drill at the wall and fired again, creating an escape route back to the surface.

"Come on!" Izzy yelled. "Let's get out of here!"

Moving as one, the team **bound**ed out of the tunnel, up and over the **ravine ledge**, and slid down the **hillside** toward the Armadillo.

In the dark sky above, **pinpoint**s of light grew large. It was a **legion** of **enemy** ships descending toward their location. A battle was **imminent**.

Everyone **race**d aboard the Armadillo and strapped in.

"Ready yourselves for **launch**!" Buzz directed them. "Operation Surprise Party is back on!"

"What? With us?" Izzy exclaimed, excitement and **terror comingling** in her voice.

Buzz looked back at the Junior **Patrol** with new admiration. They had saved him not just once, but twice. And besides, there was no safe place to take them anymore—not with a **barrage** of enemy **vessel**s en route and locked on target. In space or on the ground, every place was dangerous. They **were better off** facing the danger together as a team.

Buzz **banter**ed with them, the way he used to with Alisha. "What, am I going to do the whole mission alone?"

"We can't launch yet," Sox reminded him. "I still need five minutes to **install** the **coil**."

"We can't sit here for five minutes!" Darby cried **desperate**ly as she watched an army of robots emerging from their **pod**s.

"The ship still has hover **capabilities**," said Sox.

"Then let's use them!" Buzz exclaimed.

He **punch**ed the hover throttle, and the ship began **zip**ping just above the ground, **dodging** enemy robots left and right.

"We might lose them in the fire geysers,[3]" Izzy suggested.

"Point the way," Buzz agreed. He turned to Darby and Mo. "You two, blast some robots!"

Darby smiled and opened the weapon cases.

"But we haven't even finished our **munition**s training," Mo whispered to Darby.

---

3 **geyser** 간헐천. 화산 활동이 있는 곳에서 많이 나타나는 형태의 온천으로 뜨거운 물이나 수증기를 일정한 간격을 두고 주기적으로 분출한다.

"Shhh!" said Darby. "How hard can it be? Look. We got these **spiky** things, and these ones probably explode. Just do whatever feels right."

"What?" said Mo **skeptical**ly. "What are *you* going to do?"

Darby **hoist**ed a bazooka onto her shoulder with **satisfaction**. "I'm gonna dance with Mr. Boom."

She moved to the back door of the ship and kicked it open. As a robot flew toward the door, Darby fired the bazooka and blasted it away.

Explosions lit the dark side of the planet like **firework**s. One by one, the robots dropped as Mo and Darby hit their targets. Some accidentally activated their own **transport disc**s upon **impact**, causing them to **vanish** into thin air. Surprisingly, none of the robots seemed to be **retaliating** with firepower. Instead, they steadily **swarm**ed the ship, each attempting to attach a transport disc to the hull.

Meanwhile, the bubbling **lava** of the fire **pit**s loomed dead ahead.

"Don't worry," Izzy told Buzz. "I know every last **inch** of—watch out!" She pointed at a stalagmite[4] just in time. The

Armadillo **clip**ped it, sending a chunk of rock into a **pursuing** robot.

"Repair fifty-percent complete," Sox announced.

"Left!" Izzy yelled to Buzz. He did as she directed, narrowly missing a **blazing** geyser of fire that caught an **unsuspect**ing robot in the blast.

"Here we go," Buzz said. He pushed the throttle forward, and they flew across the **molten terrain**.

A dozen more robots **zoom**ed toward the Armadillo, **closing in** fast. Darby rained lasers upon them, blasting them down into the bubbling lava—all except one. It managed to **evade** her long enough to reach the hull and **slap** a transport disc on the side.

"Quick! Give me something!" Buzz shouted to Darby.

He reached his arm back, and Darby **swift**ly **fasten**ed a white laser gauntlet[5] she found onto his wrist. He slammed a button to open the side window and blasted the alien robot away. The Armadillo **sail**ed forward, free and clear of the lava

---

4   **stalagmite** 석순(石筍). 탄산칼슘이 녹아 있던 지하수가 석회암 동굴의 천장에서 바닥으로 떨어지는 과정에서 침전이 일어나 기둥 모양으로 자라 올라온 생성물.
5   **gauntlet** 손목 부분을 강조하거나 장식이 달린 긴 장갑으로 팔꿈치 위까지 올라와 팔을 보호한다.

pits, and back over **stable** terrain.

"Ninety-percent complete!" Sox announced.

"Izzy." Buzz turned and locked eyes with her. "Do you know how to **transfer** power on the fly?"

"I've done it in the **simulator**," Izzy said, a little uncertain.

Buzz threw a few switches. "Well, it's about to get real. Ready, thrusters!"

Izzy searched the console, doubt clouding her expression.

"Green button," Buzz said, guiding her.

Izzy found it and pressed it hard. "Done!"

Meanwhile, a robot was closing in on the ship. Darby tried to line up her shot, but it kept **swerving back and forth**, evading her.

"Ninety-nine percent complete!" Sox called.

"Izzy, transfer to—"

"**Oscillating** power!" Izzy completed Buzz's thought, pushing the correct button. "Done!"

The robot was getting closer, its transport disc **outstretch**ed. Darby squinted through her weapon's **scope**. She had the robot in her crosshairs.[6]

"One-hundred percent complete!" Sox announced. The

repair was finished!

"Okay, not yet . . . ," Buzz said to Izzy as he watched a **gauge** on the **dash**.

Izzy's hand hovered nervously over the console, close to the buttons.

"Fuel check!" Buzz called.

"Fuel **eject**!" Izzy replied.

Suddenly, with a **sicken**ing lurch, the Armadillo ground to a halt, dropping **unceremonious**ly to the planet's surface. Darby was knocked off-balance and fired her shot into dead air while the tracking bot zipped past. The **dashboard flash**ed a warning: FUEL CELL EJECT.

Izzy looked at Buzz, her heart sinking. "Oh, no."

Buzz hurried to the window and spied the ship's fuel cell lying on the ground outside.

"Blast!" he cried.

Buzz kicked open the side door, and he and Izzy sprinted across the rocky terrain to where the fuel cell lay. The robot that had been tailing them **bore down**, heading for it as well.

---

6 **crosshairs** 십자선. 현미경이나 망원경 등에서 손쉽게 방향을 맞출 수 있도록 하기 위해 렌즈에 부착하는 십(十)자 모양의 표시.

Buzz aimed his wrist blaster.

"**Grab** the crystal!" he yelled to Izzy.

Buzz fired at the robot, blowing off its arm. But the robot sailed over him, heading straight for the glowing fuel source.

Buzz turned to aim again, but the bot was in front of Izzy now. He didn't have a clear shot. Izzy dove for the crystal just as the bot **snatch**ed it up.

"No!" she cried.

Immediately, the robot pressed its transport disc and vanished. It was gone. And so was the fuel crystal.

"No," Buzz **groan**ed, sinking to his knees.

He couldn't believe it. Without the crystal, they had nothing. No way to reach the Zurg ship. No way to get it back. That fuel crystal had been their only hope. And just like that, the mission was over.

"Buzz?" Izzy said, her voice near tears as she walked over to him. "I'm so sorry. Everything was happening so fast, and I just—I made a mistake."

Buzz looked at her. He wasn't even sure what he felt right now.

"Yeah," he said, **defeat**ed.

Izzy looked **crestfallen**. "But we're not done. We can still do something, right?"

"Izzy, look around!" Buzz spread his arms out over the **vast wasteland**. "There's nothing *to* do. The mission . . . it's over."

Saying that out loud was like a punch to the **gut**. Accepting defeat was something Buzz had never done before. Something he'd never allowed himself to do. But he had failed in every sense of the word. He had **let down** his old team. He had been wrong to trust a band of **volunteer** rookies to help him. The **culmination** of everything he had **dedicate**d his life and others' lives to meant nothing now.

Buzz slowly got up and started to walk away.

"Buzz?" Izzy asked, **frighten**ed. "Buzz! Where are you going?"

"I just need to . . . be by myself," Buzz said.

He **plod**ded forward, dust **billow**ing under his footsteps as the rest of the team watched, **heartbroken**.

That was when something grabbed Buzz through the darkness. It was a giant mechanical hand, extending from the robot **cloak**ed in shining purple metal. The robot's eyes burned **fiery** red.

"No!" Izzy cried.

Buzz **struggle**d as the robot lifted him off the ground. Its eyes flashed in the direction of the team for a moment. Then it reached for a large transport disc on its chest.

"Buzz!" the team shouted.

The robot pressed the button, and they vanished.

Buzz was gone.

Chapter 13

A low mechanical **hum** filled the transport room, **odd**ly **serene** amid the **pile** of deactivated robots that lay in a **heap** on the **teleport**ation pad. Suddenly, there was a flash of light, and Buzz appeared—still trapped in the robot's **clutch**es.

Straining, Buzz fired his **wrist** laser at the robot, taking it by surprise just long enough to **wriggle** free from its **grasp** and roll out of reach. Buzz fired his laser again, but this time, the robot just **absorb**ed the **blast**, chuckling a deep, **throaty** noise that **rumble**d through its **metallic chamber**s.

"What is this?" Buzz **demand**ed. "Where are we? Who are you?"

The robot simply shook its head, as if denying the truth to a young child. "Everything will **make sense. In due time.** For now, you can call me Zurg."

"All right, *Zurg*," Buzz said, still **track**ing the **menacing foe** with his wrist laser. "Then tell me what you want."

"I want the same thing you want, Buzz." Zurg took a step closer. "I want to help you. I want you to finish the mission."

"This mission?" Buzz **echo**ed, **take**n **aback**. "What do you know about the mission?"

"I know everything," Zurg said. "I know about the crash on T'Kani Prime. About the mistake *you* made. I want to help you fix it."

Buzz shook his head, confused. "That doesn't make sense—how could you know that?"

"Because *I'm* from the future," Zurg revealed. "Where the **machinery** is so **advance**d, it can do anything, even travel through time. You don't understand now—there's no way you could. But your **crew** crashing on T'Kani Prime changed everything. All I want is a chance to help you fix your mistake, Buzz. To go back in time—to set things right."

"But why?" Buzz asked. "Why do you want to help me?"

Zurg **paused**. "Let's just say—our interests are **aligned**."

Buzz shook his head, confusion clouding his **judgment**. "I don't understand."

"You don't need to." Zurg took a step closer. "All you need to see is that together, we can go back in time to change things."

"You mean . . ." Buzz **trail**ed **off, process**ing what Zurg was suggesting. "You mean I can stop my crew from ever landing on that planet?"

Zurg nodded. "You can stop yourself from ever hitting that mountain."

Slowly, Buzz lowered his wrist laser. He knew he couldn't—shouldn't—trust this mysterious Zurg. But this offer was a possibility Buzz had never imagined.

"We can just continue the mission home," Buzz said, the truth **dawn**ing on him.

"And none of this will have ever happened," Zurg added. The robot held up Buzz's **glow**ing fuel cell. "This crystal is the key to it all. With this, we can travel through time."

"But you said you've already traveled through time," Buzz pointed out. "So, don't you already have a crystal?"

Zurg chuckled. "Well . . . sort of."

Zurg led Buzz down a long hall to a room surrounded by screens. Various robots worked busily around the **perimeter**, operating the consoles. In the center was a plasma engine, powered by a **dim**ly glowing fuel crystal, just like Buzz's.

"See, I **wore** my crystal **out** testing the time travel," Zurg explained. "But then I **realize**d I could just get a brand-new crystal from you."

Buzz eyed the engine curiously. Its **setup** looked **vague**ly familiar, as though he **intuitive**ly knew how to control it. But was any of this truly possible? Could he really travel back in time and stop the crash? He wanted so badly to believe what Zurg was saying, that his mistake could be fixed before it ever happened. But none of this made sense.

"Tell me why you want to help me," Buzz **insist**ed. "Why do you want to change the past?"

The robot held its arms wide. "I can't give you all the answers you want, Buzz. But trust me when I say, we want the same thing. Just a chance to make things right. You spent a lifetime trying to fix your mistake without the right tools. I'm giving you those tools. I'm giving you that chance."

Buzz thought about it. All this time, he had been so focused on finding a **stable** fuel source. But what if the answer had never been hyperspeed in the first place? What if time travel was the only true option for success, the missing piece to the puzzle for which he had been searching so long?

"It's a good plan," he said quietly.

Together, they began working at the engine console, **flip**ping switches in **unison** like a well-oiled machine, preparing to **swap** in the fresh fuel crystal.

"You know," Buzz said, **reminiscing**. "There's an old friend of mine who will finally get her wish because of this." He thought **fond**ly of Alisha. "She'll get to be a Space Ranger again." Buzz's hand paused **midair** over a switch, the multicolored glow of the fuel crystal **reflect**ing off his white gauntlet. "Though . . . ," he said slowly, "she won't have her family. She won't have Izzy."

Zurg removed the old crystal from the fuel housing[1] before **noticing** that Buzz had stopped his work. "Buzz," Zurg said in a deep voice. "Nobody's going to remember any of this.

---

1 **housing** 하우징. 기계의 부품이나 특정 부분을 받치는 틀.

The only thing anybody's going to know is that you finished your mission."

Zurg **toss**ed the used crystal aside and held out a robotic hand.

"Here, hand me your crystal," Zurg directed.

Buzz **furrow**ed his **brow**. Was it fair to **erase** all those people down there so that his crew might have the chance to go home? Was it fair to erase Izzy?

"I don't know," Buzz said, unsure. "Maybe . . . maybe we should think about this."

"Think about what?" Zurg **spat**. "You just said your friend would get her wish."

"Yeah, but . . . she had a whole life down there," Buzz replied.

"Believe me, you don't want to live like this," Zurg said. "Reliving the nightmare. **Haunt**ed by your mistake. You can finally **let go of** that. Starting right now."

Zurg held out a hand for the crystal again. And Buzz studied it for a long moment.

It was true: Buzz had made mistakes. A lot of them. But the life Alisha built hadn't been a mistake. Her smile in Sox's hologram and all the times Buzz had returned from his missions hadn't been because she was dreaming of what couldn't be. She had been smiling for what *was*. Her life, her family, everything she had built with her own two hands. Crashing on T'Kani Prime may not have been the plan. But maybe, just maybe, it wasn't a mistake after all.

Buzz looked up at Zurg with **renew**ed confidence.

"You're right," said Buzz. "I can." He lowered the fuel crystal to his side and walked toward the door.

"Where are you going?" Zurg demanded.

"I've spent far too long trapped in the past. Maybe my mission is to make a better future for the people down there, now." Buzz **square**d his shoulders. "I won't help you."

Zurg's eyes glowed a deeper red than Buzz thought possible.

"Then you leave me no choice."

Far below on T'Kani Prime, Izzy, Darby, and Mo sat **forlorn**ly by the powerless Armadillo.

"Hey, cat," Darby called to Sox. "Do you know how to

fly this thing?"

"Um, there's no fuel," Sox replied.

Mo pulled at his hair. "See, *this* is why we should have never **gotten in over our heads**."

"What did *you* want to do?" Darby **snap**ped. "Wait at the outpost until the robots found us?"

"Well, that's better than being **strand**ed out here, where no one's *ever* going to find us!" Mo shouted back.

While they **bicker**ed, Izzy simply sat. She'd never felt emptiness like this before. Not only had she **let down** her team, but she had let down her grandmother's best friend and gotten him **capture**d in the process. She was supposed to be a leader, like her grandmother. Some Hawthorne she'd turned out to be.

Frustrated, Izzy **rip**ped the Hawthorne nameplate off her suit and tossed it on the ground.

Sox **pad**ded up to her. "I've completely lost Buzz," he said sadly. "He's too far away to track."

Izzy **sigh**ed. Buzz was probably up on that Zurg ship right now, **enduring** who knew what. She stared **blank**ly at the nameplate on the ground, the wind picking it up and carrying it away, toward the Armadillo. At that moment, she noticed something on the ship. What she saw made her **gasp**.

"Everybody! Inside!" she ordered.

"What?" Darby asked, stopping in the middle of a **verbal tirade** against Mo.

"What's after us now?" Mo looked around nervously as they all **clamber**ed up and into the ship.

"We don't have any more weapons!" Darby pointed out.

"That's okay," Izzy said, her voice **fuel**ed with renewed confidence. "We're getting out of here."

"Where are we going?" Sox asked.

Izzy **lean**ed out the Armadillo window, looking at the transport disc one of the robots had slapped on it.

"We're going to space."

She took a deep breath and **slam**med a **fist** against the button. The ship disappeared.

Chapter 14

"**N**o, you can't do this!" Buzz **resist**ed as two robots **restrain**ed him. "You're going to **erase** it all!"

Zurg's eyes **flash**ed as the robot **strode** over and picked up the glowing fuel crystal. "Exactly."

"You're going to take away people's families!" Buzz **exclaim**ed. "Their friends. *My* friends. They have lives on that planet. Everyone does!"

"I hardly recognize you, Buzz," said Zurg. "All these new ideas . . . you know what? We'll go ahead and erase those, too."

Zurg's hand reached toward the launch button.

"No!" screamed Buzz.

At that moment, he broke free from the robots and blasted them with his laser. One robot **topple**d into Zurg, causing the **foe** to drop the fuel crystal and **crash** into the control **panel**.

Buzz **sprang** forward, grabbed hold of the fuel crystal, and **sprint**ed out of the room.

He had to make his way to the bridge. **Operation** Surprise Party was back on.

He was going to **blow up** the ship.

In the transport room, an **unlikely quartet** appeared in a **blind**ing flash of light. Izzy, Mo, Darby, and Sox had all **teleport**ed in the Armadillo up to Zurg's ship.

"Operation Surprise Party, here we go!" Izzy said eagerly as they climbed out. She looked at her team.

"Hup, hup!" they all said in **unison**.

"We need to protect our escape ship," Izzy directed, taking control like a real Space **Ranger**, feeling the strength of her grandma coursing through her. "If the robots get to it, we'll never get out alive. So nothing comes through that door."

Darby pointed to herself and Mo. "Don't worry. We'll **seal** it off."

"You go find Buzz," Mo said, their confidence **inspiring** him, too.

"I'll **track** the chip in his dog tags," Sox **confirm**ed, his ears tracking the signal. "Come on!"

"And I've got us a **shortcut** back." Izzy grabbed a transport disc from the wall and **slap**ped it on her back.

With that, she and Sox **slip**ped out of the transport room and **stealthily** hurried down the long **corridor** in the direction of Buzz's signal.

"Meow, meow, meow, meow," Sox repeated softly as he continued **homing in on** his target. "Oh! The signal is tighter now. He has to be straight this way!"

He led Izzy to a glass-windowed **observatory**, giving her a first real **glimpse** of the **vast**ness of space outside the ship. Izzy stopped and **gulp**ed.

"*Bguhhh*. That's a lot of space." She felt a **knot** forming in her stomach and looked down at the floor so she wouldn't **throw up**. "**Keep it together** . . . keep it together," she **whisper**ed to herself.

Suddenly, alarms sounded. Something had **trigger**ed the ship's **security** system! Izzy heard robots **thunder**ing toward the transport room just as the door behind them **slid** shut with a **resound**ing *thunk*. They were trapped!

"No, no, no!" Izzy **pound**ed on the door.

Sox looked around, confused. "I don't understand. The signal says Buzz is fifty meters away."

Izzy **begrudging**ly turned her **gaze** back toward the windows, breathing **rhythmic**ally to keep herself calm. It was like being trapped in a fishbowl surrounded by her greatest fear. Beyond the glass **barrier** of the observatory windows was nothing but the **immense** black **void** of space—except for a **portion** of the ship that **jut**ted out directly across from them. Izzy **press**ed her hands against the glass and gasped.

"He's over there!" She pointed to the bridge, where Buzz was standing at the control panel.

And he wasn't alone.

Over on the bridge, Buzz tried to **make sense** of the futuristic **command console**. Unlike the plasma engine from before, none of it looked familiar. "I don't know any of this technology," he said, **frustrate**d. For the first time in his life, he wished he had an auto**pilot** to tell him what to do.

"Computer, is there an autopilot?" he asked hopefully.

"Affirmative," the computer replied. "You may call me IVAN."

"IVAN—" Buzz whispered. What were the **odds** that Zurg's ship ran on exactly the same autopilot that Star Command used?

What was Zurg not telling him?

"IVAN," Buzz **instruct**ed, taking a chance. "**Initiate self-destruct sequence** in two minutes."

"Self-destruct **countdown** initiated," IVAN replied.

Buzz turned—and was immediately caught in a **chokehold** by Zurg.

"Enough!" Zurg **bellow**ed, pulling Buzz painfully close. "Just tell me where the crystal is."

Zurg **flung** Buzz across the room, slamming the Space Ranger hard into a console. Buzz's head **throb**bed upon **impact**. He rolled down to the floor, and suddenly realized he wasn't rolling at all—he was **hover**ing.

Dazed, he looked over at the control panel. He'd **accidentally** hit the antigravity[1] button. Now everything was starting to float up and around the bridge, including the fuel crystal, which Zurg caught **sight** of. The **menacing** robot **chuckled**.

"No!" **yell**ed Buzz. He fired his wrist laser, but his focus was still **woozy**. He missed, instead hitting an energy transformer behind Zurg, which **explode**d like a shock wave.[2] Both Zurg and Buzz were blasted to **opposite** sides of the bridge. Zurg's red eyes **flicker**ed, and Buzz slammed into a window. He felt his **vision dim**ming as he floated **listless**ly beside a glass panel that offered a glimpse into the vast darkness of space.

"Buzz?"

The voice seemed to be coming from outside. No—his communicator.

"Are you okay?" the voice asked.

Buzz **blink**ed and looked out the window in a **stupor**. He

---

1 **antigravity** 반(反)중력. 중력과 반대되는 힘으로 중력과 같은 형태의 힘에 의해 한 물체가 다른 물체를 밀어 낸다.

2 **shock wave** 충격파. 화약 등이 폭발할 때 공기 중에 생기는 압축파로 이 과정에서 압력과 온도, 밀도 등이 급격하게 변화한다.

couldn't make sense of what he was seeing. Across the way was a glass observatory jutting out from the ship, and pressed against the glass window, watching him, was Alisha.

"No, Alisha." His own voice sounded **distant**. "I—I need help."

"Buzz, I'm not my grandma," the woman said.

Buzz shook the **cobweb**s from his brain. He **squint**ed. The woman watching him wasn't Alisha at all, but Izzy. Somehow, she had made it to the ship. Somehow, she had made it there to help him—all on her own.

"Izzy," Buzz said, "I don't need your grandma. I need *you*."

Chapter 15

In the **observatory**, Izzy **desperate**ly searched for escape options. "How do we get over there?"

Sox **scan**ned the room. "Through the air lock.[1]"

Izzy looked to where Sox **indicate**d and felt her **chest seize up** in panic. The cat wanted her to walk through a door leading into space! "Through *there*?" she exclaimed. "There's *nothing* out there!"

"Exactly," explained Sox. "Nothing in your way. You just go straight across."

---

1 **air lock** 우주선 등에서 기체 성분이나 압력이 다른 두 공간 사이를 이동하기 위해 설치하는 공간.

Izzy **stared** across to the other section of the ship. Sox was right—an **identical** air lock was on that side. **Theoretical**ly, if she jumped out from this one, she would float straight across to the other. Unless she missed, and just kept **drift**ing out into space—forever.

Izzy looked back at Buzz. He was still **float**ing **limp**ly near the glass window on the bridge. It looked like his eyes were closed.

He needs me, Izzy thought, pushing down the fear rising in her. *I have to do this—he's **running out of** time!*

Taking deep, **rhythmic** breaths, Izzy and Sox climbed into the air lock, and she sealed the door to the observatory behind them. Then Izzy lowered her helmet's face **shield** and Sox climbed up onto her back. With a shaking hand, she pressed the **release** button for the outer air lock door.

WHOOOOSH.

Her worst fear lay **stretch**ed before her: an **infinite abyss** of simply—nothing. Nothing to **grab** hold of. Nothing to save her if she drifted off-course. **Endless** emptiness.

"Just don't look down," Sox **instruct**ed.

Izzy looked up, and the same view **greet**ed her above. It

was a **void** so black, she felt it could **suck** her in if she stared too long.

"Or up," Sox said quickly. "It's all space. It's everywhere. All around you. I'm sorry. I'm probably not helping. Just go straight. Once you push off, that's the direction you'll go."

Izzy **gulp**ed. "But what if I miss?"

"Don't miss," Sox said.

With a final deep breath, Izzy aimed for the bridge air lock, ready to push off.

Every **fiber** of her being told her not to do this. But this wasn't about her. It was about her friend. Only she could save him.

Don't let go, her pounding heart seemed to say.

Izzy let go.

Back on the bridge, Buzz saw the fuel cell floating an arm's length away. He pushed past the pain and **force**d himself to **regain** focus. Using the window as **leverage**, he **propel**led himself forward and swam toward the fuel cell.

Buzz just barely managed to grab hold of the fuel cell as

he drifted past the main console. From the corner of his eye, he could see the **countdown**: only twenty-five seconds left. Somehow, he had to get away from Zurg, reach Izzy, and get them off this ship before it was too late.

Twisting in the air, he pushed himself toward the bridge door. He was halfway there when he felt an **unexpected lurch** in his stomach and **slam**med to the ground.

"Ugh!" Buzz landed heavily on his arm. He managed to hold on to the fuel cell, but his wrist blaster broke off and **skid**ded across the floor. He lifted his head and saw Zurg standing **triumphant**ly by the main console, the **artificial** gravity **reinstate**d.

Zurg pushed another few buttons and the computer **chime**d, "**Manual override activate**d."

Zurg **chuckle**d as Buzz realized that the **self-destruct** sequence had paused with only ten seconds remaining.

Suddenly, the air lock door at their side crashed open. Zurg **whip**ped around to face it. But no one was there—the air lock was empty.

In that moment of **confusion**, Buzz reached out to grab his wrist blaster. But he wasn't quick enough. Zurg saw what was happening and **extend**ed a robotic hand to **snare** Buzz in a **squeeze** so tight, he could barely breathe.

Then something **inexplicable** happened. A **figure materialize**d **out of thin air** in the middle of the bridge. Buzz watched in **disbelief** as Izzy became **visible**, leaving **stealth** mode, with Sox on her shoulder, and they were right next to his fallen wrist blaster. She had made it across—and they had one shot.

"Now!" Buzz **gasp**ed.

Knowing exactly what to do, Izzy **snatch**ed up the wrist blaster and threw it just as Buzz stretched out his hand. It was the perfect throw and catch. Buzz **grip**ped the blaster and fired down at the **cord** attaching Zurg's hand to the bot's arm. In a **spray** of **spark**s, the cord **sever**ed, and the **recoil** sent Zurg **reel**ing back over the main console. Buzz **somersault**ed down to the floor, still **cradling** the precious fuel crystal. Without so much as a breath, he sprinted forward and grabbed Izzy.

"Come on!" he shouted. "Let's get out of here!"

Izzy pointed to the console. "We have to **blow up** the ship!"

"There's no time!" Buzz shook his head. "We'll never

make it."

"Oh yes, we will," Izzy said with the confidence of a true Space Ranger, producing the **transport disc** she'd found.

Buzz felt a **surge** of pride. With a **nod**, he aimed his wrist blaster at the self-destruct button on the main console and fired.

"Self-destruct sequence reactivated," IVAN announced. "**Resuming** countdown. Ten . . . nine . . ."

Behind the console, Zurg rose like a **monolith**, **livid** at what was happening. "IVAN?" the robot **bellow**ed, **intend**ing to **shut down** the self-destruct again. But IVAN didn't respond.

Zurg's eyes burned like **lava** as they **peer**ed down and the robot realized the console **panel** was **ruin**ed, and the self-destruct sequence was locked in.

"IVAN!" Zurg **roar**ed.

But Buzz, Izzy, and Sox weren't there to **witness** the full **wrath** of Zurg, because they had already used the transport disc to disappear.

Chapter 16

"**W**hat happened in here?" Izzy **exclaim**ed as she, Buzz, and Sox reappeared on top of the Armadillo in the **transport** room and **slid** down the side. Darby and Mo stood before a smoking **pile** of robot **wreckage** that blocked the entry door to the transport room.

"I **seal**ed the door," Darby said bluntly. "Like you asked."

"See, we **trigger**ed the alarm," Mo explained **hurried**ly. "And then all the robots came. But Darby then found three things, and—"

"**Boom**." Darby nodded.

"Well, there's about to be an even bigger boom," Buzz

urged. "Everyone, get in!"

Izzy, Darby, Mo, and Sox **clamber**ed aboard the ship as Buzz **hastily** went to **insert** the fuel crystal. He had just opened the fuel door, when—

KA-BOOM!

They were too late! The **self-destruct** sequence had started. An **explosion** rocked Zurg's ship, and the entire **vessel list**ed to one side. Buzz lost his **grip** on the Armadillo and began sliding down toward an open **cargo bay** door. He just barely managed to **grab** hold of the fuel crystal and activate his Space Ranger helmet before he passed through the pressurization[1] **force** field and out into open space. Everything from the transport room—the deactivated robots, the Armadillo, Buzz's XL-15 ship—all **tumble**d out into the **void** and began to **drift**.

The force of the **blast** sent everything **hurtling** down toward T'Kani Prime, including Buzz. Free-falling[2] through space, he **collide**d with the XL-15, **bouncing** off the **hull**.

---

1 **pressurization** 여압(與壓). 항공기 내부의 공기 압력을 높여 지상에 가까운 기압 상태를 유지하는 일.
2 **free-fall** 자유 낙하. 높은 곳에서 어떤 물체를 놓았을 때 물체가 땅을 향해 속도가 점점 빨라지며 떨어지는 현상. 여기서는 '자유 낙하하다'라는 뜻의 동사로 쓰였다.

Buzz reached out wildly and **snag**ged the edge of the ship's wing just before he went flying off into deep space. **Strain**ing with every **fiber** in his body, Buzz **heave**d himself up and onto the ship, **cling**ing to it **for dear life**. He could see the fuel port.

Inch by inch, he pulled himself toward the small door, even while all about him **fiery debris** from the **crash sail**ed by, threatening to **knock** him loose at any moment. His fingers closed around the fuel door handle, and he **pried** it open, **shoving** the fuel crystal into place. It activated with a **hum** of energy, powering up the ship. Breathing hard, Buzz pulled himself to the **cockpit** and climbed inside. The canopy **whoosh**ed closed, and the ship pressurized. Sweat **drench**ed the inside of Buzz's Space Ranger suit. He had done it.

Now he had to save his friends. Without a fuel source, they were **helpless** against the **gravitational** pull of the planet. They would get **suck**ed into the upper **atmosphere** and crash down to the surface if he didn't get to them and **transfer** over the fuel crystal in time.

Buzz fired up the ship's engines and locked on course for the **plummet**ing Armadillo.

"Come on," he said through **grit**ted teeth, pushing full

throttle toward his friends.

Suddenly, the back of the ship **pitch**ed downward, like something heavy had sat on it. At first, Buzz thought he must have collided with a piece of falling wreckage. But when he turned to look, a **pit** formed deep in his stomach.

"Going somewhere?" a deep **mechanical** voice asked him.

It was Zurg! Somehow, the robot had managed to survive the self-destruct and was **latch**ed onto Buzz's ship!

Zurg laughed, **rip**ping off the back wing and **hurl**ing it into space. Inside, Buzz **struggle**d to keep control, but it was no use. The ship started **spiral**ing. Zurg reached the fuel port and **wrench**ed the fuel cell from it, which **shut down** the thrusters and the weapons. Buzz was out of power and out of **defense**s. Only the ship's **emergency** lights **retain**ed **residual** energy—along with one **glow**ing red button Buzz recognized all too well.

An **eject** button.

"Don't be scared, Buzz," Zurg's voice **echo**ed as the **foe crept** along the hull to face Buzz, its burning red eyes **practically sear**ing a hole through the wind**shield**. "I'm going to **erase** all this, remember? You could have used this crystal to matter again. Instead, it will be like you were never here. So . . . prepare to die."

Buzz locked eyes with Zurg—and hit the glowing red eject button. The back of his seat **strap**ped around him, and the ship's canopy **burst** open, **launch**ing Buzz from the cockpit. The seat back opened to **reveal** a jet pack[3] with wings! Buzz **flip**ped up and over Zurg, flying out in front of the **careen**ing ship. Zurg turned just in time to see Buzz take aim with his **wrist** blaster at the glowing crystal **clutch**ed in Zurg's hands.

"Not today, Zurg!" Buzz exclaimed.

With that, Buzz fired his laser and blasted the crystal.

"No!" Zurg screamed.

The crystal exploded in a **blaze** of color that was brighter than Buzz had ever **witness**ed, **engulf**ing Zurg along with it. The **culmination** of a hundred years of work—gone in one **brilliant** explosion.

But all that was in the past now. Buzz had a new mission.

He aimed himself toward the Armadillo and **engage**d his jet pack, shooting forward on an intercept course to save his friends.

---

3 **jet pack** 제트팩. 등에 맨 상태에서 가스나 물을 뿜어내어 하늘을 날 수 있게 하는 개인용 비행 장치.

"We've entered the planet's gravitational pull," Sox **alert**ed everyone as the Armadillo careened toward certain **doom**.

"Are we gonna crash?" Mo asked.

"I'm afraid so," Sox replied.

Izzy, Darby, and Mo exchanged **frighten**ed **whimper**s. This wasn't looking good.

Then like a miracle, Buzz Lightyear sailed in front of the ship!

"Buzz!" Izzy cried, **press**ing against the windshield. She couldn't believe it—Buzz was alive!

Buzz positioned himself in front of the Armadillo and pushed his jet pack to full power. Without a fuel crystal, his only hope for getting the ship under control was to slow its **descent**. But even he knew that the **odds** of success were **slim**. One little jet pack hardly had the firepower to **match up to** the gravitational pull of T'Kani Prime. He pushed with all his **might**, the metal nose of the Armadillo **crush**ing under the **pressure**. But the ship didn't slow.

Buzz looked at his friends through the windshield. Their

expectant faces **plain**ly showed all their hopes were **pin**ned on him. He wanted so badly not to **let** them **down**.

"I—" His voice broke. "I can't do it."

Izzy studied his face for a long beat, and then, **inexplicably**, she smiled.

"Hey! That's all right," she told him. "*We* can!"

Now it was Buzz's turn to look hopeful.

"Can you keep the ship **steady**?" Izzy asked him.

"Affirmative," Buzz replied. He **zoom**ed under the Armadillo's hull and grabbed two handholds, using the power of his jet pack to guide the ship more steadily. "Sox," he said into his communicator. "Use your emergency battery to power up flight controls!"

"Got it!" Sox replied. The robotic cat lifted his tail and the end **pop**ped off, revealing the flash drive. He inserted the drive into the main console, activating the emergency battery. The ship's controls **sprang** to life.

"I'll need a co**pilot**," Izzy said, looking at Mo.

"Okay . . . I've only done this in the **simulator**," Mo said **hesitant**ly.

"Well, it's about to get real," Izzy told him as they took

their seats. She reminded him to pull back on the control wheel nice and easy.

Mo **yank**ed the control wheel back much too hard, and a **flap** on the right wing ripped off, **whiz**zing past Buzz's head.

Izzy shot Mo a look, and he **grimace**d. "Yep, sorry. Nice and easy from now on."

All around them, the ship began to glow from the heat of re**entry** into the planet's atmosphere. Not for the first time, Buzz was **grateful** for the protection of his Space Ranger suit. But their efforts still weren't enough. Buzz turned to his last remaining hope.

"IVAN?" he called out.

"Yes, captain?" said IVAN, full of **static**.

"We're going too fast!"

"Congratulations!" IVAN exclaimed. Confetti shot out of the **dash**.

"We don't need confetti! We need brakes!" Mo exclaimed.

"The air brake!⁴" Izzy and Buzz shouted in **realization**.

"IVAN, is there an air brake?" Izzy asked.

---

4 **air brake** 공기 제동기. 높은 압력을 가하여 부피를 줄인 공기를 이용하여 항공기나 차량 등의 속도를 조절하거나 멈추게 하는 장치.

"Certainly," IVAN replied. "The air brake is located on the floor."

Izzy looked around and spotted the air brake under a cover on the floor. "Darby!" she exclaimed.

Darby bent down and hit a button to open the air brake cover. But it was jammed.

"The cover! It's stuck! I need a screwdriver . . . or a hair clip . . . or some sort of a small wedge."

Mo's eyes brightened with a sudden realization. "The pen! I've got the pen!"

He popped the pen out of his suit and wielded it like a sword. He leaned over and pried open the cover, allowing Darby to pull on the air brake with force and fury.

Finally, the ship began to slow. Its descent was still incredibly fast. But with everyone working together, they had a chance.

The wind whipped past as the ground raced up to meet the ship. Buzz let go at the last possible second, watching the Armadillo sail forward mere feet above the ground before it scraped across the surface in a massive wave of dirt, rock, and burned metal.

Slowly, the Armadillo **skid**ded to a stop, coming to a rest long before the team's **pound**ing hearts did.

Buzz used his jet pack to **loop** overhead and touch down.

"Is everyone okay?" he shouted, **sprint**ing up to the door. Shaking, Izzy, Darby, Mo, and Sox **emerg**ed from the ship. Then they all **embrace**d Buzz in a group hug that was **fiercer** than any **alien** force in the universe.

Suddenly, the sound of sirens broke through the team's **emotional** moment.

"The **cop**s! Everyone run!" Darby cried.

"Wait . . . it's just the **rescue** team," Buzz said.

"Oh, right. Okay," said Darby, **relieve**d.

"You know, you seem like a **decent** citizen," Buzz said. "What led to your **incarceration**?"

"I stole a ship," Darby replied.

"Oh. I see," Buzz said, uncomfortable. "Well, you know, who among us hasn't stolen a ship in a moment of **relative desperation**?"

Mo walked over to them, holding his pen **aloft**. "I am a man of **resource**s! My weapon is **ingenuity**! I can do anything!"

"Can you not shout in my ear?" Darby said.

Buzz **glance**d over at Izzy, who was looking up at the sky with a soft smile on her face.

"You okay?" Buzz asked.

Izzy pointed up. "I was in space."

Buzz **squeeze**d Izzy's shoulder. "Your grandma would be proud."

Izzy looked at Buzz **appreciative**ly. His praise meant more to her than anything in the world, because coming from him, she knew she'd earned it.

"She'd be proud of you, too," Izzy said. "She always was." Then Izzy realized Buzz was missing something very important. "Wait, where's your crystal?"

Buzz simply shook his head. "It's gone."

"But your mission . . . ," Izzy **insist**ed. "You wanted to go home."

"You know," said Buzz, looking at his team, "for the first time in a long time, I feel like I *am* home."

Chapter 17

"Lightyear!" **Command**er Burnside said **stern**ly.

Buzz stood at **attention** as the commander **pace**d in front of him. The Space **Ranger** was prepared for a **dressing-down** that was twenty-two years in the making.

"You **abscond**ed with Star Command **property**, stole an **experimental spacecraft**, and **defied** a direct order from your commander. I ought to throw you in the stockade.[1]"

Buzz **hung his head**. Commander Burnside was right—his **conduct** had been **unbecoming** of a Space Ranger. Even if he

---

1 **stockade** 영창. 군법을 위반한 군인들을 가두기 위해 군대 내에 설치한 감옥.

had saved the entire T'Kani Prime **colony** from **annihilation**.

"But I have other plans for you," Burnside told Buzz.

Burnside **gesture**d to the de**activate**d robots on the ground. "We want you to start a new version of the Space Ranger **Corps**: Universe Protection **Division**. You're going to be a Space Ranger again, Buzz. You can hand-select your team from the very best of the Zap **Patrol** and train them **to your liking**."

The **security** patrol **salute**d Buzz. "Hup, hup!"

Buzz smiled as he took in the news. To be a Space Ranger again, out among the stars. It felt like coming home. But his smile quickly **fade**d.

"Well, that's very kind of you, sir," he said. "But . . . I'm afraid I'm going to have to **decline**."

Everyone looked at Buzz in shock.

"I already have my team," Buzz said, turning to look at Izzy, Darby, Mo, and Sox.

The doors of the **launch bay** opened, **reveal**ing a team of Space Rangers **outfit**ted in new, **state-of-the-art** suits. As members of the Universe Protection Division of Space Ranger Corps, this elite group protected the **galaxy** from any **sworn** enemies of the **Galactic Alliance**. They were headed to gamma quadrant[2] section four to **investigate** an unknown signal.

Darby held up her arm blaster. "I can't believe I'm allowed to carry this. I wish I had two of them."

"You got a clean record[3] and you're free and **arm**ed," Mo said. "How are you still **complain**ing?"

"I got off for good behavior, not good **attitude**," Darby replied.

"You know, I never wear pants," Sox said, looking at his new space **vest**, "but suddenly it feels **weird** not to be wearing pants. Does it look weird without pants?"

"Nah, you look good," Mo **reassure**d him.

As the group approached a **statue** of Commander Alisha Hawthorne, Izzy stopped and **puff**ed out her **chest** like she once did as a child in her homemade Space Ranger costume.

"Look, Grandma. I'm a Space Ranger, too. Just like you."

---

2 **gamma quadrant** 감마 사분면. 공상 과학 소설이나 영화에서 은하계를 크게 4개로 나눈 구역 중 하나로, 감마 분면은 미지의 영역을 의미한다.
3 **clean record** 전과(前科)나 범죄 경력이 없는 깨끗한 이력을 의미한다.

"She really is," Buzz said quietly to Alisha. He gave her a salute and caught up to his team.

They prepared for launch with Buzz in the pilot's seat. Behind him, Darby and Mo were **strap**ped in, ready for **takeoff**. Sox was positioned in a perfect-fitting **compartment** on top of the **console**, able to plug in directly to the computer. And Izzy was the copilot at Buzz's side.

"Do we have everything?" Buzz asked. "**Munition**s?"

"Check," Darby said.

"**Sustenance**?"

"I brought sandwiches," Mo replied.

Buzz turned to Izzy, **concern**ed. "I don't know. Am I forgetting anything?"

Izzy smiled and shook her head confidently. "I think we're ready."

Buzz **nod**ded and **insert**ed IVAN into the control console.

"Hello," said IVAN. "I am your **Internal** Voice-Activated **Navigator**."

Buzz smiled. "Good to have you back, IVAN."

A message from the control room came over the radio. "Captain Lightyear, ready for launch."

"IVAN," Buzz said, "**initiate** hyperlaunch."

"Certainly," IVAN replied. "Hyperlaunch initiating."

The ship's engines **flare**d to life as the launch **sequence** initiated.

"All right, Space Rangers," Buzz **declare**d. "Here we go."

Izzy held out a finger to Buzz with a knowing smile. "To **infinity** . . ."

Buzz **tap**ped a finger to hers. ". . . and beyond."

CONTENTS

QR코드를 스마트폰으로 인식하여 『LIGHTYEAR』
오디오북과 한국어 번역 파일을 확인해 보세요!

<토이 스토리> 시리즈의 우주 영웅,
버즈 라이트이어의 또 다른 이야기!

전설적인 스페이스 레인저 버즈 라이트이어는 자신의 사령관이자 가장 친한 친구인 앨리샤 호손을 비롯한 많은 동료들과 함께 우주를 누비며 특별 임무를 수행하는 중입니다. 하지만 버즈의 실수로 그들은 지구로부터 수백만 광년 떨어진 적대적인 외계 행성에 모두 고립되고 맙니다. 버즈는 자신의 실수를 바로잡고 동료들을 집으로 돌려보내는 것을 자신의 절대적인 임무로 받아들입니다. 그리고 이어지는 실패에 굴하지 않고 수십 년에 걸쳐 시험 비행을 계속하죠. 하지만 버즈가 홀로 우주 시공간을 넘나드는 동안, 외계 행성에 남은 동료들의 시간은 버즈를 기다려 주지 않고 흐릅니다.
마침내 버즈는 귀여운 로봇 고양이 삭스, 의욕만 넘치는 좌충우돌 신입 대원들과 한 팀을 이룹니다. 대원들 중에는 할머니를 쏙 빼닮은, 앨리샤의 손녀인 이지도 있죠. 그리고 노익장 폭발 전문가 다비와 허술하고 수수께끼 같은 모도 있습니다. 버즈와 팀원들이 드디어 임무를 완수하려는 찰나, 무시무시한 로봇 군대를 거느린 저그가 나타나 버즈의 팀과 그들의 행성을 위협합니다. 과연 저그의 정체는 무엇일까요? 버즈와 동료들은 각종 위협을 물리치고 무사히 행성을 탈출할 수 있을까요?
우주를 배경으로 펼쳐지는 버즈와 동료들의 흥미진진한 모험과 우정의 이야기, <버즈 라이트이어>를 지금 영화로 읽는 영어원서를 통해 읽어 보세요!

한국인을 위한 맞춤형 영어원서!

원서 읽기는 모두가 인정하는 최고의 영어 공부법입니다. 하지만 영어 구사력이 뛰어나지 않은 보통 영어 학습자들에게는 원서 읽기를 선뜻 시작하기가 부담되는 것도 사실이지요.

이 책은 영어 초보자들도 쉽게 원서 읽기를 시작하고, 꾸준한 읽기를 통해 '영어 원서 읽기 습관'을 형성할 수 있도록 만들어진 책입니다. 남녀노소 누구나 좋아할 만한 내용의 원서를 기반으로 내용 이해와 영어 실력 향상을 위한 다양한 콘텐츠를 덧붙였고, 리스닝과 낭독 훈련에 활용할 수 있는 오디오북까지 함께 제공하여, 원서를 부담 없이 읽으면서 자연스럽게 영어 실력이 향상되도록 도와줍니다.

특히 원서와 워크북을 분권하여 휴대와 학습이 효과적으로 이루어지도록 배려했습니다. 일반 원서에서 찾아볼 수 없는 특장점으로, 워크북과 오디오북을 적절히 활용하면 더욱 쉽고 재미있게 영어 실력을 향상시킬 수 있습니다. ('원서'와 '워크북' 및 '오디오북 MP3 파일'의 3가지 패키지가 이상 없이 갖추어져 있는지 다시 한번 확인해 보세요!)

이런 분들께 강력 추천합니다!

- 영어원서 읽기를 처음 시작하는 독자
- 쉽고 재미있는 원서를 찾고 있는 영어 학습자
- 영화 『버즈 라이트이어』를 재미있게 보신 분
- 특목고 입시를 준비하는 초·중학생
- 토익 600~750점, 고등학교 상위권 수준의 영어 학습자
- 엄마표 영어를 위한 교재를 찾고 있는 부모님

이 책의 구성

본문 텍스트

내용이 담긴 본문입니다.
원어민이 읽는 일반 원서와 같은 텍스트지만, 암기해야 할 중요 어휘들은 볼드체로 표시되어 있습니다. 이 어휘들은 지금 들고 계신 워크북에 챕터별로 정리되어 있습니다.

학습 심리학 연구 결과에 따르면, 한 단어씩 따로 외우는 단어 암기는 거의 효과가 없다고 합니다. 대신 단어를 제대로 외우기 위해서는 문맥(Context) 속에서 단어를 암기해야 하며, 한 단어당 문맥 속에서 15번 이상 마주칠 때 완벽하게 암기할 수 있다고 합니다.

이 책의 본문은 중요 어휘를 볼드로 강조하여, 문맥 속의 단어들을 더 확실히 인지(Word Cognition in Context)하도록 돕고 있습니다. 또한 대부분의 중요한 단어들은 다른 챕터에서도 반복해서 등장하기 때문에 이 책을 읽는 것만으로도 자연스럽게 어휘력을 향상시킬 수 있습니다.

또한 본문에는 내용 이해를 돕기 위해 '각주'가 첨가되어 있습니다. 각주는 굳이 암기할 필요는 없지만, 알아 두면 내용을 더 깊이 있게 이해할 수 있어 원서를 읽는 재미가 배가됩니다.

워크북(Workbook)의 구성

Check Your Reading Speed

해당 챕터의 단어 수가 기록되어 있어, 리딩 속도를 측정할 수 있습니다. 특히 리딩 속도를 중시하는 독자들이 유용하게 사용할 수 있습니다.

Build Your Vocabulary

본문에 볼드 표시되어 있는 단어들이 정리되어 있습니다. 리딩 전, 후에 반복해서 보면 원서를 더욱 쉽게 읽을 수 있고, 어휘력도 빠르게 향상됩니다.

단어는 〈빈도 − 스펠링 − 발음기호 − 품사 − 한글 뜻 − 영문 뜻〉 순서로 표기되어 있으며 빈도 표시(★)가 많을수록 필수 어휘입니다. 반복 등장하는 단어는 빈도 대신 '복습'으로 표기되어 있습니다. 품사는 아래와 같이 표기했습니다.

n. 명사 ｜ a. 형용사 ｜ ad. 부사 ｜ v. 동사

conj. 접속사 ｜ prep. 전치사 ｜ int. 감탄사 ｜ idiom 숙어 및 관용구

Comprehension Quiz

간단한 퀴즈를 통해 읽은 내용에 대한 이해력을 점검해 볼 수 있습니다.

영어원서 읽기, 이렇게 시작해 보세요!!

아래와 같이 프리뷰(Preview) → 리딩(Reading) → 리뷰(Review) 세 단계를 거치면서 원서를 읽으면, 더욱 효과적으로 영어 실력을 향상할 수 있습니다!

1. 프리뷰(Preview): 오늘 읽을 내용을 먼저 점검한다!

- 워크북을 통해 오늘 읽을 Chapter에 나와 있는 단어들을 쭉 훑어봅니다. 어떤 단어들이 나오는지, 내가 아는 단어와 모르는 단어가 어떤 것들이 있는지 가벼운 마음으로 살펴봅니다.
- 평소처럼 하나하나 쓰면서 암기하려고 하지는 마세요! 그렇게 해서는 원서를 읽기도 전에 지쳐 쓰러져버릴 것입니다. 익숙하지 않은 단어들을 주의 깊게 보되, 어차피 리딩을 하면서 점차 익숙해질 단어라는 것을 잊지 말고 빠르게 훑어봅니다.
- 뒤 Chapter로 갈수록 '복습'이라고 표시된 단어들이 늘어나는 것을 알 수 있습니다. '복습' 단어인데도 여전히 익숙하지 않다면 더욱 신경을 써서 봐야겠죠? 매일매일 꾸준히 읽는다면, 익숙한 단어들이 점점 많아진다는 것을 몸으로 느낄 수 있습니다.

2. 리딩(Reading): 내용에 집중하며 빠르게 읽어 가자!

- 프리뷰를 마친 후 바로 리딩을 시작합니다. 방금 살펴봤던 어휘들을 문장 속에서 다시 만나게 되는데 이 과정에서 단어의 쓰임새와 어감을 자연스럽게 익히게 됩니다.
- 모르는 단어, 이해 가지 않는 문장이 나오더라도 멈추지 말고 전체적인 맥락을 잡아 가면서 스피디하게 읽어 가세요. 특히 영화를 먼저 보고 책을 읽으면 맥락을 통해 읽을 수 있어 훨씬 수월합니다.
- 이해 가지 않는 문장들은 따로 표시를 하되, 일단 넘어가서 계속 읽는 것이 좋습니다. 뒷부분을 읽다 보면 자연히 이해가 되는 경우도 있고, 정 이해가 되지 않는 부분은 리딩을 마친 이후에 따로 리뷰하는 시간을 가지면 됩니다. 문제집을 풀듯이 모든 문장을 분석하면서 원서를 읽는 것이 아니라, 리딩할 때는 리딩에만, 리뷰할 때는 리뷰에만 집중하는 것이 필요합니다.
- 볼드 처리된 단어의 의미가 궁금하더라도, 워크북을 바로 펼치지 마세요. 정 궁금하다면 한 번씩 참고하는 것도 나쁘진 않지만, 워크북과 원서를 번갈아

보면서 읽는 것은 리딩의 흐름을 끊고 단어 하나하나에 집착하는 좋지 않은 리딩 습관을 만들 수 있습니다.

- 초보자라면 분당 150단어의 리딩 속도를 목표로 잡아서 리딩을 합니다. 분당 150단어는 원어민이 말하는 속도로, 영어 학습자들이 리스닝과 스피킹으로 넘어가기 위해 가장 기초적으로 달성해야 하는 단계입니다. 분당 50~80단어 정도의 낮은 리딩 속도를 가지고 있는 경우는 대부분 영어 실력이 부족해서라 기보다 '잘못된 리딩 습관'을 가지고 있어서 그렇습니다. 이해력이 조금 떨어진 다고 하더라도 분당 150단어까지는 속도에 대한 긴장감을 놓치지 말고 스피디하게 읽어 나가도록 하세요.

- 이미 150단어 이상의 리딩 속도에 도달한 상태라면, 각자의 상황에 맞게 원서를 보다 다양한 방식으로 활용해 보세요. 이에 대한 자세한 조언이 워크북 말미에 실려 있습니다.

3. 리뷰(Review): 이해력을 점검하고 꼼꼼하게 다시 살펴보자!

- 해당 Chapter의 Comprehension Quiz를 통해 이해력을 점검해 봅니다.
- 오늘 만난 어휘도 다시 한번 복습합니다. 읽으면서 중요하다고 생각했던 단어를 연습장에 써 보면서 꼼꼼하게 외우는 것도 좋습니다.
- 이해가 되지 않는다고 표시해 뒀던 부분도 주의 깊게 분석해 봅니다. 다시 한번 문장을 꼼꼼히 읽고, 어떤 이유에서 이해가 되지 않았는지 생각해 봅니다. 따로 메모를 남기거나 노트를 작성하는 것도 좋은 방법입니다.
- 사실 꼼꼼히 리뷰하는 것은 매우 고된 과정입니다. 원서를 읽고 리뷰하는 시간을 가지는 것은 영어 실력 향상에 많은 도움이 되긴 하나, 이 과정을 철저히 지키려다가 원서 읽기의 재미를 반감시키는 것은 바람직하지 않습니다. 그럴 때는 차라리 리뷰를 가볍게 하는 것이 좋을 수 있습니다. '내용에 빠져서 재미있게', 문제집에서는 상상도 못할 '많은 양'을 읽으면서, 매일매일 조금씩 꾸준히 실력을 향상하는 것이 원서를 활용하는 기본적인 방법이며, 영어 공부의 왕도입니다. 문제집 풀듯이 원서 읽기를 시도하고 접근해서는 실패할 수밖에 없습니다.

1 & 2

1. **What did Buzz think of Commander Alisha Hawthorne?**
   A. She was a nice teacher.
   B. She teased him too much.
   C. She followed the rules too strictly.
   D. She was a good friend.

2. **Why didn't Buzz take the rookie with him at first?**
   A. He did not think it would be helpful.
   B. He thought the rookie was with Alisha.
   C. He wanted the rookie to take a rest.
   D. He was worried that the mission was dangerous.

3. How did Buzz help the rookie on the T'Kani Prime planet?

   A. By saving him from vines and a bug

   B. By teaching him how to use a laser

   C. By protecting him in the engine room

   D. By pulling him out of the mud

4. Why didn't Buzz use the ship's autopilot?

   A. He wanted the rookie to try it instead.

   B. The autopilot was not working.

   C. He thought he could fly the ship himself.

   D. Alisha told him not to use it.

5. What happened because of the crash?

   A. The wheels of the ship came off.

   B. Alisha lost her wrist laser.

   C. The fuel cell got broken.

   D. Some crew members got injured.

CHAPTER 1

Check Your Reading Speed
1분에 몇 단어를 읽는지 리딩 속도를 측정해 보세요.

$$\frac{1{,}087 \text{ words}}{\text{reading time ( ) sec}} \times 60 = (\ ) \text{ WPM}$$

Build Your Vocabulary

haze [heiz] n. 희부연 것; 실안개; v. 흐릿해지다 (hazy a. 흐릿한)
Hazy weather conditions are those in which things are difficult to see, because of light mist, hot air, or dust.

⚹ **mist** [mist] n. 엷은 안개; v. 부옇게 되다; 눈물이 맺히다
Mist consists of a large number of tiny drops of water in the air, which make it difficult to see very far.

⋆ **alien** [éiljən] a. 외계의; 생경한; 이질적인; n. 외계인
Alien means coming from another world, such as an outer space.

⋆ **swamp** [swamp] n. 늪, 습지; v. (일 등이) 쇄도하다 (swampland n. (넓은) 습지대)
Swampland is an area of land that is always very wet.

⋆ **obscure** [əbskjúər] v. 보기 어렵게 하다; a. 잘 알려져 있지 않은; 모호한
If one thing obscures another, it prevents it from being seen or heard properly.

vegetation [vèdʒətéiʃən] n. 초목, 식물
Plants, trees, and flowers can be referred to as vegetation.

lurk [ləːrk] v. (불쾌한 일·위험이) 도사리다; (나쁜 짓을 하려고) 숨어 있다
If something such as a danger, doubt, or fear lurks somewhere, it exists but is not obvious or easily recognized.

slither [slíðər] v. (매끄럽게) 스르르 나아가다; 미끄러지듯 나아가다; n. 스르르 미끄러짐
If an animal such as a snake slithers, it moves along in a curving way.

ranger [réindʒər] n. 경비 대원; 기습 공격대원
A ranger is an armed guard who patrols a region.

footprint [fútprìnt] n. (사람·동물의) 발자국
A footprint is a mark in the shape of a foot that a person or animal makes in or on a surface.

terrestrial [təréstriəl] **a.** 지구(상)의; 육지의; 현세의; **n.** 인간
(extraterrestrial **a.** 지구 밖의, 외계의)
Extraterrestrial means happening, existing, or coming from somewhere beyond the planet Earth.

goop [guːp] **n.** 끈적거리는 것
Goop is a thick, slimy substance.

⋆ **wrist** [rist] **n.** 손목, 팔목
Your wrist is the part of your body between your hand and your arm which bends when you move your hand.

⋆ **log** [lɔːg] **n.** (비행·항해 등의) 일지, 기록; 통나무; **v.** 일지에 기록하다; 비행하다, 항해하다
A log is an official written account of what happens each day, for example on board a ship.

galactic [gəlǽktik] **a.** 은하계의, 성운의; 거대한, 막대한 (intergalactic **a.** 은하계 사이의)
Intergalactic means relating to or situated between two or more galaxies.

⋆ **survey** [sərvéi] **v.** 둘러보다, 바라보다; 조사하다; **n.** 조사
If you survey something, you look at or consider the whole of it carefully.

⋆ **expanse** [ikspǽns] **n.** 넓게 퍼진 공간; 팽창, 확장
An expanse of something, usually sea, sky, or land, is a very large amount of it.

⋆ **keen** [kiːn] **a.** 예리한, 예민한; 강한, 깊은; 열정적인
If you have a keen eye or ear, you are able to notice things that are difficult to detect.

⋆ **gaze** [geiz] **n.** 응시, (눈여겨보는) 시선; **v.** (가만히) 응시하다, 바라보다
You can talk about someone's gaze as a way of describing how they are looking at something, especially when they are looking steadily at it.

nuance [njúːaːns] **n.** 미묘한 차이, 뉘앙스; **v.** 미묘한 차이를 덧붙이다, 뉘앙스를 띠게 하다
A nuance is a small difference in sound, feeling, appearance, or meaning.

⋆ **overlook** [òuvərlúk] **v.** 못 보고 넘어가다, 간과하다; 못 본 체하다; (건물 등이) 바라보다
If you overlook a fact or problem, you do not notice it, or do not realize how important it is.

⋆ **detect** [ditékt] **v.** 발견하다, 알아내다, 감지하다
To detect something means to find it or discover that it is present somewhere by using equipment or making an investigation.

uncharted [ʌntʃáːrtid] **a.** 미지의, 잘 알지 못하는; 지도에 표시되어 있지 않은
If you describe a situation, experience, or activity as uncharted territory or waters, you mean that it is new or unfamiliar.

detour [díːtuər] n. 둘러 가는 길, 우회로; v. 둘러 가다, 우회하다
If you make a detour on a journey, you go by a route which is not the shortest way.

⁕ **investigate** [invéstəgèit] v. 조사하다, 살피다; 연구하다
To investigate is to examine, study, or inquire into systematically.

⁕ **initial** [iníʃəl] a. 처음의, 초기의; n. 이름의 첫 글자
You use initial to describe something that happens at the beginning of a process.

⁑ **evaluate** [ivǽljuèit] v. 평가하다, 어림하다 (evaluation n. 평가)
Your evaluation about something or someone refers to your judgment about them, for example about how good or bad they are.

⁕ **assess** [əsés] v. 평가하다, 가늠하다; (특성·자질 등을) 재다
When you assess a person, thing, or situation, you consider them in order to make a judgment about them.

⁕ **crew** [kruː] n. (함께 일을 하는) 팀, 조; (배·항공기의) 승무원; v. 승무원을 하다
A crew is a group of people with special technical skills who work together on a task or project.

⁕ **ghost** [goust] n. 아주 적은 양; 유령, 귀신; 기억, 환영; v. 소리 없이 움직이다
If there is a ghost of something, that thing is so faint or weak that it hardly exists.

⁕ **venture** [vénʧər] v. (위험을 무릅쓰고) 가다; 조심스럽게 말하다; n. (사업상의) 모험
If you venture somewhere, you go somewhere that might be dangerous.

⁕ **countless** [káuntlis] a. 셀 수 없는, 무수한
Countless means very many.

terrain [təréin] n. 지역, 지형
Terrain is used to refer to an area of land or a type of land when you are considering its physical features.

seasoned [síːznd] a. (사람이) 경험 많은, 노련한; (식품이) 양념을 한, 조미료를 넣은
You can use seasoned to describe a person who has a lot of experience of something.

teem with idiom ~으로 풍부하다; ~이 많이 있다
If you say that a place is teeming with certain things, you mean that it is crowded with them.

⁕ **potential** [pəténʃəl] a. 가능성이 있는, 잠재적인; n. 잠재력; 가능성
You use potential to say that someone or something is capable of developing into the particular kind of person or thing mentioned.

‡ further [fə́:rðər] v. 발전시키다, 성공시키다; a. 추가의; ad. 더; 더 멀리에; 게다가
If you further something, you help it to progress, to be successful, or to be achieved.

‡ press [pres] v. 꾹 밀어 넣다; 누르다; (무엇에) 바짝 대다; n. 언론
To press something into something else means to put it into that thing by pushing it.

bog [bag] n. 습지, 수렁; v. 꼼짝 못 하게 되다, 수렁에 빠지다
A bog is an area of land which is very wet and muddy.

squelch [skwelʧ] v. 철벅거리다; 억누르다, 진압하다; n. 철벅거리는 소리
To squelch means to make a wet, sucking sound, like the sound you make when you are walking on wet, muddy ground.

unsettle [ʌnsétəl] v. (사람을) 불안하게 하다, 동요시키다 (unsettling a. 불안하게 하는)
If you describe something as unsettling, you mean that it makes you feel rather worried or uncertain.

‡ resist [rizíst] v. 저항하다; 참다, 견디다; 굴하지 않다 (resistance n. 저항)
Resistance refers to a force which slows down a moving object.

★ stable [steibl] a. 안정된, 안정적인; 차분한; n. 마구간 (unstable a. 불안정한)
You can describe something as unstable if it is likely to change suddenly, especially if this creates difficulty or danger.

readout [rí:daut] n. (정보의) 해독, 판독; v. 정보를 송신하다
If an electronic measuring device gives you a readout, it displays information about the level of something such as a speed, height, or sound.

‡ intelligent [intéləʤənt] a. 지능이 있는; 총명한, 똑똑한
Something that is intelligent has the ability to think and understand instead of doing things automatically or by instinct.

‡ interrupt [intərʌ́pt] v. 중단시키다; (말·행동을) 방해하다; 차단하다
If someone or something interrupts a process or activity, they stop it for a period of time.

★ whirl [hwə́:rl] v. 빙그르르 돌다; (마음·생각 등이) 혼란스럽다; n. 빙빙 돌기
If something or someone whirls around or if you whirl them around, they move around or turn around in circles.

‡ command [kəmǽnd] v. 지휘하다; 명령하다; n. 지휘; 명령; 사령부 (commander n. 사령관)
A commander is an officer in charge of a military operation or organization.

narrate [nǽreit] v. 이야기하다, 말하다
If you narrate a story, you tell it from your own point of view.

disapprove [dìsəprúːv] v. 탐탁찮아 하다, 못마땅해 하다 (disapproving a. 탐탁찮아 하는)
A disapproving action or expression shows that you do not approve of something or someone.

tease [tiːz] v. 놀리다, 장난하다; 못살게 굴다; n. 장난, 놀림
To tease someone means to make jokes about someone, usually in a light-hearted way.

strict [strikt] a. 엄격한; 엄밀한
If a person in authority is strict, they regard many actions as unacceptable and do not allow them.

by the book idiom (엄격히) 규칙대로
If you do something by the book, you do it exactly as the rules tell you. A by-the-book person does something exactly according to the rules.

cadet [kədét] n. (경찰·군대 등의) 간부 후보생
A cadet is a young man or woman who is being trained in the armed services or the police.

drill [dril] n. (군사) 훈련; 반복 연습; 드릴; v. 훈련시키다, 연습시키다; 드릴로 구멍을 뚫다
A drill is repeated training for a group of people, especially soldiers, so that they can do something quickly and efficiently.

memorize [méməràiz] v. 기억하다, 암기하다
If you memorize something, you learn it so that you can remember it exactly.

code [koud] n. 규정, 법규; (컴퓨터) 코드; 암호, 부호; v. 암호로 쓰다
A code is a set of rules about how people should behave or about how something must be done.

second nature idiom (습관으로 굳어진) 제2의 천성
If a way of behaving is second nature to you, you do it almost without thinking because it is easy for you or obvious to you.

eventually [ivénʃuəli] ad. 결국, 마침내
Eventually means at the end of a situation or process or as the final result of it.

ultimate [Áltəmət] a. 궁극적인, 최종적인; 최고의, 최상의; n. 극치
You use ultimate to describe the final result or aim of a long series of events.

accomplish [əkÁmpliʃ] v. 성취하다, 완수하다, 해내다 (accomplishment n. 성취)
An accomplishment is something remarkable that has been done or achieved.

* **corps** [kɔːr] n. (특수한 임무를 띤) 부대; 군단; (특정한 활동을 하는) 단체, 집단
A Corps is a part of the army which has special duties.

* **shrug** [ʃrʌg] v. (어깨를) 으쓱하다; n. 어깨를 으쓱하기
If you shrug, you raise your shoulders to show that you are not interested in something or that you do not know or care about something.

activate [ǽktəvèit] v. 작동시키다; 활성화시키다
If a device or process is activated, something causes it to start working.

* **blade** [bleid] n. (칼·도구 등의) 날; 풀잎
The blade of a knife, axe, or saw is the flat sharp part that is used for cutting.

* **slice** [slais] v. 헤치고 나아가다; 자르다; 베다; n. (얇게 썬) 조각; 부분, 몫
If something slices through a substance, it moves through it quickly, like a knife.

gnarl [naːrl] v. 비틀다; 마디지게 하다; n. (나무) 마디, 옹이 (gnarled a. 울퉁불퉁하고 비틀린)
A gnarled tree or plant is twisted and strangely shaped.

* **patch** [pætʃ] n. 부분; (덧대는 용도의) 조각; 안대; v. 덧대다, 때우다
A patch on a surface is a part of it which is different in appearance from the area around it.

* **vine** [vain] n. 덩굴 식물; 포도나무
A vine is a plant with long thin stems that attach themselves to other plants, trees, or buildings.

forge [fɔːrdʒ] v. 서서히 나아가다, 착실히 전진하다; 위조하다; 꾸며 내다; (쇠를) 벼리다
To forge is to move at a steady and persevering pace.

* **glance** [glæns] v. 흘낏 보다; 대충 훑어보다; n. 흘낏 봄
If you glance at something or someone, you look at them very quickly and then look away again immediately.

* **transport** [trænspɔ́ːrt] n. 수송; 운송 수단; v. 수송하다; 실어 나르다
Transport is the activity of taking goods or people from one place to another.

* **outline** [áutlàin] n. 윤곽; v. 윤곽을 보여 주다; 개요를 서술하다
The outline of something is its general shape, especially when it cannot be clearly seen.

blur [bləːr] n. 흐릿한 형체; (기억이) 희미한 것; v. 흐릿해지다; 모호해지다
(blurry a. 흐릿한, 모호한)
A blurry shape is one that has an unclear outline.

bulbous [bʌ́lbəs] **a.** (보기 싫게) 둥글납작한; 구근의, 구근 모양의
Something that is bulbous is round and fat in a rather ugly way.

hoist [hɔist] **v.** 들어 올리다, 끌어올리다; **n.** 끌어올리기
If you hoist something heavy somewhere, you lift it or pull it up there.

★ **cluster** [klʌ́stər] **n.** 무리, 집단; **v.** 무리를 이루다, (소규모로) 모이다
A cluster of people or things is a small group of them close together.

rookie [rúki] **n.** 신참, 초보자; (스포츠 팀의) 신인 선수
A rookie is someone who has just started doing a job and does not have much experience, especially someone who has just joined the army or police force.

hack [hæk] **v.** (마구·거칠게) 자르다, 난도질하다; (컴퓨터) 해킹하다
If you hack something or hack at it, you cut it with strong, rough strokes using a sharp tool such as an axe or knife.

★ **complicate** [kámpləkèit] **v.** 복잡하게 하다 (overcomplicate v. 과하게 복잡하게 하다)
To overcomplicate something means to make it more difficult to understand or deal with, often in an excessive way.

be better off idiom (상태가) 더 낫다; 더 부자이다
If you say someone is better off, you mean that they are or would be happier or more satisfied if they were in a particular position or did a particular thing.

‡ **notice** [nóutis] **v.** 알아채다, 인지하다; 주의하다; **n.** 신경 씀, 주목, 알아챔
If you notice something or someone, you become aware of them.

‡ **figure** [fígjər] **n.** (멀리서 흐릿하게 보이는) 사람; 수치; (중요한) 인물; **v.** 생각하다; 중요하다
You describe someone as a figure when you cannot see them clearly.

‡ **inch** [intʃ] **v.** 조금씩 움직이다; **n.** 조금, 약간
To inch somewhere or to inch something somewhere means to move there very slowly and carefully, or to make something do this.

★ **cautious** [kɔ́ːʃəs] **a.** 조심스러운, 신중한 (cautiously ad. 조심스럽게)
If someone behaves cautiously, they act very carefully in order to avoid possible danger.

muck [mʌk] **n.** 진흙, 진창; 배설물
Muck is dirt or some other unpleasant substance.

‡ **awkward** [ɔ́ːkwərd] **a.** 어색한; (처리하기) 곤란한; 불편한
Someone who feels awkward behaves in a shy or embarrassed way.

gangly [gǽŋgli] **a.** 호리호리하게 큰
If you describe someone as gangly, you mean that they are tall and thin and have a slightly awkward or clumsy manner.

dress-up [drés-ʌp] **n.** 변장
Dress-up refers to a game or activity that involves dressing up in special clothing or costumes.

⋆ **meek** [miːk] **a.** 온순한, 온화한
If you describe a person as meek, you think that they are gentle and quiet, and likely to do what other people say.

protocol [próutəkɔːl] **n.** (군대·궁전 등의) 의례, 관습
Protocol is a system of rules about the correct way to act in formal situations.

‡ **insist** [insíst] **v.** 고집하다, 주장하다, 우기다
If you insist that something is the case, you say so very firmly and refuse to say otherwise, even though other people do not believe you.

⋆ **judgment** [dʒʌ́dʒmənt] **n.** 판단, 평가; 재판, 심판; 판단력
A judgment is an opinion that you have or express after thinking carefully about something.

⋆ **stare** [stɛər] **v.** 빤히 쳐다보다, 응시하다; **n.** 빤히 쳐다보기, 응시
If you stare at someone or something, you look at them for a long time.

pitiful [pítifəl] **a.** 측은한, 가련한; 한심한
Someone or something that is pitiful is so sad, weak, or small that you feel sorry for them.

⋆ **groan** [groun] **v.** (고통·짜증으로) 신음 소리를 내다, 끙끙거리다; **n.** 신음, 끙 하는 소리
If you groan, you make a long, low sound because you are in pain, or because you are upset or unhappy about something.

squint [skwint] **v.** 눈을 가늘게 뜨고 보다; 사시이다; **n.** 잠깐 봄; 사시
If you squint at something, you look at it with your eyes partly closed.

make heads or tails of idiom ~을 알아보다, ~을 이해하다, ~을 구별하다
When you make heads or tails of something or someone, you attempt to understand them.

‡ **stamp** [stæmp] **v.** (도장·스탬프 등을) 찍다; 밟다; **n.** 도장; (발을) 쿵쾅거리기
If you stamp a mark or word on an object, you press them onto the object using a stamp or other device.

* galaxy [gǽləksi] n. 은하계; 은하수
A galaxy is an extremely large group of stars and planets that extends over many billions of light years.

huff [hʌf] v. (화가 나서) 씩씩거리다; n. 발끈 화를 냄
If you huff, you indicate that you are annoyed or offended about something.

triumphant [traiʌ́mfənt] a. 의기양양한; 크게 성공한, 큰 승리를 거둔
A triumphant event is one in which someone has been successful or has won a victory.

‡ chest [ʧest] n. 가슴, 흉부; 상자, 궤
Your chest is the top part of the front of your body where your ribs, lungs, and heart are.

* panel [pænl] n. 계기판; 판; 패널, 자문단
A panel is a board or surface which contains switches and controls to operate a machine or piece of equipment.

* fade [feid] v. 서서히 사라지다; (색깔이) 바래다, 희미해지다
When the volume of a sound fades, it decreases slowly.

* sway [swei] n. (전후·좌우로) 흔들림; v. (전후·좌우로) 흔들리다; (마음을) 동요시키다
A sway refers to a swinging or leaning movement.

* mock [mak] v. 놀리다, 조롱하다; 무시하다; a. 거짓된, 가짜의
If someone mocks you, they show or pretend that they think you are foolish or inferior, for example by saying something funny about you, or by imitating your behavior.

* amused [əmjúːzd] a. 재미있어하는, 즐거워하는 (unamused a. 재미없어하는)
When someone is unamused, they are not entertained, diverted, or laughing.

supportive [səpɔ́ːrtiv] a. 지원하는, 도와주는, 힘을 주는
If you are supportive, you are kind and helpful to someone at a difficult or unhappy time in their life.

rebuke [ribjúːk] v. 꾸짖다, 비난하다; n. 비난, 힐책
If you rebuke someone, you speak severely to them because they have said or done something that you do not approve of.

ominous [ámənəs] a. 불길한, 나쁜 징조의 (ominously ad. 불길하게, 기분 나쁘게)
When someone or something moves ominously, it worries you because it makes you think that something unpleasant is going to happen.

Check Your Reading Speed
1분에 몇 단어를 읽는지 리딩 속도를 측정해 보세요.

$$\frac{1,405 \text{ words}}{\text{reading time ( ) sec}} \times 60 = (\quad) \text{ WPM}$$

Build Your Vocabulary

vine [vain] n. 덩굴 식물; 포도나무
A vine is a plant with long thin stems that attach themselves to other plants, trees, or buildings.

swamp [swamp] n. 늪, 습지; v. (일 등이) 쇄도하다 (swampland n. (넓은) 습지대)
Swampland is an area of land that is always very wet.

spring [spriŋ] v. (sprang-sprung) 갑자기 ~하다; 휙 움직이다; 튀다; n. 생기, 활기; 봄; 샘
If things or people spring into action or spring to life, they suddenly start being active or suddenly come into existence.

squelch [skwelʧ] n. 철벅거리는 소리; v. 철벅거리다; 억누르다, 진압하다 (squelchy a. 철벅거리는)
Something that is squelchy makes a wet, sucking sound, like the sound you make when you are walking on wet, muddy ground.

terrestrial [təréstriəl] a. 지구(상)의; 육지의; 현세의; n. 인간
(extraterrestrial a. 지구 밖의, 외계의)
Extraterrestrial means happening, existing, or coming from somewhere beyond the planet Earth.

hum [hʌm] n. 웅성거리는 소리; v. 웅웅거리다; (노래를) 흥얼거리다
Hum refers to a low and continuous murmuring sound.

vibrate [váibreit] v. 진동하다, (가늘게) 떨다
If something vibrates or if you vibrate it, it shakes with repeated small, quick movements.

haze [heiz] n. 희부연 것; 실안개; v. 흐릿해지다 (hazy a. 흐릿한)
Hazy weather conditions are those in which things are difficult to see, because of light mist, hot air, or dust.

mist [mist] n. 엷은 안개; v. 부옇게 되다; 눈물이 맺히다
Mist consists of a large number of tiny drops of water in the air, which make it difficult to see very far.

★ **swarm** [swɔ:rm] **n.** (곤충의) 떼, 무리; 군중; **v.** 무리를 지어 다니다; 많이 모여들다
A swarm of bees or other insects is a large group of them flying together.

★ **descend** [disénd] **v.** 불시에 습격하다; 내려오다, 내려가다; (아래로) 경사지다
To descend means to swoop or pounce down as in a sudden attack.

★ **whip** [hwip] **v.** 격렬하게 움직이다; 휙 빼내다; **n.** 채찍
If something or someone whips somewhere, they move there or go there very quickly.

‡ **realize** [ríːəlàiz] **v.** 깨닫다, 알아차리다; 실현하다, 달성하다
If you realize that something is true, you become aware of that fact or understand it.

‡ **flash** [flæʃ] **n.** (감정이나 생각이) 갑자기 떠오름; 번쩍임; **v.** 불현듯 들다; 번쩍이다; 휙 나타나다
A flash of something is a particular feeling or idea that suddenly comes into your mind or shows on your face.

★ **alarm** [əláːrm] **n.** 불안, 공포; **v.** 불안하게 하다
Alarm is a feeling of fear or anxiety that something unpleasant or dangerous might happen.

‡ **suck** [sʌk] **v.** (특정한 방향으로) 빨아들이다; 빨아 먹다; **n.** 빨기, 빨아 먹기
If something sucks a liquid, gas, or object in a particular direction, it draws it there with a powerful force.

복습 **command** [kəmǽnd] **v.** 명령하다; 지휘하다; **n.** 명령; 지휘; 사령부
If someone in authority commands you to do something, they tell you that you must do it.

sprint [sprint] **v.** (짧은 거리를) 전력 질주하다; **n.** 전력 질주; 단거리 경기
If you sprint, you run or ride as fast as you can over a short distance.

★ **overtake** [òuvərtéik] **v.** (overtook-overtaken) 앞지르다, 추월하다; 불시에 닥치다
If you overtake a vehicle or a person that is ahead of you and moving in the same direction, you pass them.

‡ **engage** [ingéidʒ] **v.** 사용하다; 약혼시키다; 관계를 맺다; 교전을 벌이다
To engage is to bring a mechanism into operation.

stealth [stelθ] **n.** 살며시 함, 몰래 함, 잠행
If you use stealth when you do something, you do it quietly and carefully so that no one will notice what you are doing.

★ **exclaim** [ikskléim] **v.** 소리치다, 외치다
If you exclaim, you cry out suddenly in surprise, strong emotion, or pain.

press [pres] **v.** 누르다; 꾹 밀어 넣다; (무엇에) 바짝 대다; **n.** 언론
If you press a button or switch, you push it with your finger in order to make a machine or device work.

run out of idiom ~을 다 써버리다; ~이 없어지다
If you run out of something like money or time, you have used up all of it.

unison [júːnisn] **n.** 조화, 화합, 일치 (in unison idiom 합심하여)
If two or more people do something in unison, they do it together at the same time.

ignite [ignáit] **v.** 불을 켜다, 불을 붙이다, 점화하다
When you ignite something or when it ignites, it starts burning or explodes.

blade [bleid] **n.** (칼·도구 등의) 날; 풀잎
The blade of a knife, axe, or saw is the flat sharp part that is used for cutting.

slice [slais] **v.** 헤치고 나아가다; 자르다; 베다; **n.** (얇게 썬) 조각; 부분, 몫
If something slices through a substance, it moves through it quickly, like a knife.

predator [prédətər] **n.** 포식자, 포식 동물; 약탈자
A predator is an animal that kills and eats other animals.

have one's back idiom ~을 지키다; ~을 지지하다; ~을 보살피다
When you have someone's back, you look out for them to help or defend them.

swoop [swuːp] **v.** (공격을 하기 위해) 급강하하다, 위에서 덮치다; 급습하다; **n.** 급강하; 급습
To swoop is to come down upon something in a sudden, swift attack.

blast [blæst] **v.** 발사하다; 폭발시키다, 폭파하다; 확 뿌리다; **n.** 폭발; (한 줄기의) 강한 바람
To blast a person or animal means to shoot them.

wrist [rist] **n.** 손목, 팔목
Your wrist is the part of your body between your hand and your arm which bends when you move your hand.

sever [sévər] **v.** 자르다, 절단하다; 끊어지다, 갈라지다; (관계·연락을) 끊다, 단절하다
To sever something means to cut completely through it or to cut it completely off.

grasp [græsp] **v.** 꽉 잡다; 완전히 이해하다, 파악하다; **n.** 움켜잡기; 통제; 이해
If you grasp something, you take it in your hand and hold it very firmly.

outstretch [àutstrétʃ] **v.** 펴다, 뻗다, 확장하다 (outstretched a. 쭉 뻗은)
If a part of the body of a person or animal is outstretched, it is stretched out as far as possible.

* **precise** [prisáis] a. 정확한, 정밀한; 엄밀한, 꼼꼼한
You use precise to emphasize that you are referring to an exact thing, rather than something vague.

복습 **ranger** [réindʒər] n. 경비 대원; 기습 공격대원
A ranger is an armed guard who patrols a region.

duck [dʌk] n. (머리나 몸을) 휙 수그림; [동물] 오리; v. 휙 수그리다; 급히 움직이다
A duck is a movement in which you move your head or the top half of your body quickly downward to avoid something that might hit you, or to avoid being seen.

* **slam** [slæm] v. 세게 치다, 놓다; 쾅 닫다, 닫히다; n. 쾅 하고 닫기; 쾅 하는 소리
If you slam into somewhere, you enter there quickly and with great force.

shoulder to shoulder idiom 힘을 모아, 협력하여; 서로 어깨를 맞대고
If people work or stand shoulder to shoulder, they work together in order to achieve something, or support each other.

* **circuit** [sə́:rkit] n. 전기 회로; 순환로, 순회 노선 (short-circuit v. 전기 회로에 합선이 생기다)
If an electrical device short-circuits, a wrong connection or damaged wire causes electricity to travel along the wrong route and damage the device.

‡ **operate** [ápərèit] v. 조작하다; 작전을 벌이다; 작동하다; 작업하다; 수술하다
When you operate a machine or device, you make it work.

splatter [splǽtər] v. 튀다, 튀기다; n. 튀기기; 철벅철벅 소리
If a thick wet substance splatters on something or is splattered on it, it drops or is thrown over it.

복습 **panel** [pǽnl] n. 계기판; 판; 패널, 자문단
A control panel or instrument panel is a board or surface which contains switches and controls to operate a machine or piece of equipment.

‡ **route** [ru:t] v. 보내다, 전송하다; n. 길, 경로; 방법 (reroute v. 경로를 변경하다)
If vehicles or planes are rerouted, they are directed along a different route because the usual route cannot be used.

* **rip** [rip] v. (재빨리·거칠게) 뜯어 내다; (갑자기) 찢다, 찢어지다; n. (길게) 찢어진 곳
If you rip something away, you remove it quickly and forcefully.

rewire [riwaíər] v. (집·기계·라디오 등의) 철사를 갈아 달다; 전보를 다시 치다
If someone rewires a building or an electrical appliance, a new system of electrical wiring is put into it.

LIGHTYEAR

grateful [gréitfəl] a. 고마워하는, 감사하는
If you are grateful for something that someone has given you or done for you, you have warm, friendly feelings toward them and wish to thank them.

collected [kəléktid] a. 아주 침착한
If you say that someone is collected, you mean that they are very calm and self-controlled, especially when they are in a difficult or serious situation.

rookie [rúki] n. 신참, 초보자; (스포츠 팀의) 신인 선수
A rookie is someone who has just started doing a job and does not have much experience, especially someone who has just joined the army or police force.

pause [pɔːz] v. (말·일을 하다가) 잠시 멈추다; 정지시키다; n. (말·행동 등의) 멈춤
If you pause while you are doing something, you stop for a short period and then continue.

simultaneous [sàiməltéiniəs] a. 동시에 일어나는, 동시의 (simultaneously ad. 동시에)
If two things happen simultaneously, they take place at the same time.

drag [dræg] v. 끌다, 끌고 가다; 힘들게 움직이다; n. 끌기, 당기기; 장애물
If you drag something, you pull it along the ground, often with difficulty.

tug [tʌg] n. (갑자기 세게) 잡아당김; v. (세게) 잡아당기다; 끌어당기다 (tug-of-war n. 줄다리기)
A tug-of-war is a sports event in which two teams test their strength by pulling against each other on opposite ends of a rope.

grab [græb] v. (와락·단단히) 붙잡다; 급히 ~하다; n. 와락 잡아채려고 함
If you grab something, you take it or pick it up suddenly and roughly.

give up idiom 포기하다; 그만두다; 단념하다
If you give up, you stop trying to do something, usually because it is too difficult.

flick [flik] v. 잽싸게 움직이다; (손가락 등으로) 튀기다; n. 재빨리 움직임
If you flick something, you move or make it move with a sudden quick movement.

iridescent [ìrədésnt] a. 보는 각도에 따라 색깔이 변하는, 무지갯빛의
Something that is iridescent has many bright colors that seem to keep changing.

knock [nak] v. 치다, 부딪치다; (문 등을) 두드리다; n. 부딪침; 문 두드리는 소리
If you knock something, you touch or hit it roughly, especially so that it falls or moves.

waist [weist] n. 허리; (옷의) 허리 부분
Your waist is the middle part of your body where it narrows slightly above your hips.

hoist [hɔist] v. 들어 올리다, 끌어올리다; n. 끌어올리기
If you hoist something heavy somewhere, you lift it or pull it up there.

creature [kríːʧər] n. 생물, 생명체; 사람
You can refer to any living thing that is not a plant as a creature, especially when it is of an unknown or unfamiliar kind.

shriek [ʃriːk] v. (날카로운) 소리를 내다; 악을 쓰며 말하다; n. (날카로운) 비명
If something shrieks, it makes a loud, high-pitched voice.

ooze [uːz] v. (액체가) 흐르다; (특징·자질 등을) 줄줄 흘리다; n. (아주 조금씩) 스며 나오는 것
When a thick or sticky liquid oozes from something or when something oozes it, the liquid flows slowly and in small quantities.

bog [bag] n. 습지, 수렁; v. 꼼짝 못 하게 되다, 수렁에 빠지다
A bog is an area of land which is very wet and muddy.

stretch [streʧ] v. 뻗어 있다; (팔·다리를) 뻗다; 이어지다, 계속되다; 늘어나다; n. (길게) 뻗은 구간
Something that stretches over an area or distance covers or exists in the whole of that area or distance.

encircle [insə́ːrkl] v. 둘러싸다, 두르다
To encircle something or someone means to surround or enclose them, or to go round them.

demise [dimáiz] n. 죽음, 사망; 종말
The demise of something or someone is their end or death.

hurl [həːrl] v. (거칠게) 던지다; (욕·비난 등을) 퍼붓다
If you hurl something, you throw it violently and with a lot of force.

burst [bəːrst] v. (burst-burst) 불쑥 움직이다; 갑자기 ~하다; 터지다; n. (갑자기) ~을 함; 파열, 폭발
To burst into or out of a place means to enter or leave it suddenly with a lot of energy or force.

pile [pail] n. 무더기, 더미; 쌓아 놓은 것; v. 쌓다; (차곡차곡) 포개다; 우르르 가다
A pile of things is a mass of them that is high in the middle and has sloping sides.

glow [glou] v. 빛나다, 타다; (얼굴이) 상기되다; n. (은은한) 불빛; 홍조
If something glows, it produces a dull, steady light.

triumph [tráiəmf] n. 승리감, 환희; 승리, 업적; v. 승리를 거두다, 이기다
Triumph is a feeling of great satisfaction and pride resulting from a success or victory.

* **heroic** [hiróuik] a. 영웅적인, 용감무쌍한; 영웅의 (heroically ad. 영웅적으로)
If something is done heroically, it is admired because it shows extreme bravery.

‡ **swing** [swiŋ] v. (swung-swung) 휙 움직이다; (전후·좌우로) 흔들다; 휘두르다; n. 휘두르기; 흔들기
If something swings in a particular direction or if you swing it in that direction, it
moves in that direction with a smooth, curving movement.

* **exhaust** [igzɔ́:st] v. 기진맥진하게 하다; 다 써 버리다; n. (자동차 등의) 배기가스
(exhausted a. 기진맥진한)
When you are exhausted, you are depleted of energy and extremely tired.

‡ **charge** [ʧa:rdʒ] v. 급히 가다; 돌격하다; (요금·값을) 청구하다; 충전하다; n. 책임, 담당; 요금
If you charge toward someone or something, you move quickly and aggressively
toward them.

* **leap** [li:p] v. 뛰다, 뛰어오르다; (서둘러) ~하다; n. 높이뛰기, 도약; 급증
If you leap somewhere, you move there suddenly and quickly.

‡ **pilot** [páilət] n. 조종사, 비행사; v. 조종하다 (autopilot n. (항공기·배의) 자동 조종 장치)
An autopilot is a device in an aircraft or a ship that keeps it on a fixed course without
the need for a person to control it.

* **instant** [ínstənt] a. 즉각적인; n. 순간, 아주 짧은 동안 (instantly ad. 즉각, 즉시)
If something happens instantly, it happens without any delay.

* **chime** [ʧaim] v. (노래하듯) 말하다; (종이나 시계가) 울리다; n. 차임, 종
To chime is to speak or recite in a musical or rhythmic manner.

cheery [ʧíəri] a. 쾌활한 (cheerily ad. 쾌활하게)
When someone behaves cheerily, they are cheerful and happy.

복습 **groan** [groun] v. (고통·짜증으로) 신음 소리를 내다, 끙끙거리다; n. 신음, 끙 하는 소리
If you groan, you make a long, low sound because you are in pain, or because you are
upset or unhappy about something.

console [kánsoul] n. 제어반, 계기반; v. 위로하다, 위안을 주다
A console is a panel with a number of switches or knobs that is used to operate a
machine.

* **crucial** [krú:ʃəl] a. 결정적인, 중대한
If you describe something as crucial, you mean it is extremely important.

* **monitor** [mánətər] v. 지켜보다, 감시하다; 추적 관찰하다; n. (텔레비전·컴퓨터의) 화면; 감시 장치
If you monitor something, you regularly check its development or progress, and
sometimes comment on it.

rely on idiom ~에 의지하다; ~을 신뢰하다
If you rely on someone or something, you need them and depend on them in order to live or work properly.

slack [slæk] n. 느슨한 부분; a. 느슨한; 한산한; 해이한; v. 해이해지다
(pick up the slack idiom 부족한 부분을 보충하다)
To pick up the slack means to do or provide something that another person or organization is no longer doing or providing.

hostile [hastl] a. 적대적인; 강력히 반대하는
In a war, you use hostile to describe your enemy's forces and activities.

timid [tímid] a. 소심한, 용기가 없는 (timidly ad. 소심하게)
If someone is timid, they are too cautious or slow to act, because they are nervous about the possible consequences of their actions.

smack [smæk] v. 찰싹 소리가 나게 치다; 세게 부딪치다; n. 찰싹 때리는 소리, 때리기; ad. 정통으로
If you smack someone or something, you hit them with your hand.

simulate [símjulèit] v. 모의실험하다; 가장하다 (simulation n. 모의실험)
In a simulation, you create a set of conditions artificially, for example in order to conduct an experiment.

status [stéitəs] n. 상황; 신분, 자격
The status of something is its state of affairs at a particular time.

static [stætik] n. (수신기의) 잡음; 정전기; a. 고정된; 정지 상태의 (staticky a. 잡음 섞인)
A staticky sound includes a series of loud noises which spoils the sound.

punch [pʌnʧ] v. (자판·번호판 등을) 치다; 주먹으로 치다; n. 주먹으로 한 대 침
If you punch something such as the buttons on a keyboard, you touch them in order to give the machine a command to do something.

launch [lɔ:nʧ] n. 발사; 시작; 개시; v. 던지다; 발사하다; 맹렬히 덤비다
A launch refers to the action of sending a rocket, missile, or satellite into the air or into space.

unsettle [ʌnsétəl] v. (사람을) 불안하게 하다, 동요시키다 (unsettling a. 불안하게 하는)
If you describe something as unsettling, you mean that it makes you feel rather worried or uncertain.

shudder [ʃʌdər] v. 마구 흔들리다; (공포·추위 등으로) 몸을 떨다; n. 크게 흔들림; 몸이 떨림, 전율
If something such as a machine or vehicle shudders, it shakes suddenly and violently.

resist [rizíst] v. 저항하다; 참다, 견디다; 굴하지 않다 (resistance n. 저항)
Resistance refers to a force which slows down a moving object.

awkward [ɔ́ːkwərd] a. 어색한; (처리하기) 곤란한; 불편한 (awkwardly ad. 어설프게)
If something moves awkwardly, it moves in a clumsy and uncomfortable way.

trajectory [trədʒéktəri] n. 궤적, 궤도, 탄도
The trajectory of a moving object is the path that it follows as it moves.

unsound [ʌnsáund] a. 불안정한, 견고하지 못한; 부적절한
If a system or structure is unsound, it is in poor condition and is likely to collapse.

kick in idiom 효과가 나타나기 시작하다
If something kicks in, it starts to have an effect.

⁎ **altitude** [ǽltətjùːd] n. (해발) 고도; 고도가 높은 곳, 고지
If something is at a particular altitude, it is at that height above sea level.

⁎ **bead** [biːd] n. (구슬 같은) 방울; 구슬
A bead of liquid or moisture is a small drop of it.

⁎ **drip** [drip] v. (액체를) 뚝뚝 흘리다; 가득 담고 있다; n. (액체가) 뚝뚝 떨어짐; 방울
When something drips, drops of liquid fall from it.

⁎ **temple** [templ] n. 관자놀이; 신전, 사원, 절
Your temples are the flat parts on each side of the front part of your head, near your forehead.

‡ **parallel** [pǽrəlèl] ad. 평행하게; a. 평행한; 아주 유사한; n. ~와 아주 유사한 것; v. ~와 유사하다
Two or more lines that run parallel to each other are the same distance apart at every point.

⁎ **massive** [mǽsiv] a. 거대한; 엄청나게 심각한
Something that is massive is very large in size, quantity, or extent.

⁎ **collide** [kəláid] v. 부딪치다, 충돌하다; (의견 등이) 상충하다 (collision n. 충돌)
A collision occurs when a moving object crashes into something.

imminent [ímənənt] a. 금방이라도 닥칠 듯한, 목전의, 임박한
If you say that something is imminent, especially something unpleasant, you mean it is almost certain to happen very soon.

abort [əbɔ́ːrt] v. 중단시키다, 중도 하차하다
If someone aborts a process, plan, or activity, they stop it before it has been completed.

★ **cling** [kliŋ] v. 꼭 붙잡다, 매달리다; 들러붙다; 애착을 갖다
If you cling to someone or something, you hold onto them tightly.

lurch [ləːrtʃ] v. (갑자기) 휘청하다, 휘청거리다; (공포·흥분으로) 떨리다; n. 휘청함; 요동침
To lurch means to make a sudden movement, especially forward, in an uncontrolled way.

grit [grit] v. 이를 악물다; 이를 갈다; 잔모래를 뿌리다; n. 투지, 기개; 모래
If you grit your teeth, you press your upper and lower teeth tightly together, usually because you are angry about something.

‡ **crash** [kræʃ] n. 요란한 소리; (자동차·항공기) 사고; v. 추락하다; 부딪치다; 충돌하다; 굉음을 내다
A crash is a sudden, loud noise.

★ **belly** [béli] n. 배, 복부 (underbelly n. 아랫배 부분)
The underbelly of an animal or a vehicle is the underneath part of it.

snag [snæg] v. (날카롭거나 튀어나온 것에) 걸리다; 잡아채다, 낚아채다; n. 날카로운 것; 문제
If something snags on a sharp or rough object, it gets caught on the object and tears.

★ **peak** [piːk] n. (산의) 봉우리; 뾰족한 끝; 절정, 정점; v. 최고조에 달하다
A peak is a mountain or the top of a mountain.

★ **screech** [skriːtʃ] v. 꽥 하는 소리를 내다; 끼익 하는 소리를 내다; n. 꽥; 끼익 (하는 날카로운 소리)
When something screeches, it makes a loud, unpleasant, high-pitched noise.

★ **boom** [buːm] n. 쾅 (하는 소리); v. 쾅 하는 소리를 내다; 굵은 목소리로 말하다
A boom refers to a loud, deep sound that lasts for several seconds.

★ **pit** [pit] n. (신체의) 우묵한 곳; (크고 깊은) 구덩이; v. 자국을 남기다, 구멍을 남기다
If you have a feeling in the pit of your stomach, you have a tight or sick feeling in your stomach, usually because you are afraid or anxious.

★ **chaos** [kéias] n. 혼돈; 혼란
Chaos is a state of complete disorder and confusion.

erupt [irʌpt] v. 분출되다; 터뜨리다
If violence or fighting erupts, it suddenly begins or gets worse in an unexpected, violent way.

engulf [ingʌlf] v. 완전히 에워싸다, 휩싸다; (강한 감정 등이) 사로잡다
If one thing engulfs another, it completely covers or hides it, often in a sudden and unexpected way.

cacophony [kækáfəni] n. 불협화음; 잡음, 소음; 불쾌한 음조
You can describe a loud, unpleasant mixture of sounds as a cacophony.

⋆ **strive** [straiv] v. 분투하다
If you strive to do something or strive for something, you make a great effort to do it
or get it.

⋆ **regain** [rigéin] v. 되찾다, 회복하다; 되돌아오다
If you regain something that you have lost, you get it back again.

hurtle [hə:rtl] v. 돌진하다
If someone or something hurtles somewhere, they move there very quickly, often in a
rough or violent way.

race [reis] v. 쏜살같이 가다; 경주하다; (머리·심장 등이) 바쁘게 돌아가다; n. 경주; 인종, 종족
If you race somewhere, you go there as quickly as possible.

rupture [rʌ́ptʃər] n. 파열; 결렬; v. 파열시키다; 터지게 하다; 불화를 일으키다
A rupture refers to the act of breaking or bursting.

複습 **muck** [mʌk] n. 진흙, 진창; 배설물
Muck is dirt or some other unpleasant substance.

⋆ **emerge** [imə́:rdʒ] v. 나오다, 모습을 드러내다; (어려움 등을) 헤쳐 나오다
To emerge means to come out from an enclosed or dark space such as a room or a
vehicle, or from a position where you could not be seen.

⋆ **wreck** [rek] v. 망가뜨리다, 파괴하다; n. 충돌; 난파선; 사고 잔해 (wreckage n. 잔해)
When something such as a plane, car, or building has been destroyed, you can refer to
what remains as the wreckage.

soot [sut] n. 그을음, 검댕; v. 검댕으로 더럽히다
Soot is black powder which rises in the smoke from a fire and collects on the inside
of chimneys.

⋆ **shatter** [ʃǽtər] v. 산산이 부서지다, 산산조각 나다; 엄청난 충격을 주다
If something shatters or is shattered, it breaks into a lot of small pieces.

複습 **stare** [stɛər] v. 빤히 쳐다보다, 응시하다; n. 빤히 쳐다보기, 응시
If you stare at someone or something, you look at them for a long time.

⋆ **numb** [nʌm] a. 멍한, 망연자실한; (신체 부위가) 감각이 없는; v. 망연자실하게 하다; 감각이 없게 하다
If you are numb with shock, fear, or grief, you are so shocked, frightened, or upset that
you cannot think clearly or feel any emotion.

crew [kruː] n. (함께 일을 하는) 팀, 조; (배·항공기의) 승무원; v. 승무원을 하다
A crew is a group of people with special technical skills who work together on a task or project.

emergency [imə́ːrdʒənsi] n. 비상, 비상 사태
An emergency is an unexpected and difficult or dangerous situation, especially an accident, which happens suddenly and which requires quick action to deal with it.

evacuate [ivǽkjuèit] v. 떠나다, 피난하다; 대피시키다 (evacuation n. 대피)
Evacuation refers to the act of sending people to a place of safety, away from a dangerous situation.

protocol [próutəkɔ̀ːl] n. (군대·궁전 등의) 의례, 관습
Protocol is a system of rules about the correct way to act in formal situations.

pod [pad] n. 유선형 공간; (콩이 들어 있는) 꼬투리; (우주선·선박의 본체에서) 분리 가능한 부분
A pod is a long narrow container that is hung under an aircraft and used to carry fuel, equipment, or weapons.

maroon [mərúːn] v. 고립시키다, 섬에 버리다; n. 고립된 사람; 밤색, 고동색
If someone is marooned somewhere, they are left in a place that is difficult for them to escape from.

sink in idiom 충분히 이해되다, 인식되다
If an unpleasant or surprising fact or idea sinks in, you gradually start to believe it, understand it, or realize the effect it will have on you.

assign [əsáin] v. (일·책임 등을) 맡기다; (사람을) 배치하다; ~의 탓으로 하다 (assignment n. 임무)
An assignment is a task or piece of work that you are given to do, especially as part of your job or studies.

dejected [didʒéktid] a. 실의에 빠진, 낙담한 (dejectedly ad. 맥없이, 낙담하여)
When someone behaves dejectedly, they appear miserable or unhappy.

confuse [kənfjúːz] v. (사람을) 혼란시키다; 혼동하다 (confused a. 혼란스러운)
If you are confused, you do not know exactly what is happening or what to do.

relieve [rilíːv] v. 해임하다; 덜어 주다, 없애 주다; 완화하다; 안도하다
If someone is relieved of their duties or post, they are told that they are no longer required to continue in their job.

protest [proutést] v. 이의를 제기하다, 항의하다; n. 항의; 시위
If you protest that something is the case, you insist that it is true, when other people think that it may not be.

‡ **mine** [main] v. (광물질을) 캐다, 채굴하다; n. 광산; 지뢰
When a mineral such as coal, diamonds, or gold is mined, it is obtained from the
ground by digging deep holes and tunnels.

★ **frown** [fraun] v. 얼굴을 찡그리다; 눈살을 찌푸리다; n. 찡그림, 찌푸림
When someone frowns, their eyebrows become drawn together, because they are
annoyed or puzzled.

fusion [fjúːʒən] n. 융합, 결합
In physics, fusion is the process in which atomic particles combine and produce a large
amount of nuclear energy.

복습 **stable** [steibl] a. 안정된, 안정적인; 차분한; n. 마구간 (unstable a. 불안정한)
You can describe something as unstable if it is likely to change suddenly, especially if
this creates difficulty or danger.

★ **counter** [káuntər] v. 반박하다; 대응하다; n. (식당 등의) 계산대, 카운터; 반작용
If you counter something that someone has said, you say something which shows that
you disagree with them or which proves that they are wrong.

‡ **manufacture** [mænjufǽktʃər] v. 제조하다, 생산하다; n. 제조, 생산; 상품
To manufacture is to process or make something from a raw material.

lasso [lǽsou] v. 올가미 밧줄로 잡다; n. 올가미 밧줄
If you lasso something, you catch it by throwing a long rope round it and pulling it
tight.

oblivion [əblíviən] n. 흔적도 없이 사라짐; 의식하지 못하는 상태; 망각
If you say that something is blown into oblivion, you are emphasizing that it is
completely destroyed.

smirk [sməːrk] v. 능글맞게 웃다; n. 능글맞은 웃음
If you smirk, you smile in a smug way, often because you believe that you have gained
an advantage over someone else or know something that they do not know.

catch on idiom 이해하다
If you catch on to something, you understand it, or realize that it is happening.

★ **slap** [slæp] v. 털썩 놓다; (손바닥으로) 철썩 때리다; n. 철썩 때리기, 치기
If you slap something onto a surface, you put it there quickly, roughly, or carelessly.

★ **furrow** [fə́ːrou] v. (미간을) 찡그리다; (밭에) 고랑을 만들다; n. 깊은 주름; 고랑
If someone furrows their brow or forehead or if it furrows, deep folds appear in it
because the person is annoyed, unhappy, or confused.

* **brow** [brau] n. 이마; 눈썹
Your brow is your forehead.

* **determination** [ditə̀:rmənéiʃən] n. 결심, 결단; 결정
Determination is the quality that you show when you have decided to do something and you will not let anything stop you.

3 & 4

1. **How long did it take for the crew to be ready for the first hyperspeed test flight?**
   A. One month
   B. Six months
   C. One year
   D. Four years

2. **Why did Buzz's ship go off course?**
   A. Because of an explosion
   B. Because Buzz changed his mind
   C. Because the autopilot was outdated
   D. Because the ship was too heavy

3. **Why was Buzz confused when he landed?**
   A. He forgot who Díaz was.
   B. He had been gone longer than he realized.
   C. He could not find Alisha.
   D. He went to the wrong place.

4. **What was Alisha's surprising news?**
   A. She found the fuel.
   B. She got engaged.
   C. She had a baby.
   D. She wanted to quit being a Space Ranger.

5. **What did Alisha leave in the box for Buzz?**
   A. A mission log
   B. A new flight suit
   C. A robotic cat
   D. A birthday cake

CHAPTER 3

Check Your Reading Speed
1분에 몇 단어를 읽는지 리딩 속도를 측정해 보세요.

$$\frac{1,646 \text{ words}}{\text{reading time ( ) sec}} \times 60 = (\quad) \text{ WPM}$$

Build Your Vocabulary

복습 **log** [lɔːg] n. (비행·항해 등의) 일지, 기록; 통나무; v. 일지에 기록하다; 비행하다, 항해하다
A log is an official written account of what happens each day, for example on board a ship.

복습 **maroon** [mərúːn] v. 고립시키다, 섬에 버리다; n. 고립된 사람; 밤색, 고동색
If someone is marooned somewhere, they are left in a place that is difficult for them to escape from.

* **specialize** [spéʃəlàiz] v. 전문화하다; 특수화하다 (specialized a. 전문적인, 전문화된)
Someone or something that is specialized is trained or developed for a particular purpose or area of knowledge.

* **assistant** [əsístənt] n. 조수, 보조원
Someone's assistant is a person who helps them in their work.

‡ **vast** [væst] a. 어마어마한, 방대한, 막대한
Something that is vast is extremely large.

* **incredible** [inkrédəbl] a. 믿을 수 없는, 믿기 힘든
If you describe something or someone as incredible, you like them very much or are impressed by them, because they are extremely or unusually good.

복습 **blast** [blæst] v. 확 뿌리다; 폭발시키다, 폭파하다; 발사하다; n. 폭발; (한 줄기의) 강한 바람
If something blasts light or water somewhere, it sends out a sudden, powerful stream of it.

* **hop** [hap] v. 급히 움직이다; 깡충깡충 뛰다; n. 깡충깡충 뛰기
If you hop somewhere, you move there quickly or suddenly.

복습 **launch** [lɔːnʧ] n. 발사; 시작; 개시; v. 던지다; 발사하다; 맹렬히 덤비다 (launchpad n. 발사대)
A launchpad is a platform from which a spacecraft or rocket is launched.

^복_습 **gaze** [geiz] v. (가만히) 응시하다, 바라보다; n. 응시, (눈여겨보는) 시선
If you gaze at someone or something, you look steadily at them for a long time.

⋆ **perimeter** [pərímitər] n. (어떤 구역의) 주위, 주변; 방어선
The perimeter of an area of land is the whole of its outer edge or boundary.

encampment [inkǽmpmənt] n. 진영, 진지; 야영지, 캠프장
An encampment is a group of tents or other shelters in a particular place, especially when they are used by soldiers or refugees.

^복_습 **vine** [vain] n. 덩굴 식물; 포도나무
A vine is a plant with long thin stems that attach themselves to other plants, trees, or buildings.

⋆ **patrol** [pətróul] n. 순찰대; 순찰; v. 순찰을 돌다
A patrol is a group of soldiers or vehicles that are moving around an area in order to make sure that there is no trouble there.

livable [lívəbl] a. 살기에 적합한; 살 만한
If you describe a place as livable, you mean that the place is pleasant enough to live in.

⋆ **hospitable** [háspitəbl] a. (기후·환경이) 쾌적한, 알맞은; (손님·방문객을) 환대하는, 친절한
A hospitable climate or environment is one that encourages the existence or development of particular people or things.

^복_습 **grab** [græb] n. 와락 잡아채려고 함; v. (와락·단단히) 붙잡다; 급히 ~하다 (grabby a. 꽉 붙잡는)
Something that is grabby has a tendency toward holding, grasping, or sticking.

measurable [méʒərəbl] a. 측정할 수 있는; 주목할 만한 (immeasurable a. 측정할 수 없는)
If you describe something as immeasurable, you are emphasizing how great it is.

^복_습 **mine** [main] v. (광물질을) 캐다, 채굴하다; n. 광산; 지뢰
When a mineral such as coal, diamonds, or gold is mined, it is obtained from the ground by digging deep holes and tunnels.

⋆ **ore** [ɔːr] n. 광물
Ore is rock or earth from which metal can be obtained.

rudimentary [rùːdəméntəri] a. 기본적인, 기본의; 초보의; 미발달의, 원시적인
Rudimentary things are very basic or simple.

‡ **quarter** [kwɔ́ːrtər] n. 숙소; 구역; 4분의 1; v. 숙소를 제공하다; 4등분하다
The rooms provided for soldiers, sailors, or servants to live in are called their quarters.

★ **await** [əwéit] v. (어떤 일이 사람 앞에) 기다리다; ~을 기다리다
Something that awaits you is going to happen or come to you in the future.

복습 **initial** [iníʃəl] a. 처음의, 초기의; n. 이름의 첫 글자
You use initial to describe something that happens at the beginning of a process.

‡ **calculate** [kǽlkjulèit] v. 추정하다, 추산하다; 계산하다, 산출하다 (calculation n. 추정, 추산)
A calculation is something that you think carefully about and arrive at a conclusion on after having considered all the relevant factors.

★ **stake** [steik] n. (내기 등에) 건 것; 지분; 말뚝; v. (돈 등을) 걸다; 말뚝을 받치다
The stakes involved in a risky action are the things that can be gained or lost.

복습 **lasso** [lǽsou] v. 올가미 밧줄로 잡다; n. 올가미 밧줄
If you lasso something, you catch it by throwing a long rope round it and pulling it tight.

★ **index finger** [índeks fíŋgər] n. 집게손가락
Your index finger is the finger that is next to your thumb.

infinity [infínəti] n. 아득히 먼 곳; 무한성
Infinity is a point that is further away than any other point and can never be reached.

★ **tap** [tæp] v. (가볍게) 톡톡 두드리다; n. (가볍게) 두드리기
If you tap something, you hit it with a quick light blow or a series of quick light blows.

복습 **boom** [buːm] v. 쾅 하는 소리를 내다; 굵은 목소리로 말하다; n. 쾅 (하는 소리)
When something such as someone's voice, a cannon, or a big drum booms, it makes a loud, deep sound that lasts for several seconds.

★ **explode** [iksplóud] v. 폭발하다; 갑자기 ~하다; (강한 감정을) 터뜨리다 (explosion n. 폭발)
An explosion is a sudden, violent burst of energy, for example one caused by a bomb.

★ **ritual** [ríʧuəl] n. 의식과 같은 일; (종교적인) 의식, 의례
A ritual is a way of behaving or a series of actions which people regularly carry out in a particular situation.

복습 **cadet** [kədét] n. (경찰·군대 등의) 간부 후보생
A cadet is a young man or woman who is being trained in the armed services or the police.

복습 **second nature** idiom (습관으로 굳어진) 제2의 천성
If a way of behaving is second nature to you, you do it almost without thinking because it is easy for you or obvious to you.

marvel [máːrvəl] v. 경이로워하다, 경탄하다; n. 경이로운 것
If you marvel at something, you express your great surprise, wonder, or admiration.

square [skwɛər] v. 똑바로 펴다; 네모지게 만들다; a. 정사각형 모양의; 직각의; ad. 똑바로
If you square your shoulders, you stand straight and push them back, usually to show your determination.

roll one's eyes idiom 눈을 굴리다
If you roll your eyes or if your eyes roll, they move round and upward to show you are bored or annoyed.

internal [intə́ːrnl] a. 내부의; 내면적인; 국내의
Internal is used to describe things that exist or happen inside a particular person, object, or place.

activate [ǽktəvèit] v. 작동시키다; 활성화시키다
If a device or process is activated, something causes it to start working.

navigate [nǽvəgèit] v. 조종하다; 길을 찾다; 항해하다 (navigator n. 자동 조종기)
A navigator is a person or device for assisting a pilot to navigate an aircraft.

pilot [páilət] n. 조종사, 비행사; v. 조종하다 (autopilot n. (항공기·배의) 자동 조종 장치)
An autopilot is a device in an aircraft or a ship that keeps it on a fixed course without the need for a person to control it.

sophisticated [səfístəkèitid] a. 정교한; 지적인, 수준 높은; 세련된
A sophisticated machine, device, or method is more advanced or complex than others.

colleague [káliːg] n. (같은 곳에서 일하는) 동료
Your colleagues are the people you work with, especially in a professional job.

combine [kəmbáin] v. 결합하다; 겸비하다
If you combine two or more things or if they combine, they join together to make a single thing.

chemical [kémikəl] n. 화학 물질; a. 화학의; 화학적인
Chemicals are substances that are used in a reaction involving changes to atoms or molecules, especially those that are derived artificially for practical use.

concoct [kankákt] v. (이것저것 섞어) 만들다; (계획·음모 등을) 꾸미다
If you concoct something, especially something unusual, you make it by mixing several things together.

formula [fɔ́ːrmjulə] n. 제조법; 화학식; 공식
In science, the formula for a substance is a list of the amounts of various elements which make up that substance, or an indication of the atoms that it is composed of.

bend [bend] v. (bent-bent) (몸·머리를) 굽히다, 숙이다; 구부리다; n. 굽은 곳
When you bend a part of your body such as your arm or leg, or when it bends, you change its position so that it is no longer straight.

glow [glou] n. (은은한) 불빛; 홍조; v. 빛나다, 타다; (얼굴이) 상기되다
A glow is a dull, steady light.

reflect [riflékt] v. 반사하다; (상을) 비추다; 깊이 생각하다
When light, heat, or other rays reflect off a surface or when a surface reflects them, they are sent back from the surface and do not pass through it.

nod [nad] v. (고개를) 끄덕이다, 까딱하다; n. (고개를) 끄덕임
If you nod, you move your head downward and upward to show that you are answering 'yes' to a question, or to show agreement, understanding, or approval.

odds [adz] n. 가능성; 역경, 곤란
You refer to how likely something is to happen as the odds that it will happen.

compartment [kəmpá:rtmənt] n. 칸; 객실
A compartment is one of the separate parts of an object that is used for keeping things in.

strap [stræp] v. 끈으로 묶다; 붕대를 감다; n. 끈, 줄, 띠
If you strap something somewhere, you fasten it there with a piece of cloth or other material.

grant [grænt] v. 승인하다, 허락하다; 인정하다; n. 보조금
If someone in authority grants you something, or if something is granted to you, you are allowed to have it.

dome [doum] n. 반구형 모양의 것; 돔, 반구형 지붕; v. 반구형으로 만들다
A dome is any object that has a similar shape to a dome.

shield [ʃi:ld] n. 보호 장치; 방패; v. 보호하다, 가리다 (windshield n. (자동차 등의) 방풍 유리)
The windshield of a car or other vehicle is the glass window at the front through which the driver looks.

brace [breis] v. (스스로) 대비를 하다; (몸에) 단단히 힘을 주다; n. 버팀대; 치아 교정기
If you brace yourself for something unpleasant or difficult, you prepare yourself for it.

sequence [sí:kwəns] n. 순서, 차례; (일련의) 연속적인 사건들
A particular sequence is a particular order in which things happen or are arranged.

initiate [iníʃièit] v. 개시되게 하다, 착수시키다; 가입시키다; n. 가입자
If you initiate something, you start it or cause it to happen.

‡ **steady** [stédi] a. 차분한, 침착한; 흔들림 없는, 안정된; 꾸준한; v. 균형을 잡다, 진정시키다
If someone's voice is steady, or they look at you in a steady way, they seem calm and do not stop speaking or looking at you.

볼수 **vibrate** [váibreit] v. 진동하다, (가늘게) 떨다
If something vibrates or if you vibrate it, it shakes with repeated small, quick movements.

* **intense** [inténs] a. 극심한, 강렬한; 치열한; 열정적인, 진지한 (intensity n. 강렬함)
Intensity is the state of being very great or extreme in strength or degree.

* **thrust** [θrʌst] v. (thrust-thrust) (거칠게) 밀다; 찌르다; n. 추진력; 찌르기
If you thrust something or someone somewhere, you push or move them there quickly with a lot of force.

‡ **force** [fɔ:rs] n. 힘; 영향력; 세력; v. 억지로 ~하다; ~을 강요하다
Force is the power or strength which something has.

* **clatter** [klǽtər] v. 달가닥달가닥하는 소리를 내다; n. 달가닥달가닥하는 소리; 떠들썩한 소리
If hard objects clatter, they knock together and make a loud noise.

볼수 **numb** [nʌm] v. 감각이 없게 하다; 망연자실하게 하다; a. (신체 부위가) 감각이 없는; 멍한, 망연자실한
If cold weather, a drug, or a blow numbs a part of your body, you can no longer feel anything in it.

‡ **pressure** [préʃər] n. 압력; 압박; 스트레스; v. 압력을 가하다; 강요하다
The pressure in a place or container is the force produced by the quantity of gas or liquid in that place or container.

볼수 **massive** [mǽsiv] a. 거대한; 엄청나게 심각한
Something that is massive is very large in size, quantity, or extent.

exhilarate [igzílərèit] v. 아주 기쁘게 만들다 (exhilarating a. 아주 신나는)
If you describe an experience or feeling as exhilarating, you mean that it makes you feel very happy and excited.

* **terrify** [térəfài] v. (몹시) 무섭게 하다 (terrifying a. 무서운)
If something is terrifying, it makes you very frightened.

makeshift [méikʃift] a. 임시변통의, 일시적인; n. 임시 수단, 미봉책
Makeshift things are temporary and usually of poor quality, but they are used because there is nothing better available.

* **atmosphere** [ǽtməsfiər] n. 대기; 공기; 분위기
A planet's atmosphere is the layer of air or other gases around it.

breathtaking [brέθtèikiŋ] a. (너무 아름답거나 놀라서) 숨이 막히는, 숨이 멎는 듯한
If you say that something is breathtaking, you are emphasizing that it is extremely beautiful or amazing.

★ **cease** [si:s] v. 중단되다, 그치다
If something ceases, it stops happening or existing.

envelop [invéləp] v. 감싸다, 뒤덮다
If one thing envelops another, it covers or surrounds it completely.

exhale [ekshéil] v. (숨·연기 등을) 내쉬다
When you exhale, you breathe out the air that is in your lungs.

fritz [frits] v. 고장나다, 망가지다
If a machine fritzes out, it becomes inoperable.

console [kánsoul] n. 제어반, 계기반; v. 위로하다, 위안을 주다
A console is a panel with a number of switches or knobs that is used to operate a machine.

‡ **replace** [ripléis] v. 교체하다; 대신하다, 대체하다
If you replace something that is broken, damaged, or lost, you get a new one to use instead.

★ **instruct** [instrʌ́kt] v. 지시하다; 가르치다; (정보를) 알려 주다
If you instruct someone to do something, you formally tell them to do it.

★ **accelerate** [æksélərèit] v. 속도를 높이다, 가속화되다
When a moving vehicle accelerates, it goes faster and faster.

slingshot [slíŋʃat] v. (갑자기) 내던지다, 내던져지다; n. 새총
If someone or something slingshots through the air, they are thrown very suddenly, quickly, and violently through it.

decelerate [di:sélərèit] v. 속도를 줄이다; 속도가 줄어들다 (deceleration n. 감속)
Deceleration refers to a process in which the speed of a vehicle or machine is reduced.

lurch [ləːrtʃ] v. (갑자기) 휘청하다, 휘청거리다; (공포·흥분으로) 떨리다; n. 휘청함; 요동침
To lurch means to make a sudden movement, especially forward, in an uncontrolled way.

★ **streak** [stri:k] n. 줄무늬; v. 줄무늬를 넣다; 전속력으로 가다
A streak is a long stripe or mark on a surface which contrasts with the surface because it is a different color.

^복_습 **slice** [slais] **v.** 헤치고 나아가다; 자르다; 베다; **n.** (얇게 썬) 조각; 부분, 몫
If something slices through a substance, it moves through it quickly, like a knife.

^복_습 **readout** [rí:daut] **n.** (정보의) 해독, 판독; **v.** 정보를 송신하다
If an electronic measuring device gives you a readout, it displays information about the level of something such as a speed, height, or sound.

throttle [θrɑtl] **n.** (자동차 등의 연료) 조절판; **v.** 목을 조르다
The throttle of a motor vehicle or aircraft is the device, lever, or pedal that controls the quantity of fuel entering the engine and is used to control the vehicle's speed.

^복_습 **hum** [hʌm] **v.** 웅웅거리다; (노래를) 흥얼거리다; **n.** 웅성거리는 소리
If something hums, it makes a low continuous noise.

momentum [mouméntəm] **n.** 가속도; 기세
If a process or movement gains momentum, it keeps developing or happening more quickly and keeps becoming less likely to stop.

⋆ **brilliant** [bríljənt] **a.** 눈부신; 훌륭한, 멋진; (재능이) 뛰어난
You describe light, or something that reflects light, as brilliant when it shines very brightly.

⋆ **pound** [paund] **v.** (가슴이) 쿵쿵 뛰다; (요란한 소리로 여러 차례) 두드리다; 쿵쾅거리며 걷다
If your heart is pounding, it is beating with an unusually strong and fast rhythm, usually because you are afraid.

^복_습 **whip** [hwip] **v.** 격렬하게 움직이다; 휙 빼내다; **n.** 채찍
If something or someone whips somewhere, they move there or go there very quickly.

‡ **gravity** [grǽvəti] **n.** 중력; 심각성, 중대성; 엄숙함 (gravitational **a.** 중력의)
Gravitational means relating to or resulting from the force of gravity.

⋆ **confirm** [kənfɔ́:rm] **v.** 사실임을 보여주다, 확인해 주다; 더 분명히 해 주다
If you confirm something that has been stated or suggested, you say that it is true because you know about it.

‡ **grip** [grip] **v.** 움켜잡다; (마음·흥미·시선을) 끌다; **n.** 꽉 붙잡음, 움켜쥠; 통제, 지배
If you grip something, you take hold of it with your hand and continue to hold it firmly.

^복_습 **rip** [rip] **v.** (갑자기) 찢다, 찢어지다; (재빨리·거칠게) 뜯어 내다; **n.** (길게) 찢어진 곳
If something such as a fire, storm, or bomb rips through a place, it damages or destroys the place very quickly.

hull [hʌl] **n.** (배의) 선체; **v.** (콩 등의) 껍질을 벗기다
The hull of a boat or aircraft is the main body of it.

wail [weil] v. (길고 높은) 소리를 내다; 울부짖다, 통곡하다; 투덜거리다; n. 울부짖음, 통곡
If something such as a siren or an alarm wails, it makes a long, loud, high-pitched sound.

status [stéitəs] n. 상황; 신분, 자격
The status of something is its state of affairs at a particular time.

★ **yell** [jel] v. 고함치다, 소리 지르다; n. 고함, 외침
If you yell, you shout loudly, usually because you are excited, angry, or in pain.

trajectory [trədʒéktəri] n. 궤적, 궤도, 탄도
The trajectory of a moving object is the path that it follows as it moves.

‡ **project** [prádʒekt] v. (빛·영상 등을) 비추다; 발사하다; 계획하다; n. 계획, 프로젝트
To project is to cause an image to appear on a surface.

dashboard [dǽʃbɔːrd] n. (자동차·비행기 등의) 계기판
The dashboard in a vehicle is the panel facing the driver's seat where most of the instruments and switches are.

veer [viər] v. 방향을 홱 틀다; (성격을) 바꾸다
If something veers in a certain direction, it suddenly moves in that direction.

eject [idʒékt] v. 탈출하다; 쫓아내다; 방출하다; 튀어나오게 하다 (ejection n. 비상 탈출)
Ejection refers to a situation where a pilot leaves the aircraft quickly, usually because the plane is about to crash.

‡ **state** [steit] v. 말하다, 진술하다; n. 상태; 국가, 나라; 주(州)
If you state something, you say or write it in a formal or definite way.

★ **pop** [pap] v. 불쑥 내놓다; 불쑥 나타나다; 쏙 넣다; 펑 하는 소리가 나다; n. 펑 하는 소리
If you pop something somewhere, you put it there quickly.

slam [slæm] v. 세게 치다, 놓다; 쾅 닫다, 닫히다; n. 쾅 하고 닫기; 쾅 하는 소리
If you slam something, you strike or beat it with force and noise.

★ **grease** [griːs] n. 기름, 지방; v. 기름을 바르다 (grease pencil n. 유성 연필)
Grease refers to a thick, oily substance.

★ **crisis** [kráisis] n. 위기; 최악의 고비
A crisis is a situation in which something or someone is affected by one or more very serious problems.

^복_습 **simulate** [símjulèit] v. 모의실험하다; 가장하다 (simulation n. 모의실험)
In a simulation, you create a set of conditions artificially, for example in order to conduct an experiment.

★ **snap** [snæp] v. (화난 목소리로) 딱딱거리다; 탁 소리를 내다; 빠르게 움직이다; n. 탁 하는 소리
If someone snaps at you, they speak to you in a sharp, unfriendly way.

^복_습 **imminent** [ímənənt] a. 금방이라도 닥칠 듯한, 목전의, 임박한
If you say that something is imminent, especially something unpleasant, you mean it is almost certain to happen very soon.

^복_습 **satisfy** [sǽtisfài] v. 만족시키다; 충족시키다; 납득시키다 (satisfied a. 만족하는)
If you are satisfied with something, you are happy because you have got what you wanted or needed.

★ **maximum** [mǽksəməm] a. 최고의, 최대의; n. 최고, 최대
You use maximum to describe an amount which is the largest that is possible, allowed, or required.

advisable [ædváizəbl] a. 권할 만한, 바람직한 (inadvisable a. 현명하지 못한, 권할 만한 일이 못 되는)
A course of action that is inadvisable should not be carried out because it is not wise or sensible.

detonate [détəneit] v. 폭발하다; 폭발시키다 (detonation n. 폭발)
A detonation is a large or powerful explosion.

count on idiom ~을 기대하다, ~을 의지하다
If you count on someone or something, you hope or expect that something will happen or that someone will do something.

^복_습 **interrupt** [intərʌ́pt] v. (말·행동을) 방해하다; 중단시키다; 차단하다
If you interrupt someone who is speaking, you say or do something that causes them to stop.

controllable [kəntróuləbl] a. 지배할 수 있는; 조종 가능한 (uncontrollable a. 억제할 수 없는)
If you describe a situation or series of events as uncontrollable, you believe that nothing can be done to control them or to prevent things from getting worse.

‡ **tear** [tɛər] ① v. 찢다, 뜯다; 뜯어 내다; 질주하다; n. 찢어진 곳, 구멍 ② n. 눈물
To tear a material is to cause it to come apart.

★ **urgent** [ə́ːrdʒənt] a. 다급한; 긴급한, 시급한 (urgently ad. 다급하게)
If you speak urgently, you show that you are anxious for people to notice something or to do something.

★ **comply** [kəmplái] v. (법·명령 등에) 따르다, 준수하다
If someone or something complies with an order or set of rules, they are in accordance with what is required or expected.

복습 **spring** [spriŋ] v. (sprang-sprung) 휙 움직이다; 튀다; 갑자기 ~하다; n. 생기, 활기; 봄; 샘
If something springs in a particular direction, it moves suddenly and quickly.

volatile [válətil] a. 불안한; 변덕스러운; 휘발성의
Something that is volatile is likely to change suddenly and unexpectedly.

★ **illuminate** [ilúːmənèit] v. (불을) 비추다; 분명히 하다; (사람의 얼굴을) 환하게 하다
To illuminate something means to shine light on it and to make it brighter and more visible.

★ **flip** [flip] v. 휙 젖히다, 젖혀지다, 홱 뒤집다, 뒤집히다; 툭 던지다; n. 회전; 툭 던지기
If something flips, or if you flip it, it moves or is moved with a quick sudden movement into a different position.

★ **hover** [hʌ́vər] v. (허공을) 맴돌다; 서성이다; 주저하다; n. 공중을 떠다님
To hover means to stay in the same position in the air without moving forward or backward.

★ **label** [léibəl] v. (표에 정보를) 적다; 꼬리표를 붙이다; n. 표, 라벨; 꼬리표
If something is labeled, a label is attached to it giving information about it.

★ **smash** [smæʃ] v. (세게) 부딪치다; 박살내다; 부서지다; n. 박살내기; 요란한 소리
If something smashes or is smashed against something solid, it moves very fast and with great force against it.

복습 **knock** [nak] v. 치다, 부딪치다; (문 등을) 두드리다; n.부딪침; 문 두드리는 소리
If you knock something, you touch or hit it roughly, especially so that it falls or moves.

‡ **pin** [pin] v. 꼼짝 못 하게 하다; (핀으로) 고정시키다; 두다, 걸다; n. 핀
If someone pins you to something, they press you against a surface so that you cannot move.

복습 **hurtle** [həːrtl] v. 돌진하다
If someone or something hurtles somewhere, they move there very quickly, often in a rough or violent way.

miraculous [mirǽkjuləs] a. 기적적인 (miraculously ad. 기적적으로)
If you say that a good event has happened miraculously, you mean that it is very surprising and unexpected.

★ **vessel** [vésəl] **n.** (대형) 선박, 배; 그릇, 용기
A vessel is a ship or large boat.

★ **helpless** [hélplis] **a.** 무력한, 속수무책인
If you are helpless, you do not have the strength or power to do anything useful or to control or protect yourself.

plummet [plʌ́mit] **v.** 곤두박질치다, 급락하다
If someone or something plummets, they fall very fast toward the ground, usually from a great height.

★ **impact** [ímpækt] **n.** 충돌, 충격; (강력한) 영향; **v.** 충돌하다; 영향을 주다
An impact is the action of one object hitting another, or the force with which one object hits another.

★ **barrel** [bǽrəl] **v.** 쏜살같이 달리다; **n.** (대형) 통
If a vehicle or person is barreling in a particular direction, they are moving very quickly in that direction.

★ **scent** [sent] **n.** 냄새; 향기; **v.** 향기가 나다
The scent of something is a distinctive smell of it.

scorch [skɔːrtʃ] **v.** 태우다, 그슬리다
To scorch something means to burn it slightly.

★ **overwhelm** [òuvərhwélm] **v.** (격하게) 휩싸다; 어쩔 줄 모르게 하다
If you are overwhelmed by a feeling or event, it affects you very strongly, and you do not know how to deal with it.

visor [váizər] **n.** (헬멧의) 얼굴 가리개; (자동차 유리창에 대는) 차양
A visor is a movable part of a helmet which can be pulled down to protect a person's eyes or face.

slouch [slautʃ] **v.** 앞으로 구부리다, 수그리다; **n.** 앞으로 수그림; 수그려 걸음
If someone slouches, they sit or stand with their shoulders and head bent so they look lazy and unattractive.

cockpit [kákpit] **n.** (항공기·경주용 자동차 등의) 조종석
In an airplane or racing car, the cockpit is the part where the pilot or driver sits.

복습 **figure** [fígjər] **n.** (멀리서 흐릿하게 보이는) 사람; 수치; (중요한) 인물; **v.** 생각하다; 중요하다
You describe someone as a figure when you cannot see them clearly.

복습 **notice** [nóutis] **v.** 알아채다, 인지하다; 주의하다; **n.** 신경 씀, 주목, 알아챔
If you notice something or someone, you become aware of them.

복습 **confuse** [kənfjúːz] v. (사람을) 혼란시키다; 혼동하다 (confused a. 혼란스러운)
If you are confused, you do not know exactly what is happening or what to do.

★ **beard** [biərd] n. (턱)수염
A man's beard is the hair that grows on his chin and cheeks.

★ **stroke** [strouk] v. 어루만지다; 쓰다듬다; n. 쓰다듬기; 치기, 때리기
If you stroke someone or something, you move your hand slowly and gently over them.

‡ **chin** [tʃin] n. 턱
Your chin is the part of your face that is below your mouth and above your neck.

복습 **unsettle** [ʌnsétəl] v. (사람을) 불안하게 하다, 동요시키다 (unsettling a. 불안하게 하는)
If you describe something as unsettling, you mean that it makes you feel rather worried or uncertain.

복습 **chest** [tʃest] n. 가슴, 흉부; 상자, 궤
Your chest is the top part of the front of your body where your ribs, lungs, and heart are.

복습 **pause** [pɔːz] v. (말·일을 하다가) 잠시 멈추다; 정지시키다; n. (말·행동 등의) 멈춤
If you pause while you are doing something, you stop for a short period and then continue.

CHAPTER 4

Check Your Reading Speed
1분에 몇 단어를 읽는지 리딩 속도를 측정해 보세요.

$$\frac{1{,}643 \text{ words}}{\text{reading time ( ) sec}} \times 60 = (\quad) \text{ WPM}$$

Build Your Vocabulary

ferocity [fərásəti] n. 강렬함; 흉포함
The ferocity of something is its fierce or violent nature.

* **startle** [stɑːrtl] v. 깜짝 놀라게 하다; 움찔하다; n. 깜짝 놀람
If something sudden and unexpected startles you, it surprises and frightens you slightly.

복습 **seasoned** [síːznd] a. (사람이) 경험 많은, 노련한; (식품이) 양념을 한, 조미료를 넣은
You can use seasoned to describe a person who has a lot of experience of something.

dilate [dailéit] v. 확장하다, 팽창시키다; 키우다, 커지다 (dilation n. 팽창)
Dilation is a process in which something becomes wider or bigger.

map out idiom ~을 준비하다; ~을 계획하다
If you map out something that you are intending to do, you work out in detail how you will do it.

* **relative** [rélətiv] a. 상대적인; 비교적인; 관계가 있는; n. 친척
Relative to something means with reference to it or in comparison with it.

interject [intərdʒékt] v. 말참견을 하다
If you interject something, you say it and interrupt someone else who is speaking.

hold off idiom 미루다, 연기하다; ~을 물리치다
If you hold off doing something, you deliberately delay doing it.

figure out idiom 이해하다, 알아내다; 계산하다, 산출하다
If you figure out someone or something, you come to understand them by thinking carefully.

복습 **protest** [proutést] v. 이의를 제기하다, 항의하다; n. 항의; 시위
If you protest that something is the case, you insist that it is true, when other people think that it may not be.

‡ **willing** [wíliŋ] a. 기꺼이 하는, 자발적인; 꺼리지 않는
If someone is willing to do something, they are fairly happy about doing it and will do it if they are asked or required to do it.

crease [kri:s] n. 주름, 접은 자국; v. 주름을 잡다, 구겨지다
Creases in someone's skin are lines which form where their skin folds when they move.

etch [etʃ] v. 뚜렷이 새기다; (얼굴에 감정을) 역력히 드러내다
If a line or pattern is etched into a surface, it is cut into the surface by means of acid or a sharp tool.

복습 **brow** [brau] n. 이마; 눈썹
Your brow is your forehead.

sag [sæg] v. 축 늘어지다; 가라앉다, 꺼지다; n. 늘어짐, 처짐
When something sags, it hangs down loosely or sinks downward in the middle.

‡ **slight** [slait] a. 약간의, 조금의; 작고 여윈 (slightly ad. 약간, 조금)
Slightly means to some degree but not to a very large degree.

* **weary** [wíəri] a. 지친, 피곤한; ~에 싫증난; v. 지치게 하다; ~에 싫증나다
If you are weary, you are very tired.

복습 **frown** [fraun] n. 찡그림, 찌푸림; v. 얼굴을 찡그리다; 눈살을 찌푸리다
A frown refers to a contracting of the brows in displeasure or concentrated thought.

* **consequence** [kánsəkwèns] n. (발생한 일의) 결과; 중요함
The consequences of something are the results or effects of it.

복습 **realize** [rí:əlàiz] v. 깨닫다, 알아차리다; 실현하다, 달성하다
If you realize that something is true, you become aware of that fact or understand it.

pang [pæŋ] n. 비통, 상심; 격통, 고통
A pang is a sudden strong feeling or emotion, for example of sadness or pain.

* **grieve** [gri:v] v. 비통해 하다; 대단히 슬프게 하다 (grief n. 비탄, 비통)
Grief is a feeling of extreme sadness.

compound [kámpaund] n. (큰 건물이나 시설 등의) 구내; 복합체; a. 합성의; v. 혼합하다
A compound is an enclosed area of land that is used for a particular purpose.

복습 **code** [koud] n. 규정, 법규; (컴퓨터) 코드; 암호, 부호; v. 암호로 쓰다
A code is a set of rules about how people should behave or about how something must be done.

★ **hurdle** [həːrdl] n. 장애, 난관; (경기용) 허들; v. ~을 뛰어넘다
A hurdle is a problem, difficulty, or part of a process that may prevent you from achieving something.

복습 **quarter** [kwɔ́ːrtər] n. 숙소; 구역; 4분의 1; v. 숙소를 제공하다; 4등분하다
The rooms provided for soldiers, sailors, or servants to live in are called their quarters.

sulk [sʌlk] v. 부루퉁하다, 샐쭉하다; n. 부루퉁함
If you sulk, you are silent and bad-tempered for a while because you are annoyed about something.

glint [glint] n. 반짝임; (눈이 강하게) 번득임; v. 반짝거리다; (눈이 강하게) 번득이다
A glint is a quick flash of light.

★ **sparkle** [spaːrkl] n. 반짝거림, 광채; v. 반짝이다; 생기 넘치다 (sparkly a. 반짝이는)
Sparkly means shining with small points of reflected light.

복습 **engage** [ingéidʒ] v. 약혼시키다; 관계를 맺다; 교전을 벌이다; 사용하다 (engaged a. 약혼한)
When two people are engaged, they have agreed to marry each other.

★ **reveal** [rivíːl] v. (비밀 등을) 밝히다; (보이지 않던 것을) 드러내 보이다
To reveal something means to make people aware of it.

★ **strand** [strænd] v. 오도 가도 못 하게 하다; 발을 묶다; n. 가닥, 꼰 줄
If you are stranded, you are prevented from leaving a place, for example because of bad weather.

‡ **congratulate** [kəngrǽtʃulèit] v. 축하하다; 기뻐하다, 자랑스러워하다
(congratulation n. (pl.) 축하해요!)
You use 'congratulations' when you want to tell someone that you are pleased about their success, good luck, or happiness on a special occasion.

swipe [swaip] v. (전자 카드 등을) 인식기에 대다, 읽히다; 휘두르다; 후려치다; n. 휘두르기; 후려치기
If you swipe a card through a machine, you pass it through a narrow space in the machine so that it can read information on the card's magnetic strip.

★ **sigh** [sai] v. 한숨을 쉬다, 한숨짓다; 탄식하듯 말하다; n. 한숨
When you sigh, you let out a deep breath, as a way of expressing feelings such as disappointment, tiredness, or pleasure.

plod [plad] v. 터벅터벅 걷다; 꾸준히 일하다
If someone plods, they walk slowly and heavily.

글씨 glance [glæns] v. 흘낏 보다; 대충 훑어보다; n. 흘낏 봄
If you glance at something or someone, you look at them very quickly and then look away again immediately.

★ **kneel** [niːl] v. (knelt-knelt) 무릎을 꿇다
When you kneel, you bend your legs so that your knees are touching the ground.

★ **mechanical** [məkǽnikəl] a. 기계와 관련된; (행동이) 기계적인
Mechanical means relating to machines and engines and the way they work.

adorable [ədɔ́ːrəbl] a. 사랑스러운
If you say that someone or something is adorable, you are emphasizing that they are very attractive and you feel great affection for them.

글씨 hop [hap] v. 급히 움직이다; 깡충깡충 뛰다; n. 깡충깡충 뛰기
If you hop somewhere, you move there quickly or suddenly.

‡ **companion** [kəmpǽnjən] n. 동료; 친구; 동행
A companion is someone who shares the experiences of another, especially when these are unpleasant or unwelcome.

‡ **inform** [infɔ́ːrm] v. 알리다, 통지하다; 알아내다
If you inform someone of something, you tell them about it.

‡ **issue** [íʃuː] v. 발부하다; 발표하다; n. 문제; 주제, 사안
To issue is to give out or allocate a certificate or equipment officially to someone.

★ **emotional** [imóuʃənl] a. 감정의, 정서의; 감동적인, 감정에 호소하는
Emotional means concerned with emotions and feelings.

★ **transition** [trænzíʃən] n. (다른 상태·조건으로의) 이행; v. 변천하다
Transition is the process in which something changes from one state to another.

swish [swiʃ] v. 휙 소리를 내며 움직이다; n. 휙 하는 소리
If something swishes or if you swish it, it moves quickly through the air, making a soft sound.

★ **rhythmic** [ríðmik] a. 리드미컬한; 주기적인 (rhythmically ad. 리드미컬하게; 주기적으로)
If something moves rhythmically, its movements are repeated at regular intervals, forming a regular pattern or beat.

★ **stammer** [stǽmər] v. 말을 더듬다; n. 말 더듬기
If you stammer, you speak with difficulty, hesitating and repeating words or sounds.

considerate [kənsídərət] a. 사려 깊은, 배려하는
Someone who is considerate pays attention to the needs, wishes, or feelings of other people.

feline [fíːlain] n. 고양이; 고양잇과의 동물; a. 고양이 같은
A feline is a cat or other member of the cat family.

protocol [próutəkɔːl] n. (군대·궁전 등의) 의례, 관습
Protocol is a system of rules about the correct way to act in formal situations.

indicate [índikèit] v. 보여 주다; (계기가) 가리키다; (손가락이나 고갯짓으로) 가리키다
If a technical instrument indicates something, it shows a measurement or reading.

frost [frɔːst] v. (케이크에) 설탕을 입히다; 서리로 덮다, 서리가 앉다; n. 서리 (frosted a. 설탕을 입힌)
Frosted means covered with sugar icing.

celebrate [séləbrèit] v. 기념하다, 축하하다
If you celebrate, you do something enjoyable because of a special occasion or to mark someone's success.

cabinet [kǽbənit] n. 찬장, 보관장; (정부의) 내각
A cabinet is a cupboard used for storing things such as medicine or food or for displaying decorative things in.

freeze [friːz] n. 얼어붙음; 동결; 한파; v. (두려움 등으로 몸이) 얼어붙다; 얼다
(freeze-dried a. 냉동 건조된)
Freeze-dried food has been preserved by a process of rapid freezing and drying.

compromise [kámprəmàiz] v. ~을 위태롭게 하다; 타협하다; 양보하다; n. 타협, 절충
If someone or something is compromised, they are brought into disrepute or danger by indiscreet, foolish, or reckless behavior.

nutrition [njuːtríʃən] n. 영양, 영양 공급 (nutritional a. 영양의)
The nutritional content of food is all the substances that are in it which help you to remain healthy.

bite [bait] n. 한 입; 물기; v. 베어 물다; (곤충·뱀 등이) 물다
A bite of something, especially food, is the action of using someone's teeth to cut or break something, usually in order to eat it.

genuine [dʒénjuin] a. 진심 어린, 진실한; 진짜의, 진품의
Genuine refers to things such as emotions that are real and not pretended.

‡ sympathy [símpəθi] n. 동정, 연민; 공감
If you have sympathy for someone who is in a bad situation, you are sorry for them, and show this in the way you behave toward them.

glisten [glisn] v. 반짝이다, 번들거리다
If something glistens, it shines, usually because it is wet or oily.

‡ comfort [kʌ́mfərt] v. 위로하다; 편하게 하다; n. 편안; 위로 (comforting a. 위로가 되는)
When something is comforting to you, they make you feel less worried, unhappy, or upset.

give up idiom 포기하다; 그만두다; 단념하다
If you give up, you stop trying to do something, usually because it is too difficult.

‡ specific [spisífik] a. 특정한; 구체적인, 명확한 (specifically ad. 특별히)
You use specifically to emphasize that something is given special attention and considered separately from other things of the same kind.

‡ personality [pə:rsənǽləti] n. 성격, 개성
Your personality is your whole character and nature.

∗ profile [próufail] n. 개요; 옆모습; 인지도, (대중의) 관심; 윤곽; v. ~의 개요를 쓰다
A profile of someone is a short article or program in which their life and character are described.

∗ buddy [bʌ́di] n. 친구
A buddy is a close friend, usually a male friend of a man.

hit the rack idiom 잠을 자다
To hit the rack is to go to bed.

∗ whale [hweil] n. [동물] 고래
Whales are very large mammals that live in the sea.

∗ collapse [kəlǽps] v. 드러눕다; (의식을 잃고) 쓰러지다; 무너지다; n. 쓰러짐; (건물의) 붕괴
If you collapse onto something, you sit or lie down suddenly, especially after working hard.

nightstand [náitstænd] n. 침실용 탁자
A nightstand is a small table or cupboard that you have next to your bed.

emit [imít] v. (소리·빛·열·가스 등을) 내다, 방출하다
If something emits heat, light, gas, or a smell, it produces it and sends it out by means of a physical or chemical process.

steady [stédi] a. 꾸준한; 흔들림 없는, 안정된; 차분한, 침착한; v. 균형을 잡다, 진정시키다
A steady situation continues or develops gradually without any interruptions and is not likely to change quickly.

extraneous [ikstréiniəs] a. 외부로부터의, 밖의; 외래의, 이질적인
Extraneous means coming from outside.

parallel [pǽrəlèl] ad. 평행하게; a. 평행한; 아주 유사한; n. ~와 아주 유사한 것; v. ~와 유사하다
Two or more lines that run parallel to each other are the same distance apart at every point.

grip [grip] v. 움켜잡다; (마음·흥미·시선을) 끌다; n. 꽉 붙잡음, 움켜쥠; 통제, 지배
If you grip something, you take hold of it with your hand and continue to hold it firmly.

might [mait] n. (강력한) 힘; 권력; 세력 (with all one's might idiom 전력을 다하여, 힘껏)
If you do something with all your might, you do it using all your strength and energy.

crash [kræʃ] v. 추락하다; 부딪치다; 충돌하다; 굉음을 내다; n. 요란한 소리; (자동차·항공기) 사고
When an aircraft crashes, it falls or lands violently out of control, so as to be damaged or smashed.

desperate [déspərət] a. 필사적인; 자포자기의, 절망적인 (desperately ad. 필사적으로)
If you behave desperately, it shows that you are in such a bad situation that you are willing to try anything to change it.

altitude [ǽltətjùːd] n. (해발) 고도; 고도가 높은 곳, 고지
If something is at a particular altitude, it is at that height above sea level.

strain [strein] v. 안간힘을 쓰다; 무리하게 사용하다; 한계에 이르게 하다; n. 부담; 압박
If you strain to do something, you make a great effort to do it when it is difficult to do.

race [reis] v. (머리·심장 등이) 바쁘게 돌아가다; 쏜살같이 가다; 경주하다; n. 경주; 인종, 종족
If your heart races, it beats very quickly because you are excited or afraid.

drench [drenʃ] v. 흠뻑 적시다
When someone or something is drenched, they are completely wet or soaked.

dresser [drésər] n. 서랍장; 화장대
A dresser is a chest of drawers, usually with a mirror on the top.

sleek [sliːk] a. (모양이) 매끈한; 윤이 나는
Sleek vehicles, furniture, or other objects look smooth, shiny, and expensive.

décor [deikɔ́ːr] n. 실내 장식, 인테리어
The décor of a house or room is its style of furnishing and decoration.

gradual [grǽdʒuəl] a. 점진적인, 서서히 일어나는; 완만한 (gradually ad. 서서히)
If something changes or is done gradually, it changes or is done in small stages over a long period of time, rather than suddenly.

tilt [tilt] v. 기울이다, (뒤로) 젖히다; (의견·상황 등이) 기울어지다; n. 기울어짐, 젖혀짐
If you tilt part of your body, usually your head, you move it slightly upward or to one side.

mumble [mʌmbl] v. 중얼거리다, 웅얼거리다; n. 중얼거림
If you mumble, you speak very quietly and not at all clearly with the result that the words are difficult to understand.

wipe [waip] v. (먼지·물기 등을) 닦다; 지우다; n. 닦기
If you wipe dirt or liquid from something, you remove it, for example by using a cloth or your hand.

clammy [klǽmi] a. (기분 나쁘게) 축축한
Something that is clammy is unpleasantly damp or sticky.

moisture [mɔ́isʧər] n. 습기, 수분
Moisture is tiny drops of water in the air, on a surface, or in the ground.

forehead [fɔ́:rhèd] n. 이마
Your forehead is the area at the front of your head between your eyebrows and your hair.

clench [klenʧ] v. (주먹을) 꽉 쥐다; (이를) 악물다; ~을 단단히 붙잡다
When you clench your fist or your fist clenches, you curl your fingers up tightly.

fist [fist] n. 주먹
Your hand is referred to as your fist when you have bent your fingers in toward the palm in order to hit someone, to make an angry gesture, or to hold something.

frighten [fraitn] v. 겁먹게 하다, 놀라게 하다 (frightened a. 겁먹은, 무서워하는)
If you are frightened, you are anxious or afraid, often because of something that has just happened or that you think may happen.

helpless [hélplis] a. 무력한, 속수무책인
If you are helpless, you do not have the strength or power to do anything useful or to control or protect yourself.

illuminate [ilú:mənèit] v. (불을) 비추다; 분명히 하다; (사람의 얼굴을) 환하게 하다
To illuminate something means to shine light on it and to make it brighter and more visible.

pathway [pǽθwei] n. 길; 방향; 계획
A pathway is a particular course of action or a way of achieving something.

⚡ horizon [həráizn] n. 지평선, 수평선
The horizon is the line in the far distance where the sky seems to meet the land or the sea.

★ supplement [sʌ́pləmənt] n. 보충제; 보충, 추가; v. 보충하다
A supplement is a pill that you take or a special kind of food that you eat in order to improve your health.

★ doubtful [dáutfəl] a. 확신이 없는, 의심을 품은; 불확실한 (doubtfully ad. 미심쩍게)
When you act doubtfully about something, it shows that you feel unsure or uncertain about it.

putter [pʌ́tər] v. 빈둥거리다, 어슬렁거리다; 꾸물거리며 일하다
To putter is to move about without hurrying and in a relaxed and pleasant way.

⚡ challenge [ʧǽlindʒ] v. 도전 의식을 북돋우다; 도전하다; n. 도전; 저항
(challenging a. 도전 의식을 북돋우는, 도전적인)
A challenging task or job requires great effort and determination.

★ chew [ʧuː] v. (음식을) 씹다; 물어뜯다, 깨물다; n. 씹기, 깨물기
When you chew food, you use your teeth to break it up in your mouth so that it becomes easier to swallow.

복습 fusion [fjúːʒən] n. 융합, 결합
In physics, fusion is the process in which atomic particles combine and produce a large amount of nuclear energy.

★ gear [giər] n. (특정 활동에 필요한) 장비; 기어
The gear involved in a particular activity is the equipment or special clothing that you use.

복습 urgent [ə́ːrdʒənt] a. 다급한; 긴급한, 시급한 (urgency n. 다급함)
The urgency is the feeling or belief that something needs to be dealt with immediately.

drown out idiom (소음이) ~을 들리지 않게 하다; 떠내려 보내다
If a sound drowns out your voice, the sound is so loud that you cannot be heard.

whir [hwəːr] v. 윙 하는 소리를 내다; n. 윙윙거리는 소리
When something such as a machine or an insect's wing whirs, it makes a series of low sounds so quickly that they seem like one continuous sound.

‡ **attention** [əténʃən] n. 차려 (자세); 주의; 관심; 배려
When people stand to attention or stand at attention, they stand straight with their feet together and their arms at their sides.

복습 **determination** [ditə̀ːrmənéiʃən] n. 결심, 결단; 결정
Determination is the quality that you show when you have decided to do something and you will not let anything stop you.

elicit [ilísit] v. 이끌어 내다, 도출하다
If you elicit a response or a reaction, you do or say something which makes other people respond or react.

＊ **spark** [spaːrk] n. 아주 조금; 불꽃, 불똥; (전류의) 스파크; v. 촉발시키다; 불꽃을 일으키다
A spark of a quality or feeling, especially a desirable one, is a small but noticeable amount of it.

＊ **adapt** [ədǽpt] v. 적응하다; 조정하다
If you adapt to a new situation or adapt yourself to it, you change your ideas or behavior in order to deal with it successfully.

복습 **hostile** [hastl] a. 적대적인; 강력히 반대하는
In a war, you use hostile to describe your enemy's forces and activities.

복습 **alien** [éiljən] a. 외계의; 생경한; 이질적인; n. 외계인
Alien means coming from another world, such as an outer space.

‡ **dull** [dʌl] v. 둔하게 만들다; 둔해지다, 약해지다; a. 따분한; (소리가) 분명하지 않은; 흐릿한
If something dulls or if it is dulled, it becomes less intense, bright, or lively.

＊ **awaken** [əwéikən] v. (감정을) 불러일으키다; (잠에서) 깨우다
If something awakens an emotion, you start to feel that emotion.

＊ **resign** [rizáin] v. 체념하다; 사직하다, 물러나다 (resigned a. 체념한)
If you are resigned to an unpleasant situation or fact, you accept it without complaining because you realize that you cannot change it.

복습 **cockpit** [kákpit] n. (항공기·경주용 자동차 등의) 조종석
In an airplane or racing car, the cockpit is the part where the pilot or driver sits.

muse [mjuːz] v. (사색에 잠긴 채) 혼잣말을 하다; 골똘히 생각하다
If you muse something, you say it in a way that shows that you have been thinking carefully about it.

visor [váizər] n. (헬멧의) 얼굴 가리개; (자동차 유리창에 대는) 차양
A visor is a movable part of a helmet which can be pulled down to protect a person's eyes or face.

solid [sálid] a. 탄탄한, 확실한; (속이) 꽉 찬; 단단한; 고체의; n. 고체
Something that is solid is firm, strong, and compact.

infinity [infínəti] n. 아득히 먼 곳; 무한성
Infinity is a point that is further away than any other point and can never be reached.

5 & 6

1. Who was in the hologram recording that had been left for Buzz?

    A. Alisha and Kiko

    B. Alisha and her daughter

    C. Alisha and Sox

    D. Alisha and her granddaughter

2. What news did Commander Burnside tell Buzz about?

    A. That Sox would be turned off

    B. That the next flight test was ready

    C. That the program would be shut down

    D. That Alisha was sick

3. Who figured out how to solve the fuel problem?

    A. Sox

    B. Buzz

    C. Alisha

    D. Izzy

4. How did Buzz know that the new fuel was different?

    A. It made a bubbling sound.

    B. It felt very heavy.

    C. It filled up the fuel cell.

    D. It turned into a crystal.

5. What did Sox do when IVAN would not authorize opening the silo doors?

    A. He pushed the doors open with his paws.

    B. He overrode the system with a flash drive.

    C. He hit IVAN with his tail.

    D. He told Buzz a secret code.

CHAPTER 5

Check Your Reading Speed
1분에 몇 단어를 읽는지 리딩 속도를 측정해 보세요.

$$\frac{1,466 \text{ words}}{\text{reading time ( ) sec}} \times 60 = (\quad) \text{ WPM}$$

Build Your Vocabulary

복습 **ranger** [réindʒər] n. 경비 대원; 기습 공격대원
A ranger is an armed guard who patrols a region.

★ **predict** [pridíkt] v. 예측하다, 예견하다
If you predict an event, you say that it will happen.

복습 **determination** [ditə̀ːrmənéiʃən] n. 결심, 결단; 결정
Determination is the quality that you show when you have decided to do something and you will not let anything stop you.

let go of idiom ~을 포기하다; ~에서 손을 놓다; ~을 잊어버리다
If you let go of a feeling, attitude, or the control that you have over something, you accept that you should give it up or that it should no longer influence you.

undying [ʌndáiiŋ] a. 변하지 않는; 불멸의, 영원한
If you refer to someone's undying feelings, you mean that the feelings are very strong and are unlikely to change.

‡ **faith** [feiθ] n. 믿음, 신뢰; 신앙
If you have faith in someone or something, you feel confident about their ability or goodness.

복습 **eventually** [ivénʧuəli] ad. 결국, 마침내
Eventually means at the end of a situation or process or as the final result of it.

복습 **pound** [paund] v. (가슴이) 쿵쿵 뛰다; (요란한 소리로 여러 차례) 두드리다; 쿵쾅거리며 걷다
If your heart is pounding, it is beating with an unusually strong and fast rhythm, usually because you are afraid.

복습 **crew** [kruː] n. (함께 일을 하는) 팀, 조; (배·항공기의) 승무원; v. 승무원을 하다
A crew is a group of people with special technical skills who work together on a task or project.

represent [rèprizént] v. 상징하다; 대표하다; 보여주다, 제시하다
If a sign or symbol represents something, it is accepted as meaning that thing.

fade [feid] v. 서서히 사라지다; (색깔이) 바래다, 희미해지다
If memories, feelings, or possibilities fade, they slowly become less intense or less strong.

lone [loun] a. 고독한, 혼자의
If you talk about a lone person or thing, you mean that they are alone.

greet [gri:t] v. 환영하다; 인사하다; 반응을 보이다; (눈·귀에) 들어오다
To greet is to meet or receive with expressions of gladness or welcome.

expect [ikspékt] v. 출산 예정이다; 예상하다, 기대하다
If you say that a woman is expecting a baby, or that she is expecting, you mean that she is pregnant.

celebrate [séləbrèit] v. 기념하다, 축하하다
If you celebrate, you do something enjoyable because of a special occasion or to mark someone's success.

milestone [máilstoun] n. 중요한 사건; 이정표; 기념비
A milestone is an important event in the history or development of something or someone.

anniversary [ænəvə́:rsəri] n. 기념일
An anniversary is a date which is remembered or celebrated because a special event happened on that date in a previous year.

display [displéi] v. 전시하다; 내보이다; n. 전시, 진열; 표현; 화면
If you display something that you want people to see, you put it in a particular place, so that people can see it easily.

trudge [trʌdʒ] v. 터덜터덜 걷다; 느릿느릿 걷다; n. 터덜터덜 걷기
If you trudge somewhere, you walk there slowly and with heavy steps, especially because you are tired or unhappy.

hallway [hɔ́:lwèi] n. 복도; 통로; 현관
A hallway in a building is a long passage with doors into rooms on both sides of it.

shatter [ʃǽtər] v. 산산이 부서지다, 산산조각 나다; 엄청난 충격을 주다
If something shatters or is shattered, it breaks into a lot of small pieces.

terrific [tərífik] a. (양·정도 등이) 엄청난; 멋진, 훌륭한
Terrific means very great in amount, degree, or intensity.

explode [iksplóud] v. 폭발하다; 갑자기 ~하다; (강한 감정을) 터뜨리다 (explosion n. 폭발)
An explosion is a sudden, violent burst of energy, for example one caused by a bomb.

electronic [ilektránik] a. 전자의, 전자 장비와 관련된
An electronic device has transistors or silicon chips which control and change the electric current passing through the device.

label [léibəl] v. (표에 정보를) 적다; 꼬리표를 붙이다; n. 표, 라벨; 꼬리표
If something is labeled, a label is attached to it giving information about it.

creep [kri:p] v. 서서히 다가가다; 살금살금 움직이다; 기다; n. 너무 싫은 사람
If something creeps in or creeps back, it begins to occur or becomes part of something without people realizing or without them wanting it.

insert [insə́:rt] v. 끼우다, 넣다; n. 부속품; 삽입 광고
If you insert an object into something, you put the object inside it.

gasp [gæsp] v. 헉 하고 숨을 쉬다; 숨을 제대로 못 쉬다; n. 헉 하는 소리를 냄
When you gasp, you take a short quick breath through your mouth, especially when you are surprised, shocked, or in pain.

prop [prap] v. 떠받치다; n. 지주, 버팀목; (연극·영화에 쓰이는) 소품
If you prop an object on or against something, you support it by putting something underneath it or by resting it somewhere.

feeble [fí:bl] a. 아주 약한 (feebly ad. 희미하게)
If someone speaks feebly, they do so in a way that lacks physical or mental strength.

mist [mist] v. 눈물이 맺히다; 부옇게 되다; n. 엷은 안개
If someone's eyes mist, they cannot see easily because there are tears in their eyes.

vision [víʒən] n. 시야; 환상, 상상; 환영
Your vision is everything that you can see from a particular place or position.

bound [baund] v. 껑충껑충 달리다; a. ~할 가능성이 큰
If a person or animal bounds in a particular direction, they move quickly with large steps or jumps.

project [prádʒekt] v. (빛·영상 등을) 비추다; 발사하다; 계획하다; n. 계획, 프로젝트 (projection n. (투사된) 영상)
A projection refers to an image that is reproduced on a surface by optical means.

exclaim [ikskléim] v. 소리치다, 외치다
If you exclaim, you cry out suddenly in surprise, strong emotion, or pain.

* **sweetheart** [swíːthàːrt] n. 애야, 여보, 당신; 애인
You call someone sweetheart if you are very fond of them.

* **puff** [pʌf] v. 부풀리다; (연기·김을) 내뿜다; 숨을 헐떡거리다; n. 부푼 것
If you puff out your cheeks or your chest, you fill them with air so that they look bigger.

* **squeeze** [skwiːz] v. 꼭 껴안다; 꼭 쥐다, 짜다; 비집고 들어가다; n. 꼭 껴안기; 꼭 쥐기
To squeeze is to hug closely.

복습 **sigh** [sai] v. 한숨을 쉬다, 한숨짓다; 탄식하듯 말하다; n. 한숨
When you sigh, you let out a deep breath, as a way of expressing feelings such as disappointment, tiredness, or pleasure.

* **extend** [iksténd] v. (신체 부위를) 뻗다; 뻗어 있다; (거리·기간을) 포괄하다
To extend is to stretch forth an arm or other body parts.

pointer finger [pɔ́intər fíŋgər] n. 집게손가락
Your pointer finger is the finger that is next to your thumb.

복습 **slight** [slait] a. 약간의, 조금의; 작고 여윈 (slightly ad. 약간, 조금)
Slightly means to some degree but not to a very large degree.

meld [meld] v. 섞이다, 혼합하다
If several things meld, they combine or blend in a pleasant or useful way.

복습 **flip** [flip] v. 홱 뒤집다, 뒤집히다; 휙 젖히다; 젖혀지다; 툭 던지다; n. 회전; 툭 던지기
If something flips over, or if you flip it over or into a different position, it moves or is moved into a different position.

* **grin** [grin] v. 활짝 웃다; n. 활짝 웃음
When you grin, you smile broadly.

* **bridle** [braidl] v. 굴레를 씌우다; n. (말에게 씌우는) 굴레 (unbridled a. 억제되지 않은)
If you describe behavior or feelings as unbridled, you mean that they are not controlled or limited in any way.

optimism [áptəmìzm] n. 낙관주의, 낙관론
Optimism is the feeling of being hopeful about the future or about the success of something in particular.

carefree [kérfri] a. 근심 걱정 없는, 속 편한
A carefree person or period of time doesn't have or involve any problems, worries, or responsibilities.

★ **echo** [ékou] v. (소리가) 울리다, 메아리치다; 그대로 따라 하다; n. (소리의) 울림, 메아리; 반복
If a sound echoes, it is reflected off a surface and can be heard again after the original sound has stopped.

복습 **command** [kəmǽnd] v. 지휘하다; 명령하다; n. 지휘; 명령; 사령부 (commander n. 사령관)
A commander is an officer in charge of a military operation or organization.

복습 **pile** [pail] v. 쌓다; (차곡차곡) 포개다; 우르르 가다; n. 무더기, 더미; 쌓아 놓은 것
If you pile things somewhere, you put them there so that they form a pile.

‡ **flesh** [fleʃ] n. 육체, 몸; (사람·동물의) 살; (사람의) 피부 (in the flesh idiom 실물로, 직접)
If you meet or see someone in the flesh, you actually meet or see them.

★ **salute** [səlúːt] v. 경례를 하다; 경의를 표하다, 절하다; n. 거수 경례; 인사
If you salute someone, you greet them or show your respect with a formal sign.

‡ **gesture** [dʒésʧər] n. 몸짓; (감정·의도의) 표시; v. 몸짓을 하다; (손·머리 등으로) 가리키다
A gesture is a movement that you make with a part of your body, especially your hands, to express emotion or information.

★ **absentminded** [ǽbsəntmáindid] a. 멍하니 있는, 넋놓은, 방심 상태의
(absentmindedly ad. 멍하니)
When someone behaves absentmindedly, they forget things or do not pay attention to what they are doing, often because they are thinking about something else.

복습 **mumble** [mʌmbl] v. 중얼거리다, 웅얼거리다; n. 중얼거림
If you mumble, you speak very quietly and not at all clearly with the result that the words are difficult to understand.

daze [deiz] n. 멍한 상태; 눈이 부심; v. 멍하게 하다; 눈부시게 하다
If someone is in a daze, they are feeling confused and unable to think clearly, often because they have had a shock or surprise.

복습 **grieve** [griːv] v. 비통해 하다; 대단히 슬프게 하다
If you grieve over something, especially someone's death, you feel very sad about it.

★ **presence** [prezns] n. (특정한 곳에) 있음, 존재; 주둔군
If you are in someone's presence, you are in the same place as that person, and are close enough to them to be seen or heard.

‡ **process** [práses] v. 처리하다; 가공하다; n. 과정, 절차; 공정
To process something is to handle it.

private [práivət] a. 사적인; 사유의; 은밀한; 사생활의
(in private idiom 다른 사람이 없는 곳에서)
If you do something in private, you do it without other people being present, often because it is something that you want to keep secret.

square [skwɛər] v. 똑바로 펴다; 네모지게 만들다; a. 정사각형 모양의; 직각의; ad. 똑바로
If you square your shoulders, you stand straight and push them back, usually to show your determination.

fidget [fídʒit] v. 안절부절못하다; 꼼지락거리다; n. 안절부절못함
If you fidget, you keep moving your hands or feet slightly or changing your position slightly, for example because you are nervous, bored, or excited.

shut down idiom (기계를) 정지시키다; (공장·가게의) 문을 닫다
If a business or a large piece of equipment shuts down or someone shuts it down, it stops operating.

suck [sʌk] v. (특정한 방향으로) 빨아들이다; 빨아 먹다; n. 빨기, 빨아 먹기
If something sucks a liquid, gas, or object in a particular direction, it draws it there with a powerful force.

inform [infɔ́:rm] v. 알리다, 통지하다; 알아내다
If you inform someone of something, you tell them about it.

incredulous [inkrédʒuləs] a. 믿지 않는, 회의적인 (incredulously ad. 믿을 수 없다는 듯이)
When someone behaves incredulously, it shows that they are unable to believe something because it is very surprising or shocking.

shield [ʃi:ld] n. 보호 장치; 방패; v. 보호하다, 가리다
Something or someone which is a shield against a particular danger or risk provides protection from it.

critter [krítər] n. 생물, 가축
A critter is a living creature.

enthusiastic [inθù:ziǽstik] a. 열렬한, 열광적인 (enthusiastically ad. 열광적으로)
If you do something enthusiastically, you show how much you like or enjoy it by the way that you behave and talk.

tuck [tʌk] v. (작은 공간에) 집어 넣다, 끼워 넣다; (끝부분을) 접다; 덮다; n. (접은) 주름
If you tuck something somewhere, you put it there so that it is safe, comfortable, or neat.

make do with idiom (만족스럽지는 않지만) ~으로 견디다; 임시변통하다
To make do with something is to manage with the limited or inadequate means available.

★ **compliment** [kámpləmənt] v. 칭찬하다; n. 칭찬, 찬사
If you compliment someone, you praise or express admiration for them.

★ **stun** [stʌn] v. 깜짝 놀라게 하다; 어리벙벙하게 하다; 기절시키다 (stunned a. 깜짝 놀란)
If you are stunned by something, you are extremely shocked or surprised by it and are therefore unable to speak or do anything.

‡ **distance** [dístəns] n. 먼 곳; 거리; v. (~에) 관여하지 않다 (in the distance idiom 저 먼 곳에)
If you can see something in the distance, you can see it, far away from you.

★ **haul** [hɔːl] v. (아주 힘들여) 끌다; (몸을) 간신히 움직이다; n. 많은 양
If you haul something which is heavy or difficult to move, you move it using a lot of effort.

★ **framework** [freímwərk] n. (건물 등의) 뼈대; 틀; 체제, 체계
A framework is a structure that forms a support or frame for something.

‡ **steel** [stiːl] n. 강철; v. (~에 대비해서) 마음을 단단히 먹다
Steel is a very strong metal which is made mainly from iron.

grid [grid] n. 격자무늬; (지도의) 격자 눈금; (자동차 경주에서) 출발점
A grid is something which is in a pattern of straight lines that cross over each other, forming squares.

gusto [gʌ́stou] n. 기쁨, 즐거움, 넘치는 활기; 취미, 즐김, 기호
If you do something with gusto, you do it with energetic and enthusiastic enjoyment.

hang one's head idiom 낙심하다, 기가 죽다, 부끄러워 고개를 숙이다
When a person hangs their head, they are feeling dejected or ashamed.

복습 **companion** [kəmpǽnjən] n. 동료; 친구; 동행
A companion is someone who shares the experiences of another, especially when these are unpleasant or unwelcome.

복습 **figure out** idiom 이해하다, 알아내다; 계산하다, 산출하다
If you figure out someone or something, you come to understand them by thinking carefully.

reverie [révəri] n. 상념, 사색; 공상, 환상, 몽상
Reverie refers to the condition of being lost in thought.

variance [vɛ́əriəns] **n.** 차이, 변화
The variance between things is the difference between them.

fusion [fjúːʒən] **n.** 융합, 결합
In physics, fusion is the process in which atomic particles combine and produce a large amount of nuclear energy.

formula [fɔ́ːrmjulə] **n.** 제조법; 화학식; 공식
In science, the formula for a substance is a list of the amounts of various elements which make up that substance, or an indication of the atoms that it is composed of.

highlight [háilait] **v.** 강조하다; 강조 표시를 하다; **n.** 하이라이트, 가장 좋은 부분
If someone or something highlights a point or problem, they emphasize it or make you think about it.

disbelief [disbilíːf] **n.** 믿기지 않음, 불신감
Disbelief is not believing that something is true or real.

stable [steibl] **a.** 안정된, 안정적인; 차분한; **n.** 마구간
If something is stable, it is not likely to change or come to an end suddenly.

crystallize [krístəlàiz] **v.** 구체화하다; 결정체를 이루다
If you crystallize an opinion or idea, or if it crystallizes, it becomes fixed and definite in someone's mind.

★ **theoretical** [θìːərétikəl] **a.** 이론상의, 이론적인 (theoretically **ad.** 이론상으로는)
You use theoretically to say that although something is supposed to be true or to happen in the way stated, it may not in fact be true or happen in that way.

startle [staːrtl] **v.** 깜짝 놀라게 하다; 움찔하다; **n.** 깜짝 놀람
If something sudden and unexpected startles you, it surprises and frightens you slightly.

★ **security** [sikjúərəti] **n.** 보안, 경비; (미래를 위한) 보장; 안도감, 안심
(security guard **n.** 보안 요원)
A security guard is someone whose job is to protect a building or people.

★ **blink** [bliŋk] **v.** 눈을 깜박이다; (불빛이) 깜박거리다; **n.** 눈을 깜박거림
When you blink or when you blink your eyes, you shut your eyes and very quickly open them again.

state [steit] **v.** 말하다, 진술하다; **n.** 상태; 국가, 나라; 주(州)
If you state something, you say or write it in a formal or definite way.

decommission [dìːkəmíʃən] v. 폐기하다, 해체하다; 퇴역시키다
When something such as a machine is decommissioned, it is taken to pieces because it is no longer going to be used.

★ **grunt** [grʌnt] v. 끙 앓는 소리를 내다; 꿀꿀거리다; n. (사람이) 끙 하는 소리; (돼지가) 꿀꿀거리는 소리
If you grunt, you make a low sound, especially to show that you are in pain, annoyed, or not interested.

intimidate [intímədèit] v. (시키는 대로 하도록) 위협하다, 겁을 주다 (intimidating a. 위협적인)
If you describe someone or something as intimidating, you mean that they are frightening and make people lose confidence.

★ **equip** [ikwíp] v. 장비를 갖추다; (지식 등을 가르쳐) 준비를 갖춰 주다
If you equip a person or thing with something, you give them the tools or equipment that are needed.

복습 **gear** [giər] n. (특정 활동에 필요한) 장비; 기어
The gear involved in a particular activity is the equipment or special clothing that you use.

★ **combat** [kəmbǽt] n. 전투, 싸움; v. (적과) 싸우다, 전투를 벌이다; 방지하다 (combatant n. 전투원)
A combatant is a person, group, or country that takes part in the fighting in a war.

★ **hardware** [hárdwɛər] n. 기재, 장비; (컴퓨터) 하드웨어
Hardware refers to mechanical equipment or components.

복습 **burst** [bəːrst] v. (burst-burst) 불쑥 움직이다; 갑자기 ~하다; 터지다; n. (갑자기) ~을 함; 파열, 폭발
To burst into or out of a place means to enter or leave it suddenly with a lot of energy or force.

☆ **sight** [sait] n. 광경, 모습; 시야; 보기, 봄; v. 갑자기 보다
A sight is something that you see.

Check Your Reading Speed

1분에 몇 단어를 읽는지 리딩 속도를 측정해 보세요.

$$\frac{880 \text{ words}}{\text{reading time ( ) sec}} \times 60 = (\quad) \text{ WPM}$$

Build Your Vocabulary

indicate [índikèit] v. 보여 주다; (계기가) 가리키다; (손가락이나 고갯짓으로) 가리키다
If one thing indicates something else, it is a sign of that thing.

concern [kənsə́:rn] n. 우려, 걱정; 관심사; v. 걱정스럽게 하다; 관련되다
Concern is worry about a situation.

skid [skid] v. 미끄러지다; n. (차량의) 미끄러짐
When a person or object skids while moving, they slide without rotating.

launch [lɔ:nʧ] n. 발사; 시작; 개시; v. 던지다; 발사하다; 맹렬히 덤비다 (launchpad n. 발사대)
A launchpad is a platform from which a spacecraft or rocket is launched.

grab [græb] v. (와락·단단히) 붙잡다; 급히 ~하다; n. 와락 잡아채려고 함
If you grab something, you take it or pick it up suddenly and roughly.

activate [ǽktəvèit] v. 작동시키다; 활성화시키다
If a device or process is activated, something causes it to start working.

wrist [rist] n. 손목, 팔목
Your wrist is the part of your body between your hand and your arm which bends when you move your hand.

log [lɔ:g] n. (비행·항해 등의) 일지, 기록; 통나무; v. 일지에 기록하다; 비행하다, 항해하다
A log is an official written account of what happens each day, for example on board a ship.

possess [pəzés] v. 소유하다, 소지하다; (자질·특징을) 지니다 (possession n. 소지, 보유)
If you are in possession of something, you have it, because you have obtained it or because it belongs to you.

formula [fɔ́:rmjulə] n. 제조법; 화학식; 공식
In science, the formula for a substance is a list of the amounts of various elements which make up that substance, or an indication of the atoms that it is composed of.

CHAPTER 6

★ **sneak** [sniːk] v. (snuck/sneaked-snuck/sneaked) 살금살금 가다; 몰래 하다; a. 기습적인
If you sneak somewhere, you go there very quietly on foot, trying to avoid being seen or heard.

★ **compel** [kəmpél] v. 강요하다, 억지로 시키다, 거역하지 못하게 하는 영향력을 갖다
If a situation, a rule, or a person compels you to do something, they force you to do it.

★ **notify** [nóutəfài] v. (공식적으로) 알리다, 통지하다
If you notify someone of something, you officially inform them about it.

복습 **decommission** [dìːkəmíʃən] v. 폐기하다, 해체하다; 퇴역시키다
When something such as a machine is decommissioned, it is taken to pieces because it is no longer going to be used.

복습 **interrupt** [intərʌ́pt] v. (말·행동을) 방해하다; 중단시키다; 차단하다
If you interrupt someone who is speaking, you say or do something that causes them to stop.

복습 **freeze** [friːz] v. (froze-frozen) (두려움 등으로 몸이) 얼어붙다; 얼다; n. 얼어붙음; 동결; 한파
To freeze is to become motionless through fear or shock.

복습 **nod** [nad] v. (고개를) 끄덕이다, 까딱하다; n. (고개를) 끄덕임
If you nod, you move your head downward and upward to show that you are answering 'yes' to a question, or to show agreement, understanding, or approval.

복습 **security** [sikjúərəti] n. 보안, 경비; (미래를 위한) 보장; 안도감, 안심
(security guard n. 보안 요원)
A security guard is someone whose job is to protect a building or people.

★ **authorize** [ɔ́ːθəràiz] v. 정식으로 허가하다, 권한을 부여하다 (authorized a. 권한을 부여받은)
If something is authorized, it is officially permitted or empowered.

tranquilize [trǽŋkwəlàiz] v. (마음을) 안정시키다; 조용하게 하다, 진정하다
(tranquilizer n. 마취제, 진정제)
Tranquilizers are sometimes used to make people or animals become sleepy or unconscious.

★ **dart** [daːrt] n. (작은) 화살; 쏜살같이 달림; v. 눈길을 던지다, 흘긋 쳐다보다; 쏜살같이 움직이다
A dart is a small, narrow object with a sharp point which can be thrown or shot.

복습 **collapse** [kəlǽps] v. (의식을 잃고) 쓰러지다; 드러눕다; 무너지다; n. 쓰러짐; (건물의) 붕괴
If you collapse, you suddenly faint or fall down because you are very ill or weak.

★ **impress** [imprés] v. 깊은 인상을 주다, 감동을 주다 (impressed a. 감명을 받은)
If you are impressed by something or someone, you feel great admiration for them.

pause [pɔːz] v. (말·일을 하다가) 잠시 멈추다; 정지시키다; n. (말·행동 등의) 멈춤
If you pause while you are doing something, you stop for a short period and then continue.

get out of line idiom 방침에 반한 행동을 하다, 예상 밖의 행동을 하다; 버릇없이 행동하다
If someone gets out of line, they behave badly or break the rules.

hasty [héisti] a. 서두른; 성급한 (hastily ad. 급히, 서둘러서)
If someone acts hastily, their movement or statement is sudden, and often done in reaction to something that has just happened.

depot [díːpou] n. 저장소, 창고
A depot is a place where large amounts of raw materials, equipment, arms, or other supplies are kept until they are needed.

mechanical [məkǽnikəl] a. 기계와 관련된; (행동이) 기계적인
Mechanical means relating to machines and engines and the way they work.

sight [sait] n. 시야; 보기, 봄; 광경, 모습; v. 갑자기 보다
If something is in sight or within sight, you can see it.

instruct [instrʌ́kt] v. (정보를) 알려 주다; 가르치다; 지시하다 (instruction n. 설명)
Instructions are clear and detailed information on how to do something.

liquid [líkwid] n. 액체; a. 액체의
A liquid is a substance which is not solid but which flows and can be poured, for example water.

refract [rifrǽkt] v. (빛을) 굴절시키다
When a ray of light or a sound wave refracts or is refracted, the path it follows bends at a particular point, for example when it enters water or glass.

slam [slæm] v. 쾅 닫다, 닫히다; 세게 치다, 놓다; n. 쾅 하고 닫기; 쾅 하는 소리
If you slam a door or window or if it slams, it shuts noisily and with great force.

sweep [swiːp] v. 훑다; 휩쓸고 가다; (빗자루로) 쓸다; n. 쓸기, 비질하기
If lights or someone's eyes sweep an area, they move across the area from side to side.

flashlight [flǽʃlait] n. 손전등, 회중전등
A flashlight is a small electric light which gets its power from batteries and which you can carry in your hand.

lean [liːn] v. 기울이다, (몸을) 숙이다; ~에 기대다; a. 호리호리한
When you lean in a particular direction, you bend your body in that direction.

ᵇ knock [nak] v. 치다, 부딪치다; (문 등을) 두드리다; n. 부딪침; 문 두드리는 소리
If you knock something, you touch or hit it roughly, especially so that it falls or moves.

ᵇ gasp [gæsp] v. 헉 하고 숨을 쉬다; 숨을 제대로 못 쉬다; n. 헉 하는 소리를 냄
When you gasp, you take a short quick breath through your mouth, especially when you are surprised, shocked, or in pain.

tarp [ta:rp] n. 방수포
A tarp is a sheet of heavy waterproof material that is used as a protective cover.

ᵇ insert [insə́:rt] v. 끼우다, 넣다; n. 부속품; 삽입 광고
If you insert an object into something, you put the object inside it.

⋆ breach [bri:ʃ] n. 위반; 파괴; v. (합의나 약속을) 위반하다; (방어벽 등에) 구멍을 뚫다
A breach of an agreement, a law, or a promise is an act of breaking it.

bay [bei] n. 구역, 구간; 만(灣)
A bay is a partly enclosed area, inside or outside a building, that is used for a particular purpose.

⋆ whisper [hwíspər] v. 속삭이다, 소곤거리다; n. 속삭임, 소곤거리는 소리
When you whisper, you say something very quietly, using your breath rather than your throat, so that only one person can hear you.

ᵇ alarm [əlá:rm] v. 불안하게 하다; n. 불안, 공포 (alarmed a. 불안해하는)
If someone is alarmed, they feel afraid or anxious that something unpleasant or dangerous might happen.

ᵇ run out of idiom ~을 다 써버리다; ~이 없어지다
If you run out of something like money or time, you have used up all of it.

⋆ scan [skæn] v. (유심히) 살피다; 훑어보다; 정밀 촬영하다; 스캔하다; n. 정밀 검사
When you scan a place or group of people, you look at it carefully, usually because you are looking for something or someone.

⋆ cozy [kóuzi] a. 아늑한, 편안한; 친밀한
If you are cozy, you are comfortable and warm.

⋆ perch [pə:rʃ] n. 높은 자리; v. (무엇의 꼭대기나 끝에) 위치하다
You can refer to a high place where someone is sitting as their perch.

headrest [hédrest] n. 머리 받침
A headrest is the part of the back of a seat on which you can lean your head, especially one on the front seat of a car.

liftoff [líftɔ:f] n. (로켓 등의) 발사, 발진, 수직 이륙
Liftoff refers to the initial movement or ascent of a rocket from its launch pad.

복습 **internal** [intə́:rnl] a. 내부의; 내면적인; 국내의
Internal is used to describe things that exist or happen inside a particular person, object, or place.

복습 **navigate** [nǽvəgèit] v. 조종하다; 길을 찾다; 항해하다 (navigator n. 자동 조종기)
A navigator is a person or device for assisting a pilot to navigate an aircraft.

muffle [mʌfl] v. (소리를) 죽이다; (따뜻하게) 감싸다
If something muffles a sound, it makes the sound quieter and more difficult to hear.

thud [θʌd] v. 쿵쿵거리다; 쿵 치다; n. 쿵 (하는 소리)
If something thuds somewhere, it makes a dull sound, usually when it falls onto or hits something else.

commotion [kəmóuʃən] n. 소란, 소동
A commotion is a lot of noise, confusion, and excitement.

복습 **attention** [əténʃən] n. 주의; 관심; 배려; 차려 (자세)
If you give someone or something your attention, you look at it, listen to it, or think about it carefully.

technician [tekníʃən] n. 기술자, 기사
A technician is someone whose job involves skilled practical work with scientific equipment, for example in a laboratory.

복습 **stare** [stɛər] v. 빤히 쳐다보다, 응시하다; n. 빤히 쳐다보기, 응시
If you stare at someone or something, you look at them for a long time.

복습 **confuse** [kənfjú:z] v. (사람을) 혼란시키다; 혼동하다 (confused a. 혼란스러운)
If you are confused, you do not know exactly what is happening or what to do.

★ **superior** [səpíəriər] n. 상관, 상급자; a. 상급의; 우수한
Your superior in an organization that you work for is a person who has a higher rank than you.

복습 **initiate** [iníʃièit] v. 개시되게 하다, 착수시키다; 가입시키다; n. 가입자
If you initiate something, you start it or cause it to happen.

복습 **sequence** [sí:kwəns] n. 순서, 차례; (일련의) 연속적인 사건들
A particular sequence is a particular order in which things happen or are arranged.

★ **bang** [bæŋ] v. 쾅 하고 치다; 쾅 하고 닫다; 쿵 하고 찧다; n. 쾅 (하는 소리)
If you bang on something or if you bang it, you hit it hard, making a loud noise.

복습 **press** [pres] v. 누르다; 꾹 밀어 넣다; (무엇에) 바짝 대다; n. 언론
If you press a button or switch, you push it with your finger in order to make a machine or device work.

★ **elevate** [éləvèit] v. (들어) 올리다; (정도를) 높이다
If you elevate something, you raise it above a horizontal level.

★ **vertical** [vɔ́:rtikəl] a. 수직의, 세로의; n. 수직
Something that is vertical stands or points straight up.

★ **slide** [slaid] v. (slid-slid/slidden) 미끄러지다; 미끄러지듯이 움직이다; n. 떨어짐; 미끄러짐
When something slides somewhere or when you slide it there, it moves there smoothly over or against something.

★ **heap** [hi:p] n. 더미, 무더기; 많음; v. 수북이 담다; (아무렇게나) 쌓다
If you fall or lie in a heap, you lie without moving after you have fallen.

home stretch [hòum strétʃ] n. 최후의 단계
You can refer to the last part of any activity that lasts for a long time as the home stretch, especially if the activity is difficult or boring.

복습 **notice** [nóutis] v. 알아채다, 인지하다; 주의하다; n. 신경 씀, 주목, 알아챔
If you notice something or someone, you become aware of them.

복습 **patrol** [pətróul] n. 순찰대; 순찰; v. 순찰을 돌다
A patrol is a group of soldiers or vehicles that are moving around an area in order to make sure that there is no trouble there.

outnumber [autnʌ́mbər] v. ~보다 수가 많다, 수적으로 우세하다
If one group of people or things outnumbers another, the first group has more people or things in it than the second group.

복습 **console** [kánsoul] n. 제어반, 계기반; v. 위로하다, 위안을 주다
A console is a panel with a number of switches or knobs that is used to operate a machine.

복습 **reveal** [rivíːl] v. (보이지 않던 것을) 드러내 보이다; (비밀 등을) 밝히다
If you reveal something that has been out of sight, you uncover it so that people can see it.

override [ouvərráid] v. (overrode-overridden) 중단시키다; n. (자동 기기의) 보조 수동 장치
To override something means to interrupt the action of it that usually works by itself.

^복_습 **atmosphere** [ǽtməsfiər] n. 대기; 공기; 분위기
A planet's atmosphere is the layer of air or other gases around it.

^복_습 **flash** [flæʃ] v. 번쩍이다; 불현듯 들다; 휙 나타나다; n. 번쩍임; (감정이나 생각이) 갑자기 떠오름
If a light flashes or if you flash a light, it shines with a sudden bright light, especially as quick, regular flashes of light.

^복_습 **wail** [weil] v. (길고 높은) 소리를 내다; 울부짖다, 통곡하다; 투덜거리다; n. 울부짖음, 통곡
If something such as a siren or an alarm wails, it makes a long, loud, high-pitched sound.

★ **furious** [fjúəriəs] a. 몹시 화가 난; 맹렬한
Someone who is furious is extremely angry.

resound [rizáund] v. (소리가 가득) 울리다 (resounding a. 울려 퍼지는)
A resounding sound is loud and clear.

★ **barrier** [bǽriər] n. 장벽; 한계; 장애물
A barrier is something that restrains or obstructs progress or access.

7 & 8

1. How were things different when Buzz started approaching hyperspeed?

A. The gauge continued to climb.

B. The needle stopped moving.

C. IVAN stopped working.

D. The explosion was very small.

2. According to Izzy, when did the Zurg ship arrive?

A. About a month before Buzz landed

B. About a week before Buzz landed

C. The day before Buzz landed

D. The morning that Buzz landed

3. What did Izzy tell Buzz about the Zurg ship?

A. It will probably leave the planet soon.

B. It was much bigger than the Turnip ship.

C. It could be used to escape the planet.

D. It gives power to the robots on the ground.

4. What did Buzz learn about Izzy's group?

A. They had been on the Zurg ship before.

B. They were all rookies.

C. They previously won a medal.

D. They had new blasters.

5. How did the robot's arm get disconnected?

A. Buzz tore off its arm bolts.

B. Izzy hit it with a blaster.

C. Sox pressed some of its buttons.

D. A soldier hit it with a harpoon.

Check Your Reading Speed
1분에 몇 단어를 읽는지 리딩 속도를 측정해 보세요.

$$\frac{1,738 \text{ words}}{\text{reading time ( ) sec}} \times 60 = (\quad) \text{ WPM}$$

Build Your Vocabulary

brace [breis] v. (스스로) 대비를 하다; (몸에) 단단히 힘을 주다; n. 버팀대; 치아 교정기
If you brace yourself for something unpleasant or difficult, you prepare yourself for it.

gauge [geidʒ] n. 게이지, 측정기; 치수; 기준; v. 판단하다, 알아내다; 측정하다; 추정하다
A gauge is a device that measures the amount or quantity of something and shows the amount measured.

steady [stédi] a. 꾸준한; 흔들림 없는, 안정된; 차분한, 침착한; v. 균형을 잡다, 진정시키다
(steadily ad. 꾸준히)
If something happens steadily, it continues or develops gradually without any interruptions and is not likely to change quickly.

inch [intʃ] n. 조금, 약간; v. 조금씩 움직이다 (every inch idiom 전부 다, 속속들이)
If you talk about every inch of an area, you are emphasizing that you mean the whole of it.

rattle [rætl] v. 덜거덕거리다; 당황하게 하다; n. 덜컹거리는 소리
When something rattles, it makes short sharp knocking sounds because it is being shaken or it keeps hitting against something hard.

velocity [vəlásəti] n. 속도
Velocity is the speed at which something moves in a particular direction.

rip [rip] v. (갑자기) 찢다, 찢어지다; (재빨리·거칠게) 뜯어 내다; n. (길게) 찢어진 곳
If something such as a fire, storm, or bomb rips through a place, it damages or destroys the place very quickly.

pin [pin] v. 꼼짝 못 하게 하다; (핀으로) 고정시키다; 두다, 걸다; n. 핀
If someone pins you to something, they press you against a surface so that you cannot move.

strain [strein] v. 안간힘을 쓰다; 무리하게 사용하다; 한계에 이르게 하다; n. 부담; 압박
To strain something means to make it do more than it is able to do.

force [fɔːrs] **n.** 힘; 영향력; 세력; **v.** 억지로 ~하다; ~을 강요하다
Force is the power or strength which something has.

streak [striːk] **v.** 전속력으로 가다; 줄무늬를 넣다; **n.** 줄무늬
If something or someone streaks somewhere, they move there very quickly.

★ **array** [əréi] **n.** (인상적인) 집합체, 모음; **v.** 배열하다, 진열하다
An array of different things or people is a large number or wide range of them.

glow [glou] **v.** 빛나다, 타다; (얼굴이) 상기되다; **n.** (은은한) 불빛; 홍조
If something glows, it produces a dull, steady light.

headrest [hédrest] **n.** 머리 받침
A headrest is the part of the back of a seat on which you can lean your head, especially one on the front seat of a car.

serene [səríːn] **a.** 고요한, 평화로운, 조용한
Someone or something that is serene is calm and quiet.

shimmer [ʃímər] **v.** 희미하게 빛나다; **n.** 희미한 빛
If something shimmers, it shines with a faint, unsteady light or has an unclear, unsteady appearance.

‡ **witness** [wítnis] **v.** (사건·사고를) 목격하다; 증명하다; **n.** 목격자; 증인
If you witness something, you see it happen.

thrust [θrʌst] **v.** (thrust-thrust) (거칠게) 밀다; 찌르다; **n.** 추진력; 찌르기
If you thrust something or someone somewhere, you push or move them there quickly with a lot of force.

decelerate [diːsélərèit] **v.** 속도를 줄이다; 속도가 줄어들다 (deceleration **n.** 감속)
Deceleration refers to a process in which the speed of a vehicle or machine is reduced.

★ **orbit** [ɔ́ːrbit] **v.** 궤도를 그리며 돌다; 선회하다; **n.** (천체의) 궤도
If something such as a satellite orbits a planet, moon, or sun, it moves around it in a continuous, curving path.

churn [tʃəːrn] **v.** (속이) 뒤틀리게 하다; (액체 등이) 마구 휘돌다
(stomach-churning **a.** (속이) 뒤틀리게 하는)
If you describe something as stomach-churning, you mean that it is so unpleasant that it makes you feel physically sick.

intense [inténs] **a.** 극심한, 강렬한; 치열한; 열정적인, 진지한 (intensity **n.** 강렬함)
Intensity is the state of being very great or extreme in strength or degree.

impact [ímpækt] n. 충돌, 충격; (강력한) 영향; v. 충돌하다; 영향을 주다
An impact is the action of one object hitting another, or the force with which one object hits another.

haze [heiz] n. 희부연 것; 실안개; v. 흐릿해지다 (hazy a. 흐릿한)
Hazy weather conditions are those in which things are difficult to see, because of light mist, hot air, or dust.

unexpected [ʌnikspéktid] a. 예기치 않은, 예상 밖의 (unexpectedly ad. 뜻밖에)
If something takes place unexpectedly, it surprises you because you did not think that it was likely to happen.

celebrate [sélǝbrèit] v. 기념하다, 축하하다 (celebratory a. 축하하는)
A celebratory meal, drink, or other activity takes place to celebrate something such as a birthday, anniversary, or victory.

panel [pǽnl] n. 계기판; 판; 패널, 자문단
A control panel or instrument panel is a board or surface which contains switches and controls to operate a machine or piece of equipment.

congratulate [kǝngrǽʧulèit] v. 축하하다; 기뻐하다, 자랑스러워하다
(congratulation n. (pl.) 축하해요!)
You use 'congratulations' when you want to tell someone that you are pleased about their success, good luck, or happiness on a special occasion.

whisper [hwíspǝr] v. 속삭이다, 소곤거리다; n. 속삭임, 소곤거리는 소리
When you whisper, you say something very quietly, using your breath rather than your throat, so that only one person can hear you.

relieve [rilíːv] v. 안도하다; 해임하다; 덜어 주다, 없애 주다; 완화하다 (relief n. 안도)
If you feel a sense of relief, you feel happy because something unpleasant has not happened or is no longer happening.

grip [grip] v. 움켜잡다; (마음·흥미·시선을) 끌다; n. 꽉 붙잡음, 움켜쥠; 통제, 지배
If you grip something, you take hold of it with your hand and continue to hold it firmly.

accelerate [æksélǝrèit] v. 속도를 높이다, 가속화되다 (acceleration n. 가속)
Acceleration is the increase in speed of a moving object.

utter [ʌ́tǝr] a. 완전한; v. (말을) 하다; (어떤 소리를) 내다 (utterly ad. 완전히)
You use utterly to emphasize that something is very great in extent, degree, or amount.

terrify [térǝfài] v. (몹시) 무섭게 하다 (terrifying a. 무서운)
If something is terrifying, it makes you very frightened.

‡ **regret** [rigrét] v. 후회하다; 유감스럽게 생각하다; n. 후회; 유감, 애석
If you regret something that you have done, you wish that you had not done it.

복습 **snap** [snæp] v. 빠르게 움직이다; (화난 목소리로) 딱딱거리다; 탁 소리를 내다; n. 탁 하는 소리
To snap is to move or cause to move in a sudden or abrupt way.

whiz [hwiz] v. 빠르게 지나가다; 윙 하는 소리가 나다; n. 윙 하는 소리
If something whizzes somewhere, it moves there very fast.

runway [rʌ́nwèi] n. 활주로
At an airport, the runway is the long strip of ground with a hard surface which an
airplane takes off from or lands on.

복습 **blur** [bləːr] n. 흐릿한 형체; (기억이) 희미한 것; v. 흐릿해지다; 모호해지다
A blur is a shape or area which you cannot see clearly because it has no distinct outline
or because it is moving very fast.

복습 **crash** [kræʃ] v. 추락하다; 부딪치다; 충돌하다; 굉음을 내다; n. 요란한 소리; (자동차·항공기) 사고
When an aircraft crashes, it falls or lands violently out of control, so as to be damaged
or smashed.

technically [téknikəli] ad. 엄밀히 말하면; 기술적으로
If something is technically the case, it is the case according to a strict interpretation
of facts, laws, or rules, but may not be important or relevant in a particular situation.

careen [kəríːn] v. 위태롭게 달리다, 흔들리면서 질주하다
To careen somewhere means to rush forward in an uncontrollable way.

★ **wilderness** [wíldərnis] n. 황야, 황무지; 버려진 땅
A wilderness is a desert or other area of natural land which is not used by people.

plume [pluːm] n. (연기·먼지 등의) 기둥; (커다란) 깃털
A plume of smoke, dust, fire, or water is a large quantity of it that rises into the air in
a column.

복습 **skid** [skid] v. 미끄러지다; n. (차량의) 미끄러짐
If a vehicle skids, it slides sideways or forward while moving, for example when you
are trying to stop it suddenly on a wet road.

‡ **nerve** [nəːrv] n. 신경; 긴장, 불안; 용기 (nerve-wracking a. 신경을 건드리는, 초조하게 하는)
A nerve-wracking situation or experience makes you feel very tense and worried.

wrack [ræk] v. 몹시 괴롭히다; 고문하다, 고통을 주다; n. 고문; 파멸
To wrack someone or something is to make them suffer great physical or mental pain.

★ **tame** [teim] v. 길들이다, 다스리다; a. 길들여진 (untamed a. 야생의; 억제되지 않은)
An untamed area or place is in its original or natural state and has not been changed or affected by people.

복습 **swamp** [swamp] n. 늪, 습지; v. (일 등이) 쇄도하다
A swamp is an area of very wet land with wild plants growing in it.

복습 **perimeter** [pərímitər] n. 방어선; (어떤 구역의) 주위, 주변
The perimeter refers to a boundary strip where defenses are set up.

복습 **miraculous** [mirǽkjuləs] a. 기적적인 (miraculously ad. 기적적으로)
If you say that a good event has happened miraculously, you mean that it is very surprising and unexpected.

★ **halt** [hɔːlt] n. 멈춤, 중단; v. 멈추다, 서다; 중단시키다
A halt refers to a temporary or permanent stop.

복습 **cockpit** [kákpit] n. (항공기·경주용 자동차 등의) 조종석
In an airplane or racing car, the cockpit is the part where the pilot or driver sits.

복습 **distance** [dístəns] n. 먼 곳; 거리; v. (~에) 관여하지 않다 (in the distance idiom 저 먼 곳에)
If you can see something in the distance, you can see it, far away from you.

‡ **swear** [swɛər] v. 맹세하다; 욕을 하다; n. 맹세
If you say that you swear that something is true or that you can swear to it, you are saying very firmly that it is true.

복습 **alien** [éiljən] a. 외계의; 생경한; 이질적인; n. 외계인
Alien means coming from another world, such as an outer space.

★ **chirp** [ʧəːrp] v. 재잘거리다; 찍찍거리다
When a bird or an insect such as a cricket or grasshopper chirps, it makes short high-pitched sounds.

★ **immense** [iméns] a. 엄청난, 어마어마한
If you describe something as immense, you mean that it is extremely large or great.

‡ **gratitude** [grǽtətjùːd] n. 고마움, 감사
Gratitude refers to a feeling of thankful appreciation for favors or benefits received.

★ **renew** [rinjúː] v. (젊음·힘 등을) 되찾다; 재개하다; 갱신하다 (renewed a. 새로워진)
When something is renewed, it is happening again after a pause, especially with more vigor, energy or enthusiasm than before.

★ **rescue** [réskjuː] n. 구출, 구조, 구제; v. 구하다, 구출하다
Rescue is help which gets someone out of a dangerous or unpleasant situation.

absolve [æbzálv] v. 책임 없음을 선언하다; 용서하다
If a report or investigation absolves someone from blame or responsibility, it formally
states that they are not guilty or are not to blame.

wrongdoing [rɔ́ːŋduːiŋ] n. 죄; 나쁜 행위, 비행
Wrongdoing is behavior that is illegal or immoral.

★ **extract** [ikstrǽkt] v. (힘들여) 꺼내다; 추출하다; (억지로) 얻어내다; n. 발췌, 초록
If you extract something from a place, you take it out or pull it out.

복습 **supplement** [sʌ́pləmənt] n. 보충, 추가; 보충제; v. 보충하다 (supplemental n. 추가되는 것)
Supplementals are added to something in order to improve it.

복습 **glance** [glæns] v. 흘깃 보다; 대충 훑어보다; n. 흘깃 봄
If you glance at something or someone, you look at them very quickly and then look
away again immediately.

convoy [kánvɔi] n. 호송대; v. 호송하다, 호위하다
A convoy is a group of vehicles or ships traveling together.

복습 **route** [ruːt] n. 길, 경로; 방법; v. 보내다, 전송하다 (en route ad. (~로 가는) 도중에)
En route to a place means on the way to that place.

복습 **emergency** [imɔ́ːrdʒənsi] n. 비상, 비상 사태
An emergency is an unexpected and difficult or dangerous situation, especially an
accident, which happens suddenly and which requires quick action to deal with it.

복습 **frown** [fraun] v. 얼굴을 찡그리다; 눈살을 찌푸리다; n. 찡그림, 찌푸림
When someone frowns, their eyebrows become drawn together, because they are
annoyed or puzzled.

★ **peer** [piər] v. 유심히 보다, 눈여겨보다; n. 또래
If you peer at something, you look at it very hard, usually because it is difficult to see
clearly.

복습 **expanse** [ikspǽns] n. 넓게 퍼진 공간; 팽창, 확장
An expanse of something, usually sea, sky, or land, is a very large amount of it.

복습 **thud** [θʌd] v. 쿵쿵거리다; 쿵 치다; n. 쿵 (하는 소리)
If something thuds somewhere, it makes a dull sound, usually when it falls onto or
hits something else.

* **tackle** [tækl] v. 달려들다; (힘든 문제·상황과) 씨름하다; n. 태클
If you tackle someone, you attack them and fight them.

assail [əséil] v. 공격을 가하다; (몹시) 괴롭히다 (assailant n. 공격을 가한 사람)
Someone's assailant is a person who has physically attacked them.

sputter [spʌ́tər] v. 식식거리며 말하다; (엔진·불길 등이) 펑펑 하는 소리를 내다
If you sputter, you speak with difficulty and make short sounds, especially because you are angry, shocked, or excited.

복습 **splatter** [splǽtər] v. 튀다, 튀기다; n. 튀기기; 철벅철벅 소리
If a thick wet substance splatters on something or is splattered on it, it drops or is thrown over it.

* **hiss** [his] v. (강한 어조로) 낮게 말하다; 쉿 하는 소리를 내다; n. 쉭쉭거리는 소리
If you hiss something, you say it forcefully in a whisper.

복습 **clench** [klenʧ] v. (이를) 악물다; (주먹을) 꽉 쥐다; ~을 단단히 붙잡다
When you clench your teeth or they clench, you squeeze your teeth together firmly, usually because you are angry or upset.

boulder [bóuldər] n. 바위
A boulder is a large rounded rock.

복습 **emerge** [imə́:rdʒ] v. 나오다, 모습을 드러내다; (어려움 등을) 헤쳐 나오다
To emerge means to come out from an enclosed or dark space such as a room or a vehicle, or from a position where you could not be seen.

* **armor** [áːrmər] n. 갑옷; 철갑; 무기; v. 갑옷을 입히다
Armor is special metal clothing that soldiers wear for protection in battle.

복습 **dome** [doum] v. 반구형으로 만들다; n. 반구형 모양의 것; 돔, 반구형 지붕 (domed a. 반구형의)
Something that is domed is in the shape of a round roof.

복습 **scan** [skæn] v. (유심히) 살피다; 훑어보다; 정밀 촬영하다; 스캔하다; n. 정밀 검사
When you scan a place or group of people, you look at it carefully, usually because you are looking for something or someone.

복습 **urgent** [ə́:rdʒənt] a. 다급한; 긴급한, 시급한 (urgently ad. 다급하게)
If you speak urgently, you show that you are anxious for people to notice something or to do something.

* **metallic** [mətǽlik] a. 금속의, 금속성의
Metallic means consisting entirely or partly of metal.

★ **disc** [disk] n. 동글납작한 판, 원반; 디스크
A disc is a flat, circular shape or object.

복습 **hull** [hʌl] n. (배의) 선체; v. (콩 등의) 껍질을 벗기다
The hull of a boat or aircraft is the main body of it.

teleport [téləpɔ̀ːrt] v. (공상 과학 소설에서) 순간 이동시키다
In science fiction, if someone or something teleports, they move across a distance instantaneously.

복습★ **demand** [diménd] v. 강력히 묻다, 따지다; 요구하다; n. 요구; 수요
If you demand something such as information or action, you ask for it in a very forceful way.

복습 **hover** [hʌ́vər] v. (허공을) 맴돌다; 서성이다; 주저하다; n. 공중을 떠다님
To hover means to stay in the same position in the air without moving forward or backward.

복습 **massive** [mǽsiv] a. 거대한; 엄청나게 심각한
Something that is massive is very large in size, quantity, or extent.

spacecraft [spéiskræft] n. 우주선
A spacecraft is a rocket or other vehicle that can travel in space.

복습 **duck** [dʌk] v. 휙 수그리다; 급히 움직이다; n. (머리나 몸을) 휙 수그림; [동물] 오리
If you duck, you move your head or the top half of your body quickly downward to avoid something that might hit you, or to avoid being seen.

복습 **pod** [pad] n. 유선형 공간; (콩이 들어 있는) 꼬투리; (우주선·선박의 본체에서) 분리 가능한 부분
A pod is a long narrow container that is hung under an aircraft and used to carry fuel, equipment, or weapons.

★ **spit** [spit] v. (spat/spit-spat/spit) (말을) 내뱉다; (침·음식 등을) 뱉다; n. 침; (침 등을) 뱉기
If someone spits an insult or comment, they say it in a forceful way.

★ **swift** [swift] a. 신속한, 재빠른 (swiftly ad. 신속하게)
When someone or something moves swiftly, they move very quickly or without delay.

★ **dense** [dens] a. 빽빽한, 밀집한; (앞이 안 보이게) 짙은, 자욱한
Something that is dense contains a lot of things or people in a small area.

swivel [swívəl] v. (몸·눈·고개를) 휙 돌리다; 돌리다, 회전시키다; n. 회전 고리
If your head or your eyes swivel in a particular direction or if you swivel them in a particular direction, you quickly look in that direction.

counter [káuntər] v. 반박하다; 대응하다; n. (식당 등의) 계산대, 카운터; 반작용
If you counter something that someone has said, you say something which shows that you disagree with them or which proves that they are wrong.

scoff [skɔ:f] v. 비웃다, 조롱하다; n. 비웃음, 조롱
If you scoff at something, you speak about it in a way that shows you think it is ridiculous or inadequate.

wipe [waip] v. (먼지·물기 등을) 닦다; 지우다; n. 닦기
If you wipe dirt or liquid from something, you remove it, for example by using a cloth or your hand.

sicken [síkən] v. 메스꺼워지다, 병나다 (sickening a. 메스꺼운)
You describe something as sickening when it gives you feelings of horror or disgust, or makes you feel sick in your stomach.

realize [rí:əlàiz] v. 깨닫다, 알아차리다; 실현하다, 달성하다 (realization n. 깨달음)
Realization is the process in which you become aware of the fact that something is true.

gather [gǽðər] v. (여기저기 있는 것을) 모으다; (사람들이) 모이다; (마음·정신 등을) 가다듬다
If you gather information or evidence, you collect it.

spin [spin] v. (빙빙) 돌다, 돌리다; 돌아서다; n. 회전
If your head is spinning, you feel unsteady or confused, for example because you are ill or excited.

cove [kouv] n. 산골짜기 길, 산그늘; 작은 만; v. 아치형으로 만들다
A cove is a narrow gap or pass between hills or woods.

hillside [hílsàid] n. (산·언덕의) 비탈
A hillside is the sloping side of a hill.

generation [dʒènəréiʃən] n. 세대, 대
A generation is the period of time, usually considered to be about thirty years, that it takes for children to grow up and become adults and have children of their own.

binoculars [bainákjulərz] n. 쌍안경
Binoculars consist of two small telescopes joined together side by side, which you look through in order to look at things that are a long way away.

keen [ki:n] a. 예리한, 예민한; 강한, 깊은; 열정적인
If you have a keen eye or ear, you are able to notice things that are difficult to detect.

gaze [geiz] n. 응시, (눈여겨보는) 시선; v. (가만히) 응시하다, 바라보다
You can talk about someone's gaze as a way of describing how they are looking at something, especially when they are looking steadily at it.

brief [bri:f] a. (시간이) 짧은; 간단한; v. 보고하다
Something that is brief lasts for only a short time.

cadet [kədét] n. (경찰·군대 등의) 간부 후보생
A cadet is a young man or woman who is being trained in the armed services or the police.

precise [prisáis] a. 엄밀한, 꼼꼼한; 정확한, 정밀한
Something that is precise is exact and accurate in all its details.

practically [prǽktikəli] ad. 사실상, 거의; 현실적으로, 실제로
Practically means almost, but not completely or exactly.

furrow [fɔ́:rou] v. (미간을) 찡그리다; (밭에) 고랑을 만들다; n. 깊은 주름; 고랑
If someone furrows their brow or forehead or if it furrows, deep folds appear in it because the person is annoyed, unhappy, or confused.

brow [brau] n. 이마; 눈썹
Your brow is your forehead.

engulf [ingʌ́lf] v. 완전히 에워싸다, 휩싸다; (강한 감정 등이) 사로잡다
If one thing engulfs another, it completely covers or hides it, often in a sudden and unexpected way.

troop [tru:p] n. 병력, 군대; v. 무리를 지어 걸어가다
A troop is a group of soldiers within a cavalry or armored regiment.

valley [vǽli] n. 골짜기, 계곡
A valley is a low stretch of land between hills, especially one that has a river flowing through it.

distant [dístənt] a. 먼, (멀리) 떨어져 있는; 다정하지 않은
Distant means very far away.

glimmer [glímər] v. (희미하게) 빛나다; n. (희미하게) 깜박이는 빛; 희미한 기미
If something glimmers, it produces or reflects a faint, gentle, often unsteady light.

envelop [invéləp] v. 감싸다, 뒤덮다
If one thing envelops another, it covers or surrounds it completely.

★ **colony** [kálǝni] n. 거주지; (동·식물의) 군집; 식민지
You can refer to a place where a particular group of people lives as a particular kind of colony.

unleash [ʌnlíːʃ] v. 발사하다, 방출하다; (강력한 반응 등을) 촉발시키다; 해방하다
If you say that someone or something unleashes a powerful force, feeling, activity, or group, you mean that they suddenly start it or send it somewhere.

relentless [riléntlis] a. 수그러들지 않는, 끈질긴; 가차 없는
Something bad that is relentless never stops or never becomes less intense.

★ **assault** [ǝsɔ́ːlt] n. 공격; 도전; v. 괴롭히다; 폭행하다
An assault by an army is a strong attack made on an area held by the enemy.

복습 **count on** idiom ~을 기대하다, ~을 의지하다
If you count on someone or something, you hope or expect that something will happen or that someone will do something.

pivot [pívǝt] v. 회전하다, 선회하다
If something pivots, it balances or turns on a central point.

★ **standard** [stǽndǝrd] a. 표준의; 일반적인, 보통의; n. 기준; 수준; 규범
(standard-issue a. 표준 품목의)
Standard-issue means provided as part of the basic equipment that is given to all the members of a particular group, especially in the army or navy.

복습 **feline** [fíːlain] n. 고양이; 고양잇과의 동물; a. 고양이 같은
A feline is a cat or other member of the cat family.

복습 **pet** [pet] v. (동물·아이를 다정하게) 어루만지다; n. 애완동물
If you pet a person or animal, you touch them in an affectionate way.

purr [pǝːr] v. (기분 좋은 듯이) 가르랑거리다; 부르릉 하는 소리를 내다; n. 가르랑거리는 소리
When a cat purrs, it makes a low vibrating sound with its throat because it is contented.

복습 **companion** [kǝmpǽnjǝn] n. 동료; 친구; 동행
A companion is someone who shares the experiences of another, especially when these are unpleasant or unwelcome.

복습 **tilt** [tilt] v. 기울이다, (뒤로) 젖히다; (의견·상황 등이) 기울어지다; n. 기울어짐, 젖혀짐
If you tilt part of your body, usually your head, you move it slightly upward or to one side.

Check Your Reading Speed

1분에 몇 단어를 읽는지 리딩 속도를 측정해 보세요.

$$\frac{1,740 \text{ words}}{\text{reading time ( ) sec}} \times 60 = (\quad) \text{ WPM}$$

Build Your Vocabulary

fall in idiom (군인들이) 집합하다, 정렬하다
When a group of soldiers fall in, they take their places in the ranks.

복습 **command** [kəmǽnd] v. 명령하다; 지휘하다; n. 명령; 지휘; 사령부
If someone in authority commands you to do something, they tell you that you must
do it.

✱✱ **march** [ma:rtʃ] v. 행진하다; (단호한 태도로 급히) 걸어가다; n. 행군, 행진; 3월
When soldiers march somewhere, or when a commanding officer marches them
somewhere, they walk there with very regular steps, as a group.

복습 **impress** [imprés] v. 깊은 인상을 주다, 감동을 주다 (impressed a. 인상 깊게 생각하는)
If you are impressed by something or someone, you feel great admiration for them.

복습 **grin** [grin] v. 활짝 웃다; n. 활짝 웃음
When you grin, you smile broadly.

cohort [kóuhɔ:rt] n. 동료, 한패; 그룹
A person's cohorts are their friends, supporters, or associates.

복습 **operate** [ápərèit] v. 작전을 벌이다; 조작하다; 작동하다; 작업하다; 수술하다 (operation n. 작전)
An operation is a highly organized activity that involves many people doing different
things.

approving [əprú:viŋ] a. 찬성하는, 좋다고 여기는 (approvingly ad. 만족스러운 듯이)
If you react to something approvingly, you show support for it, or satisfaction with it.

✱ **squad** [skwad] n. (군대의) 분대; (경찰서의) 반; (특정 작업을 하는) 소집단
A squad of soldiers is a small group of them.

✱ **motion** [móuʃən] v. (손·머리로) 몸짓을 해 보이다; n. 동작, 몸짓; 운동, 움직임
If you motion to someone, you move your hand or head as a way of telling them to do
something or telling them where to go.

복습 **ranger** [réindʒər] n. 경비 대원; 기습 공격대원
A ranger is an armed guard who patrols a region.

복습 **corps** [kɔːr] n. (특수한 임무를 띤) 부대; 군단; (특정한 활동을 하는) 단체, 집단
A Corps is a part of the army which has special duties.

★ **objective** [əbdʒéktiv] n. 목표, 목적; a. 객관적인
Your objective is what you are trying to achieve.

복습 **exclaim** [ikskléim] v. 소리치다, 외치다
If you exclaim, you cry out suddenly in surprise, strong emotion, or pain.

복습 **huff** [hʌf] v. (화가 나서) 씩씩거리다; n. 발끈 화를 냄
If you huff, you indicate that you are annoyed or offended about something.

복습 **insist** [insíst] v. 고집하다, 주장하다, 우기다
If you insist that something is the case, you say so very firmly and refuse to say otherwise, even though other people do not believe you.

clear one's throat idiom 목을 가다듬다; 헛기침하다
If you clear your throat, you cough once in order to make it easier to speak or to attract people's attention.

★★ **declare** [dikléər] v. 분명히 말하다; 선언하다, 공표하다
If you declare that something is true, you say that it is true in a firm, deliberate way.

복습 **ominous** [ámənəs] a. 불길한, 나쁜 징조의 (ominously ad. 불길하게, 기분 나쁘게)
When someone or something moves ominously, it worries you because it makes you think that something unpleasant is going to happen.

★★ **conclude** [kənklúːd] v. 결론을 내리다; 끝내다, 마치다
If you conclude that something is true, you decide that it is true using the facts you know as a basis.

★ **variation** [vɛəriéiʃən] n. 변형; 변화, 차이
A variation on something is the same thing presented in a slightly different form.

debrief [diːbríːf] v. (방금 수행한 임무에 대해) 보고를 듣다
When someone such as a soldier, diplomat, or astronaut is debriefed, they are asked to give a report on an operation or task that they have just completed.

복습 **stake** [steik] n. (내기 등에) 건 것; 지분; 말뚝; v. (돈 등을) 걸다; 말뚝을 받치다
(high-stakes a. 고위험의; 고부담의)
Something that is high-stakes involves a lot of risk.

figure out idiom 이해하다, 알아내다; 계산하다, 산출하다
If you figure out someone or something, you come to understand them by thinking carefully.

blow up idiom 폭파하다, 터뜨리다
If someone blows something up or if it blows up, it is destroyed by an explosion.

★ **manipulate** [mənípjulèit] v. 다루다; (사람·사물을) 조종하다
If you manipulate something that requires skill, such as a complicated piece of equipment or a difficult idea, you operate it or process it.

‡ **rush** [rʌʃ] n. (감정이 갑자기) 치밀어 오름; 혼잡; v. 서두르다; 급히 움직이다
If you experience a rush of a feeling, you suddenly experience it very strongly.

★ **instinctive** [instíŋktiv] a. 본능에 따른, 본능적인 (instinctively ad. 본능적으로)
If you do something instinctively, you do so without thinking or reasoning.

infinity [infínəti] n. 아득히 먼 곳; 무한성
Infinity is a point that is further away than any other point and can never be reached.

tap [tæp] v. (가볍게) 톡톡 두드리다; n. (가볍게) 두드리기
If you tap something, you hit it with a quick light blow or a series of quick light blows.

bewilder [biwíldər] v. 어리둥절하게 하다, 혼란스럽게 하다 (bewildered a. 당혹한)
If you are bewildered, you are very confused and cannot understand something or decide what you should do.

★ **suspicious** [səspíʃəs] a. 의심스러워하는; 의심스러운
If you are suspicious of someone or something, you do not trust them, and are careful when dealing with them.

pull a face idiom 얼굴을 찡그리다, 인상을 찌푸리다
To pull a face is to show a feeling such as dislike or disgust by twisting your face into an ugly expression.

fluster [flʌ́stər] v. 허둥지둥하게 만들다, 어리둥절하게 만들다; n. 허둥거림, 혼란
(flustered a. 당황한)
If you are flustered, you are in a state of confusion or agitation.

regain [rigéin] v. 되찾다, 회복하다; 되돌아오다
If you regain something that you have lost, you get it back again.

composure [kəmpóuʒər] n. (마음의) 평정
Composure is the appearance or feeling of calm and the ability to control your feelings.

★ **stride** [straid] v. (strode-stridden) 성큼성큼 걷다; n. 걸음; 걸음걸이
If you stride somewhere, you walk there with quick, long steps.

munition [mju:níʃən] n. 군사 물품, 군수품
Munitions refer to materials used in war, such as weapons.

복습 **steel** [sti:l] v. (~에 대비해서) 마음을 단단히 먹다; n. 강철
If you steel yourself, you prepare to deal with something unpleasant.

복습 **combat** [kəmbǽt] n. 전투, 싸움; v. (적과) 싸우다, 전투를 벌이다; 방지하다
Combat is fighting that takes place in a war.

복습 **fist** [fist] n. 주먹
Your hand is referred to as your fist when you have bent your fingers in toward the palm in order to hit someone, to make an angry gesture, or to hold something.

복습 **spin** [spin] v. (빙빙) 돌다, 돌리다; 돌아서다; n. 회전
If something spins or if you spin it, it turns quickly around a central point.

★ **cock** [kak] v. 쫑긋 세우다, 높이 들다; 몸을 뒤로 젖히다; n. [동물] 수탉
If you cock a part of your body such as your head or your eyes, you move it upward or in a particular direction.

복습 **burst** [bə:rst] v. (burst-burst) 불쑥 움직이다; 갑자기 ~하다; 터지다; n. (갑자기) ~을 함; 파열, 폭발
To burst into or out of a place means to enter or leave it suddenly with a lot of energy or force.

★ **defend** [difénd] v. 방어하다, 수비하다; 옹호하다, 변호하다
If you defend someone or something, you take action in order to protect them.

복습 **waist** [weist] n. 허리; (옷의) 허리 부분
Your waist is the middle part of your body where it narrows slightly above your hips.

‡ **fling** [fliŋ] v. (거칠게) 내던지다, 내팽개치다; (몸이나 신체를) 내밀다; n. (한바탕) 실컷 즐기기
If you fling something somewhere, you throw it there using a lot of force.

★ **scramble** [skrǽmbl] v. 재빨리 움직이다; 서로 밀치다; n. (힘들게) 기어가기; 서로 밀치기
If you scramble to a different place or position, you move there in a hurried, awkward way.

‡ **weigh** [wei] v. 무게가 ~이다; 무게를 달다
If someone or something weighs a particular amount, this amount is how heavy they are.

disc [disk] n. 동글납작한 판, 원반; 디스크
A disc is a flat, circular shape or object.

chest [ʧest] n. 가슴, 흉부; 상자, 궤
Your chest is the top part of the front of your body where your ribs, lungs, and heart are.

teleport [télǝpɔːrt] v. (공상 과학 소설에서) 순간 이동시키다
In science fiction, if someone or something teleports, they move across a distance instantaneously.

★ lash [læʃ] v. 후려치다, 휘갈기다; (밧줄로) 단단히 묶다; n. 채찍질
If you lash out, you attempt to hit someone quickly and violently with a weapon or with your hands or feet.

captor [kǽptǝr] n. 포획자, 억류자
You can refer to the person who has captured a person or animal as their captor.

skitter [skítǝr] v. 잽싸게 나아가다
If something skitters, it moves about very lightly and quickly.

transport [trænspɔ́ːrt] n. 수송; 운송 수단; v. 수송하다; 실어 나르다
Transport is the activity of taking goods or people from one place to another.

helpless [hélplis] a. 무력한, 속수무책인
If you are helpless, you do not have the strength or power to do anything useful or to control or protect yourself.

grasp [græsp] n. 움켜잡기; 통제; 이해; v. 꽉 잡다; 완전히 이해하다, 파악하다
A grasp is a very firm hold or grip.

★ fort [fɔːrt] n. 보루, 요새
A fort is a strong building or a place with a wall or fence around it where soldiers can stay and be safe from the enemy.

pop [pap] n. 펑 하는 소리; v. 펑 하는 소리가 나다; 불쑥 내놓다; 불쑥 나타나다; 쏙 넣다
Pop is used to represent a short sharp sound, for example the sound made by bursting a balloon or by pulling a cork out of a bottle.

vision [víʒǝn] n. 시야; 환상, 상상; 환영
Your vision is everything that you can see from a particular place or position.

crate [kreit] n. (대형 나무) 상자; 한 상자 (분량)
A crate is a large box used for transporting or storing things.

^복_습 **groan** [groun] v. (고통·짜증으로) 신음 소리를 내다, 끙끙거리다; n. 신음, 끙 하는 소리
If you groan, you make a long, low sound because you are in pain, or because you are
upset or unhappy about something.

^복_습 **have one's back** idiom ~을 지키다; ~을 지지하다; ~을 보살피다
When you have someone's back, you look out for them to help or defend them.

^복_습 **extend** [iksténd] v. (신체 부위를) 뻗다; 뻗어 있다; (거리·기간을) 포괄하다
To extend is to stretch forth an arm or other body parts.

^복_습 **duck** [dʌk] v. 휙 수그리다; 급히 움직이다; n. (머리나 몸을) 휙 수그림; [동물] 오리
If you duck, you move your head or the top half of your body quickly downward to
avoid something that might hit you, or to avoid being seen.

^복_습 **explode** [iksplóud] v. 폭발하다; 갑자기 ~하다; (강한 감정을) 터뜨리다
If an object such as a bomb explodes or if someone or something explodes it, it bursts
loudly and with great force, often causing damage or injury.

pounce [pauns] v. (공격하거나 잡으려고 확) 덮치다, 덤비다
When an animal or bird pounces on something, it jumps on it and holds it, in order
to kill it.

yowl [jaul] v. 울부짖다; n. 울부짖는 소리
If a person or an animal yowls, they make a long loud cry, especially because they are
sad or in pain.

gouge [gaudʒ] v. (난폭하게) 찌르다, 박다; 도려내다; 갈취하다
If you gouge something, you make a hole or a long cut in it, usually with a pointed
object.

disorient [disɔ́:riènt] v. 방향 감각을 혼란시키다; 어리둥절하게 하다
(disoriented a. 방향 감각을 잃은)
If you are disoriented, you are confused as to time or place.

★ **stumble** [stʌmbl] v. 비틀거리다; 발을 헛디디다; (말·글 읽기를 하다가) 더듬거리다
If you stumble, you put your foot down awkwardly while you are walking or running
and nearly fall over.

^복_습 **whiz** [hwiz] v. 빠르게 지나가다; 윙 하는 소리가 나다; n. 윙 하는 소리
If something whizzes somewhere, it moves there very fast.

wince [wins] v. (통증·당혹감으로) 움찔하고 놀라다
If you wince, the muscles of your face tighten suddenly because you have felt a pain or
because you have just seen, heard, or remembered something unpleasant.

encouraging [inkə́:ridʒiŋ] a. 격려하는, 힘을 북돋아 주는 (encouragingly ad. 격려하듯이)
If you say something encouragingly, you do so in a way that gives people hope or confidence.

복습 **frighten** [fraitn] v. 겁먹게 하다, 놀라게 하다 (frightened a. 겁먹은, 무서워하는)
If you are frightened, you are anxious or afraid, often because of something that has just happened or that you think may happen.

복습 **slight** [slait] a. 약간의, 조금의; 작고 여윈 (slightly ad. 약간, 조금)
Slightly means to some degree but not to a very large degree.

lanky [lǽŋki] a. 마르고 키 큰, 호리호리한
If you describe someone as lanky, you mean that they are tall and thin and move rather awkwardly.

복습 **rookie** [rúki] n. 신참, 초보자; (스포츠 팀의) 신인 선수
A rookie is someone who has just started doing a job and does not have much experience, especially someone who has just joined the army or police force.

복습 **tear** [tɛər] ① v. (tore-torn) 찢다, 뜯다; 뜯어 내다; 질주하다; n. 찢어진 곳, 구멍 ② n. 눈물
To tear a material is to cause it to come apart.

★ **expose** [ikspóuz] v. 드러내다; 폭로하다; 경험하게 하다 (exposed a. 노출된)
If a place is exposed, it has no natural protection against bad weather or enemies.

복습 **spark** [spa:rk] n. 불꽃, 불똥; 아주 조금; (전류의) 스파크; v. 촉발시키다; 불꽃을 일으키다
A spark is a tiny bright piece of burning material that flies up from something that is burning.

wriggle [rigl] v. 꿈틀거리며 가다; (몸을) 꿈틀거리다; n. 꿈틀거리기
If you wriggle somewhere, for example through a small gap, you move there by twisting and turning your body.

★ **frantic** [frǽntik] a. (두려움·걱정으로) 제정신이 아닌; 정신없이 서두는 (frantically ad. 미친 듯이)
If you behave frantically, you are acting in a wild and uncontrolled way because you are frightened or worried.

복습 **bend** [bend] v. (몸·머리를) 굽히다, 숙이다; 구부리다; n. 굽은 곳
When you bend a part of your body such as your arm or leg, or when it bends, you change its position so that it is no longer straight.

복습 **weather** [wéðər] v. 비바람을 맞게 하다; 무사히 헤쳐 나가다; n. 날씨, 기상
(weathered a. 풍파를 맞은)
If someone's skin is weathered, it is stained, worn, or beaten by the weather or other activities.

dishevel [diʃévl] v. (머리를) 부스스하게 하다; (옷차림을) 단정치 못하게 입다 (disheveled a. 부스스한)
If you describe someone's hair, clothes, or appearance as disheveled, you mean that it is very untidy.

⋆ **violate** [váiəlèit] v. 위반하다; 침해하다; 훼손하다 (violation n. 위반, 위배)
A violation involves breaking an agreement, law, or promise.

복습 **incredulous** [inkrédʒuləs] a. 믿지 않는, 회의적인 (incredulously ad. 믿을 수 없다는 듯이)
When someone behaves incredulously, it shows that they are unable to believe something because it is very surprising or shocking.

⋆ **snatch** [snætʃ] v. 와락 붙잡다, 잡아채다; 간신히 얻다; n. 잡아 뺏음, 강탈; 조각
If you snatch something or snatch at something, you take it or pull it away quickly.

복습 **suck** [sʌk] v. (특정한 방향으로) 빨아들이다; 빨아 먹다; n. 빨기, 빨아 먹기
If something sucks a liquid, gas, or object in a particular direction, it draws it there with a powerful force.

복습 **swift** [swift] a. 신속한, 재빠른 (swiftly ad. 신속하게)
When someone or something moves swiftly, they move very quickly or without delay.

expectant [ikspéktənt] a. 기대하는 (expectantly ad. 기대하면서)
When someone acts expectantly, they are excited because they think something interesting is about to happen.

‡ **sail** [seil] v. 미끄러지듯 나아가다; 항해하다; n. 돛
If a person or thing sails somewhere, they move there smoothly and fairly quickly.

⋆ **thicket** [θíkit] n. 덤불, 잡목 숲; 복잡하게 뒤얽힌 것
A thicket is a small group of trees or bushes which are growing closely together.

복습 **wail** [weil] v. 투덜거리다; 울부짖다, 통곡하다; (길고 높은) 소리를 내다; n. 울부짖음, 통곡
If you wail something, you say it in a loud, high-pitched voice that shows that you are unhappy or in pain.

복습 **hostile** [hastl] a. 적대적인; 강력히 반대하는
In a war, you use hostile to describe your enemy's forces and activities.

복습 **count on idiom** ~을 기대하다, ~을 의지하다
If you count on someone or something, you hope or expect that something will happen or that someone will do something.

⋆ **reckless** [réklis] a. 무모한, 신중하지 못한; 난폭한
If you say that someone is reckless, you mean that they act in a way which shows that they do not care about danger or the effect their behavior will have on other people.

predictable [pridíktəbl] a. 예상할 수 있는; 너무 뻔한 (unpredictable a. 예측 불가능한)
If you describe someone or something as unpredictable, you mean that you cannot tell
what they are going to do or how they are going to behave.

crunch [krʌnʧ] v. 윗몸을 일으키다; 저벅저벅거리며 가다; 으드득거리다; n. 으드득거리는 소리
When you crunch, you sit up from a lying position using your stomach muscles.

slump [slʌmp] v. 푹 쓰러지다; 털썩 앉다; (가치·수량 등이) 급감하다; n. 부진; 불황
To slump is to sink or fall heavily and suddenly.

★ **vanish** [vǽniʃ] v. 사라지다, 없어지다; 모습을 감추다
If someone or something vanishes, they disappear suddenly or in a way that cannot
be explained.

복습 **grunt** [grʌnt] v. 끙 앓는 소리를 내다; 꿀꿀거리다; n. (사람이) 끙 하는 소리; (돼지가) 꿀꿀거리는 소리
If you grunt, you make a low sound, especially to show that you are in pain, annoyed,
or not interested.

muster [mʌ́stər] v. (용기 등을 최대한) 내다; (지지 등을) 모으다; 소집하다; n. 소집, 집결
If you muster something such as support, strength, or energy, you gather as much of it
as you can in order to do something.

sizzle [sizl] v. 지글지글 하는 소리를 내다
If something such as hot oil or fat sizzles, it makes hissing sounds.

★ **ray** [rei] n. 광선; 약간, 소량
Rays of light are narrow beams of light.

★ **tumble** [tʌmbl] v. 굴러떨어지다; 폭삭 무너지다; 허겁지겁 나오다; n. (갑자기) 굴러떨어짐; 폭락
If someone or something tumbles somewhere, they fall there with a rolling or bouncing
movement.

★ **thunder** [θʌ́ndər] v. 우르릉거리며 질주하다; 우르릉거리다; 천둥이 치다; n. 천둥, 우레
If something or someone thunders somewhere, they move there quickly and with a
lot of noise.

복습 **sever** [sévər] v. 자르다, 절단하다; 끊어지다, 갈라지다; (관계·연락을) 끊다, 단절하다
To sever something means to cut completely through it or to cut it completely off.

복습 **triumphant** [traiʌ́mfənt] a. 의기양양한; 크게 성공한, 큰 승리를 거둔
(triumphantly ad. 의기양양하게)
Someone who acts triumphantly is very happy about a victory or success.

swing [swiŋ] v. 휘두르다; (전후·좌우로) 흔들다; 휙 움직이다; n. 흔들기; 휘두르기
If something swings in a particular direction or if you swing it in that direction, it
moves in that direction with a smooth, curving movement.

fizzle [fízl] v. 약하게 쉿 소리를 내다; 실패하다
To fizzle is to make a hissing sound, often indicating a declining momentum.

stammer [stǽmər] v. 말을 더듬다; n. 말 더듬기
If you stammer, you speak with difficulty, hesitating and repeating words or sounds.

clench [klenʧ] v. ~을 단단히 붙잡다; (주먹을) 꽉 쥐다; (이를) 악물다
If you clench something in your hand, you hold it very tightly with your hand.

ankle [ǽŋkl] n. 발목
Your ankle is the joint where your foot joins your leg.

fritz [frits] v. 고장나다, 망가지다
If a machine fritzes out, it becomes inoperable.

sputter [spʌ́tər] v. (엔진·불길 등이) 펑펑 하는 소리를 내다; 식식거리며 말하다
If something such as an engine or a flame sputters, it works or burns in an uneven way
and makes a series of soft popping sounds.

garble [ga:rbl] v. 잘못 이해하다, 혼동하다; 왜곡하다 (garbled a. 알아들을 수 없는)
A garbled message or report contains confused or wrong details, often because it is
spoken by someone who is nervous or in a hurry.

listless [lístlis] a. 무기력한, 열의가 없는
Someone who is listless has no energy or enthusiasm.

heap [hi:p] n. 더미, 무더기; 많음; v. 수북이 담다; (아무렇게나) 쌓다
If someone collapses in a heap, they fall heavily and untidily and do not move.

wrest [rest] v. 비틀어 떼다, 비틀다; 왜곡하다; n. 비틀기; 왜곡
If you wrest something from someone who is holding it, you take it from them by
pulling or twisting it violently.

cup [kʌp] v. 두 손을 동그랗게 모아 쥐다; n. 컵, 잔
If you cup your hands, you make them into a curved shape like a cup.

makeshift [méikʃift] a. 임시변통의, 일시적인; n. 임시 수단, 미봉책
Makeshift things are temporary and usually of poor quality, but they are used because
there is nothing better available.

9 & 10

1. Why did Buzz want to visit the abandoned storage depot?

    A. To destroy the robots' base

    B. To train the Junior Patrol

    C. To speak to the person in charge

    D. To get another ship

2. Why did the hibernating bugs wake up?

    A. Because of noise from the truck's alarm

    B. Because of shouting from the Junior Patrol

    C. Because of a blast from Buzz's weapon

    D. Because of a scan made by Sox

3. **Why did Darby not want a weapon at first?**

    A. Because she did not think they would work

    B. Because she was scared of weapons

    C. Because she was on parole

    D. Because she did not want to hurt the bugs

4. **What did Buzz forget to tell the Junior Patrol?**

    A. That the button can change colors

    B. That the truck had been moved

    C. That Stealth Mode had a timer

    D. That the Space Ranger suits were heavy

5. **Why did the Junior Patrol go into the ship?**

    A. They wanted to see how it worked.

    B. They were being chased by bugs.

    C. They were told to go there by Buzz.

    D. They were trying to find suits.

Check Your Reading Speed
1분에 몇 단어를 읽는지 리딩 속도를 측정해 보세요.

$$\frac{1{,}146 \text{ words}}{\text{reading time ( ) sec}} \times 60 = (\quad) \text{ WPM}$$

Build Your Vocabulary

^{복습} **dishevel** [diʃévl] v. (머리를) 부스스하게 하다; (옷차림을) 단정치 못하게 입다 (disheveled a. 부스스한)
If you describe someone's hair, clothes, or appearance as disheveled, you mean that it is very untidy.

★ **pace** [peis] v. 서성거리다; (일의) 속도를 유지하다; n. 속도; 걸음
If you pace a small area, you keep walking up and down it, because you are anxious or impatient.

smolder [smóuldər] v. (서서히) 타다; (불만 등이) 들끓다; n. 연기
If something smolders, it burns slowly, producing smoke but not flames.

^{복습} **wreck** [rek] v. 망가뜨리다, 파괴하다; n. 충돌; 난파선; 사고 잔해 (wreckage n. 잔해)
When something such as a plane, car, or building has been destroyed, you can refer to what remains as the wreckage.

^{복습} **salute** [səlúːt] v. 경례를 하다; 경의를 표하다, 절하다; n. 거수 경례; 인사
If you salute someone, you greet them or show your respect with a formal sign.

^{복습} **patrol** [pətróul] n. 순찰대; 순찰; v. 순찰을 돌다
A patrol is a group of soldiers or vehicles that are moving around an area in order to make sure that there is no trouble there.

★ **volunteer** [vàləntíər] n. 자원해서 하는 사람; 자원 봉사자; v. 자원하다; 자진해서 말하다
A volunteer is someone who offers to do a particular task or job without being forced to do it.

★ **motivate** [móutəvèit] v. 동기를 부여하다; 이유가 되다 (self-motivated a. 스스로 동기를 부여하는)
When someone is self-motivated, they are motivated or driven by themselves, without any external agency.

^{복습} **lanky** [lǽŋki] a. 마르고 키 큰, 호리호리한
If you describe someone as lanky, you mean that they are tall and thin and move rather awkwardly.

LIGHTYEAR

cook up idiom 즉흥적으로 만들다; 날조하다
To cook up is to invent something to deal with a particular situation.

sigh [sai] v. 한숨을 쉬다, 한숨짓다; 탄식하듯 말하다; n. 한숨
When you sigh, you let out a deep breath, as a way of expressing feelings such as disappointment, tiredness, or pleasure.

squad [skwad] n. (군대의) 분대; (경찰서의) 반; (특정 작업을 하는) 소집단
A squad of soldiers is a small group of them.

bunch [bʌnʧ] n. (한 무리의) 사람들; 다발, 송이, 묶음; (양·수가) 많음
A bunch of people is a group of people who share one or more characteristics or who are doing something together.

munition [mjuːníʃən] n. 군사 물품, 군수품
Munitions refer to materials used in war, such as weapons.

partial [páːrʃəl] a. 부분적인, 불완전한; ~을 매우 좋아하는
You use partial to refer to something that is not complete or whole.

tactical [tæktikəl] a. (군사) 전술의; 전략적인; 작전의
Tactical activities at the battlefront concern strategic plans to employ weapons or forces.

engage [ingéidʒ] v. 교전을 벌이다; 약혼시키다; 관계를 맺다; 사용하다 (engagement n. 교전)
A military engagement is an armed conflict between two enemies.

pending [péndiŋ] a. 곧 있을, 임박한; 결정되지 않은, 정해지지 않은, 계류 중인
Something that is pending is going to happen soon.

combat [kəmbǽt] n. 전투, 싸움; v. (적과) 싸우다, 전투를 벌이다; 방지하다
Combat is fighting that takes place in a war.

enthusiastic [inθùːziǽstik] a. 열렬한, 열광적인 (enthusiastically ad. 열광적으로)
If you do something enthusiastically, you show how much you like or enjoy it by the way that you behave and talk.

live up to idiom ~에 부끄럽지 않게 살다; ~에 부응하다
If someone or something lives up to what they were expected to be, they are as good as they were expected to be.

legacy [légəsi] n. 유산
A legacy of an event or period of history is something which is a direct result of it and which continues to exist after it is over.

replace [ripléis] v. 대신하다, 대체하다; 교체하다 (replacement n. 대체물)
Someone who takes someone else's place in an organization, government, or team can be referred to as their replacement.

crate [kreit] n. (대형 나무) 상자; 한 상자 (분량)
A crate is a large box used for transporting or storing things.

gear [giər] n. (특정 활동에 필요한) 장비; 기어
The gear involved in a particular activity is the equipment or special clothing that you use.

★ **heave** [hi:v] v. (무거운 것을) 들어 올리다; (크게 한숨 등을) 내쉬다; n. 들어올리기; 들썩거림
If you heave something heavy or difficult to move somewhere, you push, pull, or lift it using a lot of effort.

supportive [səpɔ́:rtiv] a. 지원하는, 도와주는, 힘을 주는
If you are supportive, you are kind and helpful to someone at a difficult or unhappy time in their life.

★ **initiative** [iníʃiətiv] n. 계획; 진취성; 결단력
An initiative is an important act or statement that is intended to solve a problem.

nod [nad] v. (고개를) 끄덕이다, 까딱하다; n. (고개를) 끄덕임
If you nod, you move your head downward and upward to show that you are answering 'yes' to a question, or to show agreement, understanding, or approval.

★ **abandon** [əbǽndən] v. 버리고 떠나다; 버리다; 그만두다 (abandoned a. 버려진)
An abandoned place or building is no longer used or occupied.

★ **storage** [stɔ́:ridʒ] n. 저장; 저장고, 보관소
If you refer to the storage of something, you mean that it is kept in a special place until it is needed.

depot [dí:pou] n. 저장소, 창고
A depot is a place where large amounts of raw materials, equipment, arms, or other supplies are kept until they are needed.

pause [pɔ:z] v. (말·일을 하다가) 잠시 멈추다; 정지시키다; n. (말·행동 등의) 멈춤
If you pause while you are doing something, you stop for a short period and then continue.

★ **constitute** [kánstətjù:t] v. 설립하다, 세우다; 구성하다 (reconstitute v. 재건하다)
If an organization or state is reconstituted, it is formed again in a different way.

fabricate [fǽbrikèit] v. 제작하다, 생산하다; 조립하다; (거짓말 등을) 꾸며내다
(fabrication n. 제작, 구성)
Fabrication refers to the act or process of manufacturing something.

plant [plænt] n. 시설; 식물, 초목; v. 놓다, 두다; 심다; 설치하다
A plant is a factory or a place where power is produced.

stare [stɛər] v. 빤히 쳐다보다, 응시하다; n. 빤히 쳐다보기, 응시
If you stare at someone or something, you look at them for a long time.

blank [blæŋk] a. 멍한, 무표정한; 빈; n. 빈칸, 여백; v. (갑자기) 멍해지다 (blankly ad. 멍하니)
When you act blankly, your face shows no feeling, understanding, or interest.

rumble [rʌmbl] v. 덜커덩거리며 나아가다; 웅웅거리는 소리를 내다; n. 웅웅거리는 소리
If a vehicle rumbles somewhere, it moves slowly forward while making a low continuous noise.

quarter [kwɔ́ːrtər] n. 숙소; 구역; 4분의 1; v. 숙소를 제공하다; 4등분하다
The rooms provided for soldiers, sailors, or servants to live in are called their quarters.

correctional [kərékʃənl] a. (범죄자에 대한) 교정의, 처벌의
Correctional means related to prisons.

facility [fəsíləti] n. 시설, 기관; 기능; 특징; 재능
Facilities are buildings, pieces of equipment, or services that are provided for a particular purpose.

release [rilíːs] v. 석방하다, 놓아 주다; 풀다; (감정을) 발산하다; n. 풀어 줌; 방출; 공개; 해제
If a person or animal is released from somewhere where they have been locked up or looked after, they are set free or allowed to go.

mum [mʌm] a. 아무 말도 하지 않는, 계속 잠자코 있는
If you keep mum or stay mum about something, you do not tell anyone about it.

jail [dʒeil] n. 교도소, 감옥; v. 수감하다
A jail is a place where criminals are kept in order to punish them, or where people waiting to be tried are kept.

slip [slip] v. (말이) 무심코 나오다; 미끄러지다; 슬며시 가다; n. 미끄러짐; (작은) 실수
If you let slip information, you accidentally tell it to someone, when you wanted to keep it secret.

enigma [ənígmə] n. 수수께끼 같은 인물, 불가해한 사물; 수수께끼
If you describe something or someone as an enigma, you mean they are mysterious or difficult to understand.

‡ **odd** [ad] a. 이상한, 특이한; 홀수의
If you describe someone or something as odd, you think that they are strange or unusual.

sign up for idiom ~에 가입하다, ~을 신청하다
To sign up for something is to agree to do it or join it.

lark [laːrk] n. 장난, 농담; 하찮은 일; [동물] 종달새
If you say that doing something is a lark, you mean that it is fun, although perhaps naughty or dangerous.

복습 **instant** [ínstənt] a. 즉각적인; n. 순간, 아주 짧은 동안 (instantly ad. 즉각, 즉시)
If something happens instantly, it happens without any delay.

복습 **regret** [rigrét] v. 후회하다; 유감스럽게 생각하다; n. 후회; 유감, 애석
If you regret something that you have done, you wish that you had not done it.

복습 **stake** [steik] n. (내기 등에) 건 것; 지분; 말뚝; v. (돈 등을) 걸다; 말뚝을 받치다
(at stake idiom 성패가 달린; 위태로운)
If something is at stake, it is being risked and might be lost or damaged if you are not successful.

★ **rust** [rʌst] v. 녹슬다, 부식하다; n. 녹
If something is rusted, it is covered with rust, which is a brown substance that forms on iron or steel.

‡ **appreciate** [əpríːʃièit] v. 고마워하다; 진가를 알아보다
If you appreciate something that someone has done for you or is going to do for you, you are grateful for it.

★ **alert** [ələ́ːrt] a. 기민한; 경계하는; n. 경계 태세; v. (위험 등을) 알리다
If you are alert, you are paying full attention to things around you and are able to deal with anything that might happen.

commandeer [kàməndíər] v. 제멋대로 쓰다; 징발하다
To commandeer something owned by someone else means to take charge of it so that you can use it.

복습 **blow up** idiom 폭파하다, 터뜨리다
If someone blows something up or if it blows up, it is destroyed by an explosion.

★ **squeak** [skwiːk] v. 끽 하는 소리를 내다; 간신히 해내다; n. 끼익 하는 소리
If something or someone squeaks, they make a short, high-pitched sound.

creepy [krí:pi] a. 오싹하게 하는, 으스스한; (섬뜩할 정도로) 기이한
If you say that something or someone is creepy, you mean they make you feel very nervous or frightened.

★ **occasional** [əkéiʒənəl] a. 가끔의, 때때로의
Occasional means happening sometimes, but not regularly or often.

★ **shaft** [ʃæft] n. (빛햇살 등의) 줄기, 가닥; 기다란 손잡이; (건물 지하의) 수직 통로
A shaft of light is a beam of light, for example sunlight shining through an opening.

★ **filter** [fíltər] v. 새어 들어오다; 여과하다, 거르다; n. 여과기
If light or sound filters into a place, it comes in weakly or slowly, either through a partly covered opening, or from a long distance away.

filmy [fílmi] a. 얇은, 안이 거의 다 비치는
A filmy fabric or substance is very thin and almost transparent.

recoil [rikɔ́il] v. 움찔하다, 흠칫 놀라다; 반동이 생기다; n. 반동
If something makes you recoil, you move your body quickly away from it because it frightens, offends, or hurts you.

★ **disgust** [disgʌ́st] n. 혐오감, 역겨움; v. 혐오감을 유발하다, 역겹게 하다, 넌더리나게 하다
Disgust is a feeling of very strong dislike or disapproval.

‡ **row** [rou] n. 열, 줄; 노 젓기; v. 노를 젓다
A row of things or people is a number of them arranged in a line.

chrysalis [krísəlis] n. 번데기
A chrysalis is a butterfly or moth in the stage between being a larva and an adult.

복습 **reveal** [riví:l] v. (보이지 않던 것을) 드러내 보이다; (비밀 등을) 밝히다
If you reveal something that has been out of sight, you uncover it so that people can see it.

thermal [θə́:rməl] a. 열의; 보온성이 좋은; n. 상승 온난 기류
Thermal means relating to or caused by heat or by changes in temperature.

복습 **detect** [ditékt] v. 발견하다, 알아내다, 감지하다
To detect something means to find it or discover that it is present somewhere by using equipment or making an investigation.

★ **organism** [ɔ́:rgənizm] n. 유기체; 유기적 조직체
An organism is an animal or plant, especially one that is so small that you cannot see it without using a microscope.

^{복습} **confirm** [kənfə́:rm] v. 사실임을 보여주다, 확인해 주다; 더 분명히 해 주다
If you confirm something that has been stated or suggested, you say that it is true because you know about it.

★ **hive** [haiv] n. 벌통, 벌집 비슷한 것; (사람들이 바쁘게) 북새통을 이루는 곳
A hive is where a colony of bees or other insects live.

★ **droop** [dru:p] v. 아래로 처지다; 풀이 죽다, (기가) 꺾이다
If something droops, it hangs or leans downward with no strength or firmness.

‡ **crawl** [krɔ:l] v. 근질근질하다; 기어가다; 우글거리다; n. 기어가기
If something makes your skin crawl, it makes you feel shocked or disgusted.

^{복습} **indicate** [índikèit] v. 보여 주다; (계기가) 가리키다; (손가락이나 고갯짓으로) 가리키다
If one thing indicates something else, it is a sign of that thing.

hibernate [háibərnèit] v. 동면하다, 겨울잠 자다
Animals that hibernate spend the winter in a state like a deep sleep.

^{복습} **glint** [glint] n. 반짝임; (눈이 강하게) 번득임; v. 반짝거리다; (눈이 강하게) 번득이다
A glint is a quick flash of light.

^{복습} **reflect** [riflékt] v. 반사하다; (상을) 비추다; 깊이 생각하다
When light, heat, or other rays reflect off a surface or when a surface reflects them, they are sent back from the surface and do not pass through it.

★ **hurried** [hə́:rid] a. 서둘러 하는 (hurriedly ad. 황급히, 다급하게)
If an action is done hurriedly, it is done quickly, because there is not much time in which to do it.

‡ **wheel** [hwi:l] v. (바퀴 달린 것을) 밀다; (반대 방향으로) 홱 돌다; n. (자동차 등의) 핸들; 바퀴
If you wheel an object that has wheels somewhere, you push it along.

dolly [dáli] n. 짐수레
A dolly is a low truck or cart with small wheels for moving loads that are too heavy to be carried by hand.

^{복습} **display** [displéi] n. 전시, 진열; 표현; 화면; v. 전시하다; 내보이다
A display is an arrangement of things that have been put in a particular place, so that people can see them easily.

portal [pɔ́:rtl] n. 입구; 정문
A portal can refer to any entrance or access to a place.

★ **pose** [pouz] n. 포즈, 자세; v. 자세를 취하다; (위협·문제 등을) 제기하다
When you strike a pose, you hold your body in a particular position to create an impression.

revel [révəl] v. 즐기다, 흥청대다; n. 왁자지껄한 축하
If you revel in a situation or experience, you enjoy it very much.

복습 **comfort** [kʌ́mfərt] n. 편안; 위로; v. 편하게 하다; 위로하다
If you are doing something in comfort, you are physically relaxed and contented, and are not feeling any pain or other unpleasant sensations.

복습 **hiss** [his] v. (강한 어조로) 낮게 말하다; 쉿 하는 소리를 내다; n. 쉭쉭거리는 소리
If you hiss something, you say it forcefully in a whisper.

‡ **spot** [spat] v. 발견하다, 찾다, 알아채다; n. (작은) 점; (특정한) 곳
If you spot something or someone, you notice them.

복습 **grab** [græb] v. (와락·단단히) 붙잡다; 급히 ~하다; n. 와락 잡아채려고 함
If you grab something, you take it or pick it up suddenly and roughly.

★ **accidental** [æksədéntl] a. 우연한, 돌발적인 (accidentally ad. 우연히, 뜻하지 않게)
If an event takes place accidentally, it happens by chance or as the result of an accident, and is not deliberately intended.

복습 **knock** [nak] v. 치다, 부딪치다; (문 등을) 두드리다; n. 부딪침; 문 두드리는 소리
If you knock something, you touch or hit it roughly, especially so that it falls or moves.

★ **trigger** [trígəːr] v. 촉발시키다; n. 폭파 장치; (총의) 방아쇠
To trigger a bomb or system means to cause it to work.

복습 **flash** [flæʃ] v. 번쩍이다; 불현듯 들다; 휙 나타나다; n. 번쩍임; (감정이나 생각이) 갑자기 떠오름
If a light flashes or if you flash a light, it shines with sudden brightness, especially as quick, regular flashes of light.

honk [haŋk] v. (경적을) 울리다, 빵빵거리다; n. 빵빵 (경적 소리)
If you honk the horn of a vehicle or if the horn honks, you make the horn produce a short loud sound.

★ **horn** [hɔːrn] n. (차량의) 경적; (동물의) 뿔
On a vehicle such as a car, the horn is the device that makes a loud noise as a signal or warning.

reverberate [rivə́ːrbərèit] v. (소리가) 울리다; (사람들에게) 반향을 불러일으키다
When a loud sound reverberates through a place, it echoes through it.

fumble [fʌmbl] v. (손으로) 더듬거리다; (말을) 더듬거리다; n. (손으로) 더듬거리기
If you fumble for something or fumble with something, you try and reach for it or hold it in a clumsy way.

fob [fab] n. (열쇠 등의) 고리에 달린 장식품; 시곗줄; 시곗줄이 달린 시계
A fob refers to a metal or plastic tab on a key ring.

★ **stir** [stə:r] v. 약간 움직이다; 자극하다; 젓다; n. 동요, 충격; 젓기
If you stir, you move slightly, for example because you are uncomfortable or beginning to wake up.

‡ **crack** [kræk] v. 갈라지다; 깨지다, 부서지다; n. 날카로운 소리; (갈라져 생긴) 금; (좁은) 틈
If something hard cracks, or if you crack it, it becomes slightly damaged, with lines appearing on its surface.

appendage [əpéndidʒ] n. 일부, 부속물; 첨가물
An appendage is something that is joined to or connected with something larger or more important.

grotesque [groutésk] a. 기괴한, 기이한; 터무니없는, 말도 안 되는 (grotesquely ad. 기괴하게)
If something happens grotesquely, it is so unnatural, unpleasant, and exaggerated that it upsets or shocks you.

cocoon [kəkú:n] n. 누에고치; 안식처, 보호막
A cocoon is a covering of silky threads that the larvae of moths and other insects make for themselves before they grow into adults.

★ **hideous** [hídiəs] a. 흉측한, 흉물스러운; 끔찍한
If you say that someone or something is hideous, you mean that they are very ugly or unattractive.

복습 **shriek** [ʃri:k] v. (날카로운) 소리를 내다; 악을 쓰며 말하다; n. (날카로운) 비명
If something shrieks, it makes a loud, high-pitched voice.

복습 **awaken** [əwéikən] v. (잠에서) 깨우다; (감정을) 불러일으키다
When you awaken, or when something or someone awakens you, you wake up.

sibling [síbliŋ] n. 형제, 자매
Your siblings are your brothers and sisters.

‡ **split** [split] v. 찢어지다; 분열되다; 나뉘다; n. 분열; (길게 찢어진) 틈
If something such as wood or a piece of clothing splits or is split, a long crack or tear appears in it.

Check Your Reading Speed

1분에 몇 단어를 읽는지 리딩 속도를 측정해 보세요.

$$\frac{1{,}268 \text{ words}}{\text{reading time (   ) sec}} \times 60 = (\quad) \text{ WPM}$$

Build Your Vocabulary

horrific [hɔ:rífik] **a.** 끔찍한, 무시무시한; 지독한, 불쾌한
If you describe a physical attack, accident, or injury as horrific, you mean that it is very bad, so that people are shocked when they see it or think about it.

복습 **swarm** [swɔ:rm] **n.** (곤충의) 떼, 무리; 군중; **v.** 무리를 지어 다니다; 많이 모여들다
A swarm of bees or other insects is a large group of them flying together.

복습 **descend** [disénd] **v.** 불시에 습격하다; 내려오다, 내려가다; (아래로) 경사지다
To descend means to swoop or pounce down as in a sudden attack.

복습 **unison** [jú:nisn] **n.** 조화, 화합, 일치 (in unison **idiom** 일제히)
If two or more people do something in unison, they do it together at the same time.

복습 **scramble** [skrǽmbl] **v.** 재빨리 움직이다; 서로 밀치다; **n.** (힘들게) 기어가기; 서로 밀치기
If you scramble to a different place or position, you move there in a hurried, awkward way.

복습 **rush** [rʌʃ] **v.** 급히 움직이다; 서두르다; **n.** (감정이 갑자기) 치밀어 오름; 혼잡
If you rush somewhere, you go there quickly.

복습 **slam** [slæm] **v.** 쾅 닫다, 닫히다; 세게 치다, 놓다; **n.** 쾅 하고 닫기; 쾅 하는 소리
If you slam a door or window or if it slams, it shuts noisily and with great force.

★ **claw** [klɔ:] **v.** (손톱·발톱으로) 할퀴다; 헤치며 나아가다; **n.** (동물·새의) 발톱
If an animal claws at something, it scratches or damages it with its claws.

복습 **appendage** [əpéndidʒ] **n.** 일부, 부속물; 첨가물
An appendage is something that is joined to or connected with something larger or more important.

★ **blunt** [blʌnt] **a.** 직설적인; 무딘, 뭉툭한; **v.** 약화시키다; 뭉툭하게 만들다
If you are blunt, you say exactly what you think without trying to be polite.

^복_습 **snap** [snæp] v. (화난 목소리로) 딱딱거리다; 탁 소리를 내다; 빠르게 움직이다; n. 탁 하는 소리
If someone snaps at you, they speak to you in a sharp, unfriendly way.

★ **toss** [tɔːs] v. (가볍게) 던지다; (고개를) 홱 쳐들다; n. 던지기
If you toss something somewhere, you throw it there lightly, often in a rather careless way.

^복_습 **grant** [grænt] v. 승인하다, 허락하다; 인정하다; n. 보조금
If someone in authority grants you something, or if something is granted to you, you are allowed to have it.

‡ **authority** [əθɔ́ːrəti] n. 권한; 지휘권; 권위자; (pl.) 관계자
Authority is official permission to do something.

^복_습 **blast** [blæst] v. 폭발시키다, 폭파하다; 확 뿌리다; 발사하다; n. 폭발; (한 줄기의) 강한 바람
To blast is to destroy or move earth, rock, or metal using a series of explosions.

★ **probability** [pràbəbíləti] n. 확률; 개연성
The probability of something happening is how likely it is to happen, sometimes expressed as a fraction or a percentage.

frontal [frʌntl] a. 정면의, 앞면의
Frontal means relating to or involving the front of something, for example the front of an army, a vehicle, or the brain.

^복_습 **stealth** [stelθ] n. 살며시 함, 몰래 함, 잠행
If you use stealth when you do something, you do it quietly and carefully so that no one will notice what you are doing.

hide-and-seek [haid-ənd-síːk] n. 숨바꼭질
Hide-and-seek is a children's game in which one player covers his or her eyes until the other players have hidden themselves, and then he or she tries to find them.

‡ **twist** [twist] n. 변형; 돌리기; 굽이; v. 돌리다; 구부리다; 비틀다; 왜곡하다
A twist refers to a distortion of the original or natural shape or form.

^복_습 **disorient** [disɔ́ːriènt] v. 어리둥절하게 하다; 방향 감각을 혼란시키다
If something disorients you, you lose your sense of direction, or you generally feel lost and uncertain, for example because you are in an unfamiliar environment.

^복_습 **impress** [imprés] v. 깊은 인상을 주다, 감동을 주다 (impressed a. 감명을 받은)
If you are impressed by something or someone, you feel great admiration for them.

‡ opposite [ápəzit] **a.** (정)반대의; 건너편의; 맞은편의; **n.** 반대
Opposite means situated or being on the other side or at each side of something between.

복습 notice [nóutis] **v.** 알아채다, 인지하다; 주의하다; **n.** 신경 씀, 주목, 알아챔
If you notice something or someone, you become aware of them.

복습 tuck [tʌk] **v.** (작은 공간에) 집어 넣다, 끼워 넣다; (끝부분을) 접다; 덮다; **n.** (접은) 주름
If you tuck something somewhere, you put it there so that it is safe, comfortable, or neat.

복습 attention [əténʃən] **n.** 주의; 관심; 배려; 차려 (자세)
If you pay attention to someone, you watch them, listen to them, or take notice of them.

복습 instruct [instrʌ́kt] **v.** 지시하다; 가르치다; (정보를) 알려 주다
If you instruct someone to do something, you formally tell them to do it.

복습 press [pres] **v.** 누르다; 꾹 밀어 넣다; (무엇에) 바짝 대다; **n.** 언론
If you press a button or switch, you push it with your finger in order to make a machine or device work.

복습 interrupt [intərʌ́pt] **v.** (말·행동을) 방해하다; 중단시키다; 차단하다
If you interrupt someone who is speaking, you say or do something that causes them to stop.

wave away idiom 일축하다, 물리치다; 손을 흔들어 몰아내다
To wave away something is to not accept it because you do not think it is necessary or important.

★ surrender [səréndər] **n.** 항복, 굴복; **v.** 항복하다, 투항하다; (권리 등을) 포기하다
Surrender refers to the act of stopping fighting or resisting someone and agreeing that you have been beaten.

‡ string [striŋ] **n.** 줄; 일련; (악기의) 현; **v.** 묶다, 매달다; (실 등에) 꿰다
String is thin rope made of twisted threads, used for tying things together or tying up parcels.

‡ shame [ʃeim] **n.** 수치심, 창피; 애석한 일; **v.** 창피하게 하다; 망신시키다 (shameful **a.** 수치스러운)
If you describe a person's action or attitude as shameful, you think that it is so bad that the person ought to be ashamed.

maneuver [mənú:vər] **n.** 작전, 움직임; 조종; 묘책; **v.** (조심조심) 움직이다; 계책을 부리다
A maneuver is a planned movement by a military group involving many soldiers, vehicles, ships, or planes in a particular place.

‡ **annoy** [ənɔ́i] v. 짜증나게 하다; 귀찮게 하다 (annoyed a. 짜증이 난, 약이 오른)
If you are annoyed, you are fairly angry about something.

* **frustrate** [frʌ́streit] v. 불만스럽게 하다, 좌절감을 주다; 방해하다
(frustrated a. 불만스러워하는, 좌절감을 느끼는)
If you feel frustrated, you are disappointed or dissatisfied.

jab [dʒæb] v. 쿡 찌르다; n. 쿡 찌르기; 비난
To jab is to poke or thrust, as with a sharp instrument.

복습 **cadet** [kədét] n. (경찰·군대 등의) 간부 후보생
A cadet is a young man or woman who is being trained in the armed services or the police.

복습 **hover** [hʌ́vər] v. (허공을) 맴돌다; 서성이다; 주저하다; n. 공중을 떠다님
To hover means to stay in the same position in the air without moving forward or backward.

복습 **motion** [móuʃən] v. (손·머리로) 몸짓을 해 보이다; n. 동작, 몸짓; 운동, 움직임
If you motion to someone, you move your hand or head as a way of telling them to do something or telling them where to go.

복습 **fade** [feid] v. 서서히 사라지다; (색깔이) 바래다, 희미해지다
When something that you are looking at fades, it slowly becomes less bright or clear until it disappears.

복습 **creep** [kri:p] v. (crept-crept) 살금살금 움직이다; 서서히 다가가다; 기다; n. 너무 싫은 사람
When people or animals creep somewhere, they move quietly and slowly.

‡ **entrance** [éntrəns] n. 입구, 문; 입장, 등장
The entrance to a place is the way into it, for example a door or gate.

복습 **wheel** [hwi:l] v. (바퀴 달린 것을) 밀다; (반대 방향으로) 휙 돌다; n. (자동차 등의) 핸들; 바퀴
If you wheel an object that has wheels somewhere, you push it along.

복습 **crawl** [krɔ:l] v. 기어가다; 근질근질하다; 우글거리다; n. 기어가기
When an insect crawls somewhere, it moves there quite slowly.

cram [kræm] v. (억지로) 밀어 넣다 (crammed a. 잔뜩 밀어 넣어진)
If people or things are crammed into a place or vehicle, it is full of them.

inhibit [inhíbit] v. 저해하다, 억제하다; ~하지 못하게 하다
If something inhibits an event or process, it prevents it or slows it down.

★ **visual** [víʒuəl] **n.** 시야, 보기; 시각 자료; **a.** 시각의, (눈으로) 보는
If you get a visual on someone or something, you can see them.

^복_습 **spit** [spit] **v.** (침·음식 등을) 뱉다; (말을) 내뱉다; **n.** 침; (침 등을) 뱉기
If you spit liquid or food somewhere, you force a small amount of it out of your mouth.

★ **fur** [fəːr] **n.** (동물의) 털; 모피
Fur is the thick and usually soft hair that grows on the bodies of many mammals.

★ **shift** [ʃift] **v.** 자세를 바꾸다; (장소를) 옮기다; (견해·태도를) 바꾸다; **n.** 변화
To shift means to move or change from one position or direction to another, especially slightly.

‡ **float** [flout] **v.** (물 위나 공중에서) 떠가다; (물에) 뜨다; **n.** 부표
Something that floats in or through the air hangs in it or moves slowly and gently through it.

midair [midέər] **n.** 공중, 상공
If something happens in midair, it happens in the air, rather than on the ground.

^복_습 **whisper** [hwíspər] **v.** 속삭이다, 소곤거리다; **n.** 속삭임, 소곤거리는 소리
When you whisper, you say something very quietly, using your breath rather than your throat, so that only one person can hear you.

^복_습 **insert** [insə́ːrt] **v.** 끼우다, 넣다; **n.** 부속품; 삽입 광고
If you insert an object into something, you put the object inside it.

^복_습 **glow** [glou] **v.** 빛나다, 타다; (얼굴이) 상기되다; **n.** (은은한) 불빛; 홍조
If something glows, it produces a dull, steady light.

^복_습 **satisfy** [sǽtisfài] **v.** 만족시키다; 충족시키다; 납득시키다 (satisfying **a.** 만족스러운, 만족감을 주는)
Something that is satisfying makes you feel happy, especially because you feel you have achieved something.

countdown [káuntdaun] **n.** 카운트다운; (중요한 행사의) 초읽기
A countdown is the counting aloud of numbers in reverse order before something happens, especially before a spacecraft is launched.

^복_습 **wrist** [rist] **n.** 손목, 팔목
Your wrist is the part of your body between your hand and your arm which bends when you move your hand.

^복_습 **display** [displéi] **n.** 화면; 전시, 진열; 표현; **v.** 전시하다; 내보이다
The display refers to the information that is shown on a computer screen, or the screen itself.

★ **visible** [vízəbl] a. (눈에) 보이는, 알아볼 수 있는; 뚜렷한
If something is visible, it can be seen.

복습 **hop** [hap] v. 급히 움직이다; 깡충깡충 뛰다; n. 깡충깡충 뛰기
If you hop somewhere, you move there quickly or suddenly.

복습 **fizzle** [fízl] v. 약하게 쉿 소리를 내다; 실패하다
To fizzle is to make a hissing sound, often indicating a declining momentum.

복습 **gasp** [gæsp] v. 헉 하고 숨을 쉬다; 숨을 제대로 못 쉬다; n. 헉 하는 소리를 냄
When you gasp, you take a short quick breath through your mouth, especially when you are surprised, shocked, or in pain.

★ **panic** [pǽnik] v. 어쩔 줄 모르다, 공황 상태에 빠지다; n. 극심한 공포, 공황; 허둥지둥함
(panicked a. 어쩔 줄 몰라 하는)
If you panic or if someone panics you, you suddenly feel anxious or afraid, and act quickly and without thinking carefully.

★ **hatch** [hæʧ] n. (배·항공기의) 출입구; v. 부화하다; (계획 등을) 만들어 내다
A hatch is an opening in the deck of a ship, through which people or cargo can go.

복습 **depot** [dí:pou] n. 저장소, 창고
A depot is a place where large amounts of raw materials, equipment, arms, or other supplies are kept until they are needed.

복습 **realize** [rí:əlàiz] v. 깨닫다, 알아차리다; 실현하다, 달성하다
If you realize that something is true, you become aware of that fact or understand it.

curdle [kə́:rdl] v. (공포나 충격으로) 피를 얼어붙게 하다 (blood-curdling a. 소름끼치는)
A blood-curdling sound or story is very frightening and horrible.

복습 **shriek** [ʃri:k] n. (날카로운) 비명; v. (날카로운) 소리를 내다; 악을 쓰며 말하다
A shriek is a shrill and piercing cry.

yank [jæŋk] v. 홱 잡아당기다; n. 홱 잡아당기기
If you yank someone or something somewhere, you pull them there suddenly and with a lot of force.

inflate [infléit] v. (공기나 가스로) 부풀리다; 과장하다; (가격을) 올리다
If you inflate something such as a balloon or tire, or if it inflates, it becomes bigger as it is filled with air or a gas.

legion [lí:dʒən] n. 다수, 많은 수; 군대, 군단; a. (수가) 아주 많은
A legion of people or things is a great number of them.

yelp [jelp] n. (날카롭게) 외치는 소리, 비명; v. 비명을 지르다
A yelp is a sharp or high-pitched cry or bark.

yell [jel] v. 고함치다, 소리 지르다; n. 고함, 외침
If you yell, you shout loudly, usually because you are excited, angry, or in pain.

release [rilíːs] n. 방출; 풀어 줌; 공개; 해제; v. 석방하다, 놓아 주다; 풀다; (감정을) 발산하다
A release refers to an act or device that causes gas, heat, or a substance to leave its container.

deflate [difléit] v. (타이어·풍선 등의) 공기를 빼다; 기를 꺾다
When something such as a tire or balloon deflates, or when you deflate it, all the air comes out of it.

topple [tapl] v. 넘어지다; 넘어뜨리다; 실각시키다
If someone or something topples somewhere or if you topple them, they become unsteady or unstable and fall over.

★ **scrape** [skreip] v. (상처가 나도록) 긁다; (무엇을) 긁어내다; 간신히 얻다; n. 긁기
If something scrapes against something else, they rub against it, making a noise or causing slight damage.

hull [hʌl] n. (배의) 선체; v. (콩 등의) 껍질을 벗기다
The hull of a boat or aircraft is the main body of it.

★ **pant** [pænt] v. (숨을) 헐떡이다; n. 헐떡거림
If you pant, you breathe quickly and loudly with your mouth open, because you have been doing something energetic.

adapt [ədǽpt] v. 적응하다; 조정하다
If you adapt to a new situation or adapt yourself to it, you change your ideas or behavior in order to deal with it successfully.

congratulate [kəngrǽʧulèit] v. 기뻐하다, 자랑스러워하다; 축하하다
If you congratulate yourself, you are pleased about something that you have done or that has happened to you.

wear off idiom (차츰) 사라지다
If a feeling or an effect wears off, it gradually disappears.

★ **retort** [ritɔ́ːt] n. 쏘아붙이기, 응수; v. 쏘아붙이다, 대꾸하다
A retort is a sharp, angry, or witty reply.

lurch [ləːrʧ] v. (갑자기) 휘청하다, 휘청거리다; (공포·흥분으로) 떨리다; n. 휘청함; 요동침
To lurch means to make a sudden movement, especially forward, in an uncontrolled way.

shield [ʃiːld] n. 보호 장치; 방패; v. 보호하다, 가리다 (windshield n. (자동차 등의) 방풍 유리)
The windshield of a car or other vehicle is the glass window at the front through which the driver looks.

back and forth idiom 앞뒤로; 여기저기로, 왔다갔다; 좌우로
If you move something back and forth, you repeatedly move it in one direction and then in the opposite direction.

strap [stræp] v. 끈으로 묶다; 붕대를 감다; n. 끈, 줄, 띠
If you strap something somewhere, you fasten it there with a piece of cloth or other material.

bust out idiom 도망치다; 갑자기 ~하다; 싹트다, 꽃피다
To bust out of something means to escape from it.

⋆ **old-fashioned** [òuld-fǽʃənd] a. 구식의, 유행에 뒤떨어진
An old-fashioned method or device is no longer used or done by most people, because it has been replaced by something that is more modern.

navigate [nǽvəgèit] v. 조종하다; 길을 찾다; 항해하다 (navigation n. 조종)
You can refer to the movement of ships or aircrafts as navigation.

chime [ʧaim] v. (노래하듯) 말하다; (종이나 시계가) 울리다; n. 차임, 종
To chime is to speak or recite in a musical or rhythmic manner.

belabor [biléibər] v. 오래 계속하다; 공격하다, 강타하다; 조롱하다
If something is belabored, it continues in an annoying or boring way.

metallic [mətǽlik] a. 금속의, 금속성의
Metallic means consisting entirely or partly of metal.

shatter [ʃǽtər] v. 산산이 부서지다, 산산조각 나다; 엄청난 충격을 주다
If something shatters or is shattered, it breaks into a lot of small pieces.

throttle [θratl] n. (자동차 등의 연료) 조절판; v. 목을 조르다
The throttle of a motor vehicle or aircraft is the device, lever, or pedal that controls the quantity of fuel entering the engine and is used to control the vehicle's speed.

alien [éiljən] a. 외계의; 생경한; 이질적인; n. 외계인
Alien means coming from another world, such as an outer space.

cling [kliŋ] v. (clung-clung) 들러붙다; 꼭 붙잡다, 매달리다; 애착을 갖다
Something that is clinging to something else is stuck on it or just attached to it.

^복_습 **tear** [tɛər] ① v. 찢다, 뜯다; 뜯어 내다; 질주하다; n. 찢어진 곳, 구멍 ② n. 눈물
If you tear paper, cloth, or another material, or if it tears, you pull it into two pieces or you pull it so that a hole appears in it.

^복_습 **atmosphere** [ǽtməsfiər] n. 대기; 공기; 분위기
A planet's atmosphere is the layer of air or other gases around it.

^복_습 **stammer** [stǽmər] v. 말을 더듬다; n. 말 더듬기
If you stammer, you speak with difficulty, hesitating and repeating words or sounds.

^복_습 **barrel** [bǽrəl] n. (대형) 통; v. 쏜살같이 달리다
A barrel is a large, round container for liquids or food.

⋆ **threshold** [θréʃhould] n. 문턱; 문지방; 한계점
A threshold refers to the entrance or beginning point of something.

⋆ **terror** [térər] n. 두려움, 공포; 공포의 대상
Terror is very great fear.

open fire idiom 공격을 시작하다, 발포하다
To open fire is to start firing a gun or artillery.

11 & 12

1. Why was Buzz proud of Izzy?

    A. She wanted to help with ground support.

    B. She knew how to build a coil.

    C. She was not afraid of space anymore.

    D. She figured out how to solve their problem.

2. How did the group get stuck in the control room?

    A. Star Command operators sealed the room.

    B. Mo accidentally hit the wrong button.

    C. Sox pulled out the activation coil.

    D. Some robots blocked the door.

3. What happened when Buzz started to fall from the ledge?

   A. He grabbed hold of Sox's tail.

   B. He used a jet pack to fly to safety.

   C. Izzy threw a rope to him.

   D. The Junior Patrol formed a chain to save him.

4. Why did the giant robot step over the members of the Junior Patrol?

   A. It was trying to get to Buzz.

   B. It did not see them on the ground.

   C. They ran away too quickly.

   D. They were firing at it.

5. Why did Buzz and Izzy get off the ship?

   A. To make the robot chase them

   B. To look for Sox

   C. To get the ejected fuel cell

   D. To destroy the crystal

Check Your Reading Speed
1분에 몇 단어를 읽는지 리딩 속도를 측정해 보세요.

$$\frac{2,214 \text{ words}}{\text{reading time ( ) sec}} \times 60 = (\quad) \text{ WPM}$$

Build Your Vocabulary

swerve [swəːrv] v. (갑자기) 방향을 바꾸다
If a vehicle or other moving thing swerves or if you swerve it, it suddenly changes direction, often in order to avoid hitting something.

‡ **enemy** [énəmi] n. 적; 장애물
If someone is your enemy, they hate you or want to harm you.

★ **clip** [klip] v. 스치다, 부딪치다; 자르다, 깎다; 핀으로 고정하다; n. 핀, 클립
If something clips something else, it hits it accidentally at an angle before moving off in a different direction.

복습 **plummet** [plʌmit] v. 곤두박질치다, 급락하다
If someone or something plummets, they fall very fast toward the ground, usually from a great height.

복습 **exclaim** [ikskléim] v. 소리치다, 외치다
If you exclaim, you cry out suddenly in surprise, strong emotion, or pain.

복습 **spin** [spin] v. (spun-spun) (빙빙) 돌다, 돌리다; 돌아서다; n. 회전
If something spins or if you spin it, it turns quickly around a central point.

복습 **scan** [skæn] v. (유심히) 살피다; 훑어보다; 정밀 촬영하다; 스캔하다; n. 정밀 검사
When you scan a place or group of people, you look at it carefully, usually because you are looking for something or someone.

★ **faint** [feint] a. 희미한, 약한; 소심한; v. 실신하다, 기절하다; n. 실신, 기절
A faint sound, color, mark, feeling, or quality has very little strength or intensity.

복습 **mine** [main] v. (광물질을) 캐다, 채굴하다; n. 광산; 지뢰
When a mineral such as coal, diamonds, or gold is mined, it is obtained from the ground by digging deep holes and tunnels.

operate [ápərèit] v. 작업하다; 작전을 벌이다; 조작하다; 작동하다; 수술하다 (operation n. 작업)
An operation is a highly organized activity that involves many people doing different things.

distance [dístəns] n. 먼 곳; 거리; v. (~에) 관여하지 않다 (in the distance idiom 저 먼 곳에)
If you can see something in the distance, you can see it, far away from you.

grip [grip] v. 움켜잡다; (마음·흥미·시선을) 끌다; n. 꽉 붙잡음, 움켜쥠; 통제, 지배
If you grip something, you take hold of it with your hand and continue to hold it firmly.

muster [mʌ́stər] v. (용기 등을 최대한) 내다; (지지 등을) 모으다; 소집하다; n. 소집, 집결
If you muster something such as support, strength, or energy, you gather as much of it as you can in order to do something.

steady [stédi] a. 차분한, 침착한; 흔들림 없는, 안정된; 꾸준한; v. 균형을 잡다, 진정시키다
(steadily ad. 침착히)
If you do something steadily, you do it without moving or shaking and in a controlled way.

flail [fleil] v. 마구 움직이다; (팔다리를) 마구 흔들다
If something flails, it waves about in an energetic but uncontrolled way.

terrain [təréin] n. 지역, 지형
Terrain is used to refer to an area of land or a type of land when you are considering its physical features.

plume [plu:m] n. (연기·먼지 등의) 기둥; (커다란) 깃털
A plume of smoke, dust, fire, or water is a large quantity of it that rises into the air in a column.

wince [wins] v. (통증·당혹감으로) 움찔하고 놀라다
If you wince, the muscles of your face tighten suddenly because you have felt a pain or because you have just seen, heard, or remembered something unpleasant.

wind [wind] ① v. 숨을 쉬기 어렵게 만들다; n. 바람; 숨 (winded a. 숨이 찬)
② v. 태엽을 감다; (실 등을) 감다; (도로·강 등이) 구불구불하다
If you are winded by something such as a blow, the air is suddenly knocked out of your lungs so that you have difficulty breathing for a short time.

daze [deiz] v. 멍하게 하다; 눈부시게 하다; n. 멍한 상태; 눈이 부심 (dazed a. 멍한)
If someone is dazed, they are confused and unable to think clearly, often because of shock or a blow to the head.

pitch black [pìʧ blǽk] a. 칠흑같이 어두운, 새까만
If a place or the night is pitch black, it is completely dark.

clamor [klǽmər] v. 시끄러운 소리를 내다, 와글와글 떠들다; n. 시끄러운 외침, 떠들썩함
To clamor is to make a loud and continued noise.

whoosh [hwuːʃ] n. 쉭 하는 소리; v. (아주 빠르게) 휙 하고 움직이다
A whoosh is a soft sound made by something moving fast through the air.

복습 **kneel** [niːl] v. (knelt-knelt) 무릎을 꿇다
When you kneel, you bend your legs so that your knees are touching the ground.

복습 **pant** [pænt] v. (숨을) 헐떡이다; n. 헐떡거림
If you pant, you breathe quickly and loudly with your mouth open, because you have been doing something energetic.

복습 **frustrate** [frʌ́streit] v. 불만스럽게 하다, 좌절감을 주다; 방해하다 (frustration n. 불만, 좌절감)
Frustration is a feeling of being disappointed or dissatisfied.

★ **concede** [kənsíːd] v. (마지못해) 인정하다, 시인하다, 허용하다; (권리·특권 등을) 부여하다
If you concede something, you admit, often unwillingly, that it is true or correct.

★ **clutch** [klʌʧ] v. (꽉) 움켜잡다; n. 움켜쥠
If you clutch at something or clutch something, you hold it tightly, usually because you are afraid or anxious.

pantomime [pǽntəmàim] v. 몸짓으로 나타내다; 무언극을 하다; n. 몸짓, 손짓; 무언극
If you pantomime something, you use the movement of your body and the expression of your face to communicate something or to tell a story.

복습 **float** [flout] v. (물 위나 공중에서) 떠가다; (물에) 뜨다; n. 부표
Something that floats in or through the air hangs in it or moves slowly and gently through it.

복습 **shrug** [ʃrʌg] v. (어깨를) 으쓱하다; n. 어깨를 으쓱하기
If you shrug, you raise your shoulders to show that you are not interested in something or that you do not know or care about something.

복습 **ranger** [réindʒər] n. 경비 대원; 기습 공격대원
A ranger is an armed guard who patrols a region.

★ **automatic** [ɔ̀ːtəmǽtik] a. 자동의; 무의식적인, 반사적인
If something such as an action or a punishment is automatic, it happens without people needing to think about it because it is the result of a fixed rule or method.

disqualify [diskwáləfài] v. 자격을 박탈하다, 실격시키다 (disqualification n. 자격 박탈)
Disqualification involves officially stopping someone from taking part in a particular event, activity, or competition, usually because they have done something wrong.

head-on [hed-án] ad. 정면으로; a. (차량 충돌에서) 정면으로 부딪친; 정면으로 대응하는
If you deal with something head-on, you deal with it directly, although it is difficult.

★ **conquer** [káŋkər] v. 극복하다; 정복하다; 이기다
If you conquer something such as a problem, you succeed in ending it or dealing with it successfully.

복습 **crucial** [krúːʃəl] a. 결정적인, 중대한
If you describe something as crucial, you mean it is extremely important.

★ **component** [kəmpóunənt] n. (구성) 요소, 부품
The components of something are the parts that it is made of.

복습 **corps** [kɔːr] n. (특수한 임무를 띤) 부대; 군단; (특정한 활동을 하는) 단체, 집단
A Corps is a part of the army which has special duties.

★ **tension** [ténʃən] n. 긴장 상태; 긴장, 불안; 갈등; 팽팽함
Tension is the feeling that is produced in a situation when people are anxious and do not trust each other, and when there is a possibility of sudden violence or conflict.

복습 **squint** [skwint] v. 눈을 가늘게 뜨고 보다; 사시이다; n. 잠깐 봄; 사시
If you squint at something, you look at it with your eyes partly closed.

복습 **plod** [plad] v. 터벅터벅 걷다; 꾸준히 일하다
If someone plods, they walk slowly and heavily.

복습 **shimmer** [ʃímər] n. 희미한 빛; v. 희미하게 빛나다 (shimmery a. 희미하게 빛나는)
Something that is shimmery shines softly.

복습 **strand** [strænd] v. 오도 가도 못 하게 하다, 발을 묶다; n. 가닥, 꼰 줄
If you are stranded, you are prevented from leaving a place, for example because of bad weather.

복습 **hostile** [hastl] a. 적대적인; 강력히 반대하는
In a war, you use hostile to describe your enemy's forces and activities.

복습 **force** [fɔːrs] n. 세력; 힘; 영향력; v. 억지로 ~하다; ~을 강요하다
Forces are groups of soldiers or military vehicles that are organized for a particular purpose.

roadblock [róudblak] n. 장애물; 바리케이드, 방어벽
A roadblock means a difficulty or obstacle to progress.

wallow [wálou] v. 빠져 있다; 뒹굴다; n. 뒹굴기
If you say that someone is wallowing in an unpleasant situation, you are criticizing them for being deliberately unhappy.

‡ **pity** [píti] n. 연민, 동정; v. 애석해 하다; 불쌍해하다, 동정하다 (self-pity n. 자기 연민)
Self-pity is a feeling of unhappiness that you have about yourself and your problems, especially when this is unnecessary or greatly exaggerated.

★ **discourage** [diskə́:ridʒ] v. 막다, 말리다; 낙담시키다, 용기를 잃게 하다
To discourage an action means to make people not want to do it.

복습 **groan** [groun] v. (고통·짜증으로) 신음 소리를 내다, 끙끙거리다; n. 신음, 끙 하는 소리
If you groan, you make a long, low sound because you are in pain, or because you are upset or unhappy about something.

★ **mess** [mes] n. (많은 문제로) 엉망인 상황; (지저분하고) 엉망인 상태; v. 엉망으로 만들다
If you say that a situation is a mess, you mean that it is full of trouble or problems.

복습 **assess** [əsés] v. 평가하다, 가늠하다; (특성·자질 등을) 재다 (assessment n. 평가)
An assessment is a consideration of someone or something and a judgment about them.

복습 **figure** [fígjər] v. 생각하다; 중요하다; n. (멀리서 흐릿하게 보이는) 사람; 수치; (중요한) 인물
If you figure that something is the case, you think or guess that it is the case.

★ **absorb** [æbsɔ́:rb] v. 흡수하다; (관심을) 빼앗다
If something absorbs a force or shock, it reduces its effect.

‡ **minor** [máinər] a. 중요하지 않은, 작은 쪽의
You use minor when you want to describe something that is less important, serious, or significant than other things in a group or situation.

‡ **material** [mətíəriəl] n. 재료; 소재; 제목; 자료; a. 물질적인; 중요한
A material is a solid substance from which things can be made.

복습 **specialize** [spéʃəlàiz] v. 특수화하다; 전문화하다 (specialized a. 특수화된)
Someone or something that is specialized is trained or developed for a particular purpose or area of knowledge.

thingy [θíŋi] n. (지칭하는 물건의 이름을 모르거나 잊었을 때) 뭐더라, 그거
You refer to something or someone as thingy when you do not know or cannot be bothered to use the proper word or name for them.

★ **chuckle** [ʧʌkl] v. 킬킬 웃다, 빙그레 웃다, 싱긋 웃다; n. 킬킬거림, 빙그레 웃기
To chuckle is to laugh softly or amusedly, usually with satisfaction.

★ **grumble** [grʌmbl] v. 투덜거리다, 불평하다; n. 투덜댐; 불평
If someone grumbles, they complain about something in a bad-tempered way.

^{복습} **annoy** [ənɔ́i] v. 짜증나게 하다; 귀찮게 하다 (annoyed a. 짜증이 난, 약이 오른)
If you are annoyed, you are fairly angry about something.

bicker [bíkər] v. (사소한 일로) 다투다
When people bicker, they argue or quarrel about unimportant things.

^{복습} **interject** [ìntərdʒékt] v. 말참견을 하다
If you interject something, you say it and interrupt someone else who is speaking.

reminisce [rèmənís] v. 추억에 잠기다, 추억담을 나누다
If you reminisce about something from your past, you write or talk about it, often with pleasure.

^{복습} **gesture** [dʒéstʃər] v. (손·머리 등으로) 가리키다; 몸짓을 하다; n. 몸짓; (감정·의도의) 표시
If you gesture, you use movements of your hands or head in order to tell someone something or draw their attention to something.

^{복습} **facility** [fəsíləti] n. 시설, 기관; 기능, 특징; 재능
Facilities are buildings, pieces of equipment, or services that are provided for a particular purpose.

^{복습} **wave away** idiom 손을 흔들어 몰아내다; 일축하다, 물리치다
To wave away something is to not accept it because you do not think it is necessary or important.

^{복습} **console** [kánsoul] n. 제어반, 계기반; v. 위로하다, 위안을 주다
A console is a panel with a number of switches or knobs that is used to operate a machine.

★ **coil** [kɔil] n. 전선; 고리; v. (고리 모양으로) 감다, 휘감다
A coil is a thick spiral of wire through which an electrical current passes.

predicament [pridíkəmənt] n. 곤경, 궁지
If you are in a predicament, you are in an unpleasant situation that is difficult to get out of.

trek [trek] v. (힘들게 오래) 걷다, 이동하다; 트레킹을 하다; n. 오래 걷기; 여행; 트레킹
If you trek somewhere, you go on a journey across difficult country, usually on foot.

ravine [rəvíːn] n. (좁고 험한) 산골짜기, 협곡
A ravine is a very deep narrow valley with steep sides.

^{복습} **overlook** [ouvərlúk] v. (건물 등이) 바라보다; 못 보고 넘어가다, 간과하다; 못 본 체하다
If a building or window overlooks a place, you can see the place clearly from the building or window.

★ enterprise [éntərpràiz] **n.** 기업, 회사; 산업; 진취적 정신, 모험심
An enterprise is a company or business, often a small one.

‡ whistle [hwisl] **v.** 휘파람을 불다; 기적을 울리다; **n.** 휘파람 (소리); 씩씩 하는 소리; 경적
When you whistle, you make a series of musical notes by forcing your breath out between your lips, or your teeth.

massive [mǽsiv] **a.** 거대한; 엄청나게 심각한
Something that is massive is very large in size, quantity, or extent.

★ gigantic [dʒaigǽntik] **a.** 거대한
If you describe something as gigantic, you are emphasizing that it is extremely large in size, amount, or degree.

crater [kréitər] **n.** (땅에 패인) 큰 구멍; 분화구
A crater is a very large hole in the ground, which has been caused by something hitting it or by an explosion.

excavate [ékskəvèit] **v.** 발굴하다; (구멍 등을) 파다
When people excavate a piece of land, they remove earth carefully from it and look for things which are buried there, in order to discover information about the past.

★ crust [krʌst] **n.** 딱딱한 표면, 겉껍질
A crust is a hard layer of something.

command [kəmǽnd] **n.** 사령부; 명령; 지휘; **v.** 명령하다; 지휘하다
In the armed forces, a command is a group of officers who are responsible for organizing and controlling part of an army, navy, or air force.

extend [iksténd] **v.** 뻗어 있다; (신체 부위를) 뻗다; (거리·기간을) 포괄하다
If an object extends from a surface or place, it sticks out from it.

precarious [prikέəriəs] **a.** 위태로운, 불안정한 (precariously **ad.** 위태롭게)
If something is placed somewhere precariously, it is not securely held in place and seems likely to fall or collapse at any moment.

★ ledge [ledʒ] **n.** 절벽에서 튀어나온 바위; (튀어나온) 선반
A ledge is a piece of rock on the side of a cliff or mountain, which is in the shape of a narrow shelf.

stilt [stilt] **n.** (건물을 지면·수면 위로 떠받치는) 기둥, 지주
Stilts are two long pieces of wood with pieces for the feet fixed high up on the sides so that people can stand on them and walk high above the ground.

★ **seal** [si:l] v. 봉쇄하다; 봉인하다; 확정짓다; n. 도장; [동물] 바다표범
If someone in authority seals an area, they stop people entering or passing through it, for example by placing barriers in the way.

복습 **fumble** [fʌmbl] v. (손으로) 더듬거리다; (말을) 더듬거리다; n. (손으로) 더듬거리기
If you fumble for something or fumble with something, you try and reach for it or hold it in a clumsy way.

복습 **log** [lɔːg] n. (비행·항해 등의) 일지, 기록; 통나무; v. 일지에 기록하다; 비행하다, 항해하다
A log is an official written account of what happens each day, for example on board a ship.

복습 **narrate** [nǽreit] v. 이야기하다, 말하다
If you narrate a story, you tell it from your own point of view.

복습 **slide** [slaid] v. (slid-slid/slidden) 미끄러지다; 미끄러지듯이 움직이다; n. 떨어짐; 미끄러짐
When something slides somewhere or when you slide it there, it moves there smoothly over or against something.

hot-wire [hát-wàiər] v. 부정하게 조작하다; (점화 장치를 단락시켜 자동차·비행기의) 시동을 걸다
If someone hot-wires something, they start them by short-circuiting the ignition system.

★ **convict** [kənvíkt] n. 죄수, 재소자; v. 유죄를 선고하다; (양심 등의) 가책을 받다
A convict is someone who is in prison.

복습 **slip** [slip] v. 슬며시 가다; (말이) 무심코 나오다; 미끄러지다; n. 미끄러짐; (작은) 실수
If you slip somewhere, you go there quickly and quietly.

복습 **emergency** [imə́ːrdʒənsi] n. 비상, 비상 사태
An emergency is an unexpected and difficult or dangerous situation, especially an accident, which happens suddenly and which requires quick action to deal with it.

복습 **activate** [ǽktəvèit] v. 작동시키다; 활성화시키다 (activation n. 작동; 활성화)
Activation refers to the process in which something causes a device or process to start working.

shimmy [ʃími] v. 엉덩이와 어깨를 흔들며 움직이다
If you shimmy, you move forward or backward while also quickly moving slightly from side to side.

복습 **triumphant** [traiʌ́mfənt] a. 의기양양한; 크게 성공한, 큰 승리를 거둔
(triumphantly ad. 의기양양하게)
Someone who acts triumphantly is very happy about a victory or success.

^{복습} **emerge** [imə́:rdʒ] **v.** 나오다, 모습을 드러내다; (어려움 등을) 헤쳐 나오다
To emerge means to come out from an enclosed or dark space such as a room or a
vehicle, or from a position where you could not be seen.

^{복습} **security** [sikjúərəti] **n.** 보안, 경비; (미래를 위한) 보장; 안도감, 안심
Security refers to all the measures that are taken to protect a place, or to ensure that
only people with permission enter it or leave it.

✱ **measure** [méʒər] **n.** 조치, 정책; 척도; **v.** 측정하다; 판단하다
When someone takes measures to do something, they carry out particular actions in
order to achieve a particular result.

★ **cone** [koun] **n.** 원뿔형 물체; 원뿔
A cone is a solid or hollow object that is like a cone in shape.

^{복습} **instant** [ínstənt] **a.** 즉각적인; **n.** 순간, 아주 짧은 동안 (instantly **ad.** 즉각, 즉시)
If something happens instantly, it happens without any delay.

^{복습} **whiz** [hwiz] **v.** 윙 하는 소리가 나다; 빠르게 지나가다; **n.** 윙 하는 소리
To whiz is to make the buzzing or hissing sound of something moving swiftly through
the air.

^{복습} **crash** [kræʃ] **v.** 부딪치다; 추락하다; 충돌하다; 굉음을 내다; **n.** 요란한 소리; (자동차·항공기) 사고
If something crashes somewhere, it moves and hits something else violently, making
a loud noise.

^{복습} **collide** [kəláid] **v.** 부딪치다, 충돌하다; (의견 등이) 상충하다
If two or more moving people or objects collide, they crash into one another.

★ **merge** [mə́:rdʒ] **v.** 합치다; 어우러지다
If one thing merges with another, or is merged with another, they combine or come
together to make one whole thing.

squish [skwiʃ] **v.** 찌부러뜨리다, 으깨다
If something soft squishes or is squished, it is crushed out of shape when it is pressed.

^{복습} **stumble** [stʌmbl] **v.** 비틀거리다; 발을 헛디디다; (말·글 읽기를 하다가) 더듬거리다
If you stumble, you put your foot down awkwardly while you are walking or running
and nearly fall over.

^{복습} **tuck** [tʌk] **v.** (작은 공간에) 집어 넣다, 끼워 넣다; (끝부분을) 접다; 덮다; **n.** (접은) 주름
If you tuck something somewhere, you put it there so that it is safe, comfortable, or
neat.

§ **claw** [klɔː] v. (손톱·발톱으로) 할퀴다; 헤치며 나아가다; n. (동물·새의) 발톱
If an animal claws at something, it scratches or damages it with its claws.

§ **slight** [slait] a. 약간의, 조금의; 작고 여윈
Something that is slight is very small in degree or quantity.

★ **stagger** [stǽgər] v. 비틀거리다, 휘청거리다; 큰 충격을 주다
To stagger means to walk with weak unsteady steps, as if you are about to fall.

§ **accidental** [æksədéntl] a. 우연한, 돌발적인 (accidentally ad. 우연히, 뜻하지 않게)
If an event takes place accidentally, it happens by chance or as the result of an accident, and is not deliberately intended.

★ **bump** [bʌmp] v. 부딪치다; 덜컹거리며 가다; n. 쿵 하는 소리
If you bump into something or someone, you accidentally hit them while you are moving.

flicker [flíkər] v. (불·빛 등이) 깜박거리다; 움직거리다; n. (빛의) 깜박거림; 움직거림
If a light or flame flickers, it shines unsteadily.

§ **charge** [ʧɑːrdʒ] v. 돌격하다; 급히 가다; (요금·값을) 청구하다; 충전하다; n. 책임, 담당; 요금
If you charge toward someone or something, you move quickly and aggressively toward them.

★ **bounce** [bauns] v. 튀다; 깡충깡충 뛰다; n. 튐, 튀어 오름; 탄력
If sound or light bounces off a surface or is bounced off it, it reaches the surface and is reflected back.

§ **protest** [proutést] v. 이의를 제기하다, 항의하다; n. 항의; 시위
If you protest that something is the case, you insist that it is true, when other people think that it may not be.

§ **square** [skwɛər] v. 똑바로 펴다; 네모지게 만들다; a. 정사각형 모양의; 직각의; ad. 똑바로
If you square your shoulders, you stand straight and push them back, usually to show your determination.

§ **spring** [spriŋ] v. 휙 움직이다; 튀다; 갑자기 ~하다; n. 생기, 활기; 봄; 샘
If something springs in a particular direction, it moves suddenly and quickly.

§ **recoil** [rikɔ́il] n. 반동; v. 반동이 생기다; 움찔하다, 흠칫 놀라다
Recoil refers to an action of springing back to the starting point, as in consequence of force of impact.

momentum [mouméntəm] n. 가속도; 기세
If a process or movement gains momentum, it keeps developing or happening more quickly and keeps becoming less likely to stop.

combine [kəmbáin] v. 결합하다; 겸비하다
If you combine two or more things or if they combine, they join together to make a single thing.

explode [iksplóud] v. 폭발하다; 갑자기 ~하다; (강한 감정을) 터뜨리다
If an object such as a bomb explodes or if someone or something explodes it, it bursts loudly and with great force, often causing damage or injury.

simultaneous [sàiməltéiniəs] a. 동시에 일어나는, 동시의 (simultaneously ad. 동시에)
If two things happen simultaneously, they take place at the same time.

aftermath [æftərmæθ] n. (전쟁·사고 등의) 여파, 후유증
The aftermath of an important event, especially a harmful one, is the situation that results from it.

stupor [stjú:pər] n. 멍함, 황홀함; 무감각; 인사불성
Someone who is in a stupor is unable to think or act normally because they are not completely conscious.

shift [ʃift] v. (장소를) 옮기다; 자세를 바꾸다; (견해·태도를) 바꾸다; n. 변화
To shift means to move or change from one position or direction to another, especially slightly.

give way idiom 부러지다, 무너지다; (감정에) 못 이기다; 양보하다
To give way is to collapse or break down.

croak [krouk] v. 목이 쉰 듯 말하다; (개구리나 까마귀가) 까악까악 울다; n. 꺽꺽하는 소리
If someone croaks something, they say it in a low, rough voice.

motion [móuʃən] v. (손·머리로) 몸짓을 해 보이다; n. 동작, 몸짓; 운동, 움직임
If you motion to someone, you move your hand or head as a way of telling them to do something or telling them where to go.

scramble [skræmbl] v. 재빨리 움직이다; 서로 밀치다; n. (힘들게) 기어가기; 서로 밀치기
If you scramble to a different place or position, you move there in a hurried, awkward way.

clang [klæŋ] n. 땡그랑, 쨍그랑 하는 소리; v. (서로 부딪쳐) 쨍그랑 하는 소리를 내다
A clang is a loud, resonant metallic sound or series of sounds.

★ **pitch** [pitʃ] **n.** 경사; 정점, 최고조; 음의 높이; **v.** 힘껏 던지다; 떨어지다, 떨어지게 하다
A pitch refers to the angle of descent of a downward slope.

collapse [kəlǽps] **v.** 무너지다; 드러눕다; (의식을 잃고) 쓰러지다; **n.** 쓰러짐; (건물의) 붕괴
If a building or other structure collapses, it falls down very suddenly.

sprint [sprint] **v.** (짧은 거리를) 전력 질주하다; **n.** 전력 질주; 단거리 경기
If you sprint, you run or ride as fast as you can over a short distance.

leap [li:p] **v.** 뛰다, 뛰어오르다; (서둘러) ~하다; **n.** 높이뛰기, 도약; 급증
If you leap somewhere, you move there suddenly and quickly.

crumble [krʌmbl] **v.** (건물이나 땅이) 허물어지다; 바스러지다; (힘·조직 등이) 흔들리다
If an old building or piece of land is crumbling, parts of it keep breaking off.

pivot [pívət] **v.** 회전하다, 선회하다
If something pivots, it balances or turns on a central point.

tilt [tilt] **v.** 기울이다, (뒤로) 젖히다; (의견·상황 등이) 기울어지다; **n.** 기울어짐, 젖혀짐
If something is tilted, it is sloping or inclining at an angle.

horrify [hɔ́:rəfài] **v.** 몸서리치게 하다, 소름끼치게 하다 (horrified **a.** 겁에 질린, 충격받은)
If someone is horrified, they feel shocked or disgusted, usually because of something
that they have seen or heard.

crew [kru:] **n.** (함께 일을 하는) 팀, 조; (배·항공기의) 승무원; **v.** 승무원을 하다
A crew is a group of people with special technical skills who work together on a task
or project.

crack [kræk] **n.** (갈라져 생긴) 금; 날카로운 소리; (좁은) 틈; **v.** 갈라지다; 깨지다, 부서지다
A crack is a line that appears on the surface of something when it is slightly damaged.

★ **dodge** [dadʒ] **v.** 피하다, 재빨리 움직이다; 기피하다; **n.** 몸을 홱 피함
If you dodge, you move suddenly, often to avoid being hit, caught, or seen.

debris [dəbríː] **n.** 파편, 잔해; 쓰레기
Debris is pieces from something that has been destroyed or pieces of rubbish or
unwanted material that are spread around.

propel [prəpél] **v.** 나아가게 하다; 몰고 가다
To propel something in a particular direction means to cause it to move in that
direction.

practically [prǽktikəli] **ad.** 사실상, 거의; 현실적으로, 실제로
Practically means almost, but not completely or exactly.

vertical [və́:rtikəl] a. 수직의, 세로의; n. 수직
Something that is vertical stands or points straight up.

sicken [síkən] v. 메스꺼워지다, 병나다 (sickening a. 메스꺼운)
You describe something as sickening when it gives you feelings of horror or disgust, or makes you feel sick in your stomach.

chasm [kæzm] n. 아주 깊은 틈; (사람·집단 사이의) 큰 차이
A chasm is a very deep crack in rock, earth, or ice.

split [split] n. (길게 찢어진) 틈; 분열; v. 찢어지다; 분열되다; 나뉘다
A split is a long crack or tear.

stretch [streʧ] v. (팔·다리를) 뻗다; 뻗어 있다; 이어지다, 계속되다; 늘어나다; n. (길게) 뻗은 구간
When you stretch, you put your arms or legs out straight and tighten your muscles.

clasp [klæsp] v. (꽉) 움켜쥐다; (꽉) 껴안다; 죄다; n. 악수; 포옹; 걸쇠
If you clasp someone or something, you hold them tightly in your hands or arms.

abrupt [əbrʌ́pt] a. 돌연한, 갑작스런; 퉁명스러운 (abruptly ad. 갑자기)
If something happens abruptly, its action is very sudden, often in a way which is unpleasant.

halt [hɔːlt] v. 중단시키다; 멈추다, 서다; n. 멈춤, 중단
When a person or a vehicle halts or when something halts them, they stop moving in the direction they were going and stand still.

disbelief [dìsbilíːf] n. 믿기지 않음, 불신감
Disbelief is not believing that something is true or real.

Check Your Reading Speed

1분에 몇 단어를 읽는지 리딩 속도를 측정해 보세요.

$$\frac{2{,}917 \text{ words}}{\text{reading time ( ) sec}} \times 60 = (\quad) \text{ WPM}$$

Build Your Vocabulary

collapse [kəlǽps] v. 무너지다; 드러눕다; (의식을 잃고) 쓰러지다; n. (건물의) 붕괴; 쓰러짐
If a building or other structure collapses, it falls down very suddenly.

destruction [distrʌ́kʃən] n. 파괴, 파멸; 말살
Destruction is the action or process of causing so much damage to something that it no longer exists or cannot be repaired.

stun [stʌn] v. 깜짝 놀라게 하다; 어리벙벙하게 하다; 기절시키다 (stunned a. 깜짝 놀란)
If you are stunned by something, you are extremely shocked or surprised by it and are therefore unable to speak or do anything.

stare [stɛər] v. 빤히 쳐다보다, 응시하다; n. 빤히 쳐다보기, 응시
If you stare at someone or something, you look at them for a long time.

recharge [riːʧάːrdʒ] v. (휴식으로) 재충전하다; (전지를) 충전하다, 충전되다
To recharge is to revive or restore energy or enthusiasm.

scrounge [skraundʒ] v. 얻어 내다; 슬쩍하다
If you say that someone scrounges something such as food or money, you disapprove of them because they get it by asking for it, rather than by buying it or earning it.

vending machine [véndiŋ məʃiːn] n. 자동판매기
A vending machine is a machine from which you can get things such as chocolate or coffee by putting in money and pressing a button.

cap [kæp] v. (~으로) 덮다; n. 뚜껑; 모자 (uncap v. 뚜껑을 벗기다)
To uncap is to remove a cap or top from a container.

outlet [áutlet] n. 콘센트; (액체·기체의) 배출구
An outlet is a place, usually in a wall, where you can connect electrical devices to the electricity supply.

light up idiom (두 눈·얼굴이) 환해지다, 빛이 나다
If a person's eyes or face light up, or something lights them up, they become bright with excitement or happiness.

charge [tʃaːrdʒ] v. 충전하다; 급히 가다; 돌격하다; (요금·값을) 청구하다; n. 책임, 담당; 요금
To charge a battery means to pass an electrical current through it in order to make it more powerful or to make it last longer.

distracted [distrǽktid] a. (정신이) 산만해진 (distractedly ad. 주의가 산만해져서)
When you act distractedly, you are not concentrating on something because you are worried or are thinking about something else.

★ **peel** [piːl] v. (껍질·포장 등을) 벗기다; 껍질이 벗겨지다; n. 껍질
If you peel off something that has been sticking to a surface, it comes away from the surface.

slimy [sláimi] a. 끈적끈적한, 점액질의; (사람·태도가) 지나치게 친밀한 척하는
Slimy substances are thick, wet, and unpleasant.

★ **texture** [tékstʃər] n. 질감; 감촉; 조화
The texture of food is the way that a particular type of food feels when you are eating it.

★ **juicy** [dʒúːsi] a. 즙이 많은; 재미있는; 매력적인
If food is juicy, it has a lot of juice in it and is very enjoyable to eat.

bite [bait] n. 한 입; 물기; v. 베어 물다; (곤충·뱀 등이) 물다
A bite of something, especially food, is the action of using someone's teeth to cut or break something, usually in order to eat it.

confuse [kənfjúːz] v. (사람을) 혼란시키다; 혼동하다 (confused a. 혼란스러운)
If you are confused, you do not know exactly what is happening or what to do.

★ **mutter** [mʌ́tər] v. 중얼거리다; 투덜거리다; n. 중얼거림
If you mutter, you speak very quietly so that you cannot easily be heard, often because you are complaining about something.

‡ **angle** [ǽŋgl] n. 기울기; 각도, 각; 관점; v. 비스듬히 움직이다 (at an angle idiom 비스듬히)
If something is at an angle, it is leaning in a particular direction so that it is not straight, horizontal, or vertical.

drip [drip] v. (액체를) 뚝뚝 흘리다; 가득 담고 있다; n. (액체가) 뚝뚝 떨어짐; 방울
When something drips, drops of liquid fall from it.

nod [nad] v. (고개를) 끄덕이다, 까딱하다; n. (고개를) 끄덕임
If you nod, you move your head downward and upward to show that you are answering 'yes' to a question, or to show agreement, understanding, or approval.

shrug [ʃrʌg] v. (어깨를) 으쓱하다; n. 어깨를 으쓱하기
If you shrug, you raise your shoulders to show that you are not interested in something or that you do not know or care about something.

give or take idiom 대략, 대충
Give or take is used to indicate that an amount is approximate.

suck [sʌk] v. (특정한 방향으로) 빨아들이다; 빨아 먹다; n. 빨기, 빨아 먹기
If something sucks a liquid, gas, or object in a particular direction, it draws it there with a powerful force.

moisture [mɔ́isʧər] n. 습기, 수분
Moisture is tiny drops of water in the air, on a surface, or in the ground.

rush [rʌʃ] v. 급히 움직이다; 서두르다; n. (감정이 갑자기) 치밀어 오름; 혼잡
If you rush somewhere, you go there quickly.

disorient [disɔ́:riènt] v. 어리둥절하게 하다; 방향 감각을 혼란시키다 (disoriented a. 혼란에 빠진)
If you are disoriented, you are confused as to time or place.

reboot [rì:bú:t] n. 재시동, 리부트; v. (컴퓨터를) 재시동하다
A reboot is the act of starting a computer or smartphone again immediately after you have switched it off.

comfort [kʌ́mfərt] v. 위로하다; 편하게 하다; n. 편안; 위로
When you are comforted by someone or something, you feel less worried, unhappy, or upset.

blink [bliŋk] v. 눈을 깜박이다; (불빛이) 깜박거리다; n. 눈을 깜박거림
When you blink or when you blink your eyes, you shut your eyes and very quickly open them again.

clear one's throat idiom 목을 가다듬다; 헛기침하다
If you clear your throat, you cough once in order to make it easier to speak or to attract people's attention.

slump [slʌmp] v. 푹 쓰러지다; 털썩 앉다; (가치·수량 등이) 급감하다; n. 부진; 불황
To slump is to sink or fall heavily and suddenly.

screw up idiom ~을 엉망으로 하다, ~을 망치다
If you screw up, you make a serious mistake, or spoil something, especially a situation.

* tangle [tæŋgl] v. 헝클어지다, 얽히다; n. 엉킨 것; 꼬인 상태
If something is tangled, it becomes twisted together in an untidy way.

* obstacle [ábstəkl] n. 장애물; 장애
An obstacle is an object that makes it difficult for you to go where you want to go, because it is in your way.

bull's-eye [búl-zài] n. (과녁의) 중심, 정곡; (채광용의) 둥근 창
The bull's-eye is the small circular area at the center of a target.

^복_습 **material** [mətíəriəl] n. 재목; 재료; 소재; 자료; a. 물질적인; 중요한
If you say that someone is a particular kind of material, you mean that they have the qualities or abilities to do a particular job or task.

calibrate [kǽləbrèit] v. 측정하다, 눈금을 매기다 (recalibrate v. 다시 측정하다)
If you recalibrate something, you measure it accurately once again.

* corrupt [kərʌ́pt] v. 훼손하다; 타락시키다, 매수하다; a. 타락한, 부정한
If something is corrupted, it becomes damaged or spoiled in some way.

* restore [ristɔ́:r] v. 복원하다; 회복시키다; 돌려주다
To restore someone or something to a previous condition means to cause them to be in that condition once again.

look after idiom ~을 돌보다, ~을 보살펴 주다
If you look after someone or something, you do what is necessary to keep them healthy, safe, or in good condition.

^복_습 **mine** [main] n. 광산; 지뢰; v. (광물질을) 캐다, 채굴하다
A mine is a place where deep holes and tunnels are dug under the ground in order to obtain a mineral such as coal, diamonds, or gold.

^복_습 **incredulous** [inkrédʒuləs] a. 믿지 않는, 회의적인 (incredulously ad. 믿을 수 없다는 듯이)
When someone behaves incredulously, it shows that they are unable to believe something because it is very surprising or shocking.

^복_습 **pause** [pɔ:z] v. (말·일을 하다가) 잠시 멈추다; 정지시키다; n. (말·행동 등의) 멈춤
If you pause while you are doing something, you stop for a short period and then continue.

^복_습 **swear** [swɛər] v. 맹세하다; 욕을 하다; n. 맹세
If you say that you swear that something is true or that you can swear to it, you are saying very firmly that it is true.

꿈 **absentminded** [æbsəntmáindid] a. 멍하니 있는, 넋놓은, 방심 상태의
(absentmindedly ad. 멍하니)
When someone behaves absentmindedly, they forget things or do not pay attention to
what they are doing, often because they are thinking about something else.

꿈 **tilt** [tilt] v. 기울이다, (뒤로) 젖히다; (의견·상황 등이) 기울어지다; n. 기울어짐, 젖혀짐
If you tilt part of your body, usually your head, you move it slightly upward or to one
side.

꿈 **confirm** [kənfə́:rm] v. 확인해 주다, 사실임을 보여주다; 더 분명히 해 주다
If you confirm something that has been stated or suggested, you say that it is true
because you know about it.

꿈 **flashlight** [flǽʃlait] n. 손전등, 회중전등
A flashlight is a small electric light which gets its power from batteries and which you
can carry in your hand.

꿈 **protest** [proutést] v. 이의를 제기하다, 항의하다; n. 항의; 시위
If you protest that something is the case, you insist that it is true, when other people
think that it may not be.

★ **inherit** [inhérit] v. 물려받다, 상속받다
If you inherit a characteristic or quality, you are born with it, because your parents or
ancestors also had it.

gumption [gʌ́mpʃən] n. 근성, 담력; 진취성; 상황 대처 능력
If someone has the gumption to do something, they are brave enough to do it.

꿈 **appreciate** [əprí:ʃièit] v. 고마워하다; 진가를 알아보다
If you appreciate something that someone has done for you or is going to do for you,
you are grateful for it.

꿈 **erupt** [irʌ́pt] v. 분출되다; 터뜨리다
To erupt is to start happening, suddenly and violently.

꿈 **knock** [nak] v. 치다, 부딪치다; (문 등을) 두드리다 n. 부딪침; 문 두드리는 소리
If someone knocks someone else off their feet, they make them fall over.

strew [stru:] v. 흩뿌리다; 흩어지다, 흩뿌려져 있다 (strewn a. 흩어진)
If a place is strewn with things, they are lying scattered there.

★ **rag** [ræg] n. 해진 천 (rag doll n. 봉제 인형)
A rag doll is a soft doll made of cloth.

‡ **cough** [kɔːf] v. 기침하다; 털털거리다; (기침을 하여 무엇을) 토하다; n. 기침
When you cough, you force air out of your throat with a sudden, harsh noise.

복습 **peer** [piər] v. 유심히 보다, 눈여겨보다; n. 또래
If you peer at something, you look at it very hard, usually because it is difficult to see clearly.

복습 **ominous** [ámənəs] a. 불길한, 나쁜 징조의 (ominously ad. 불길하게, 기분 나쁘게)
When someone or something moves ominously, it worries you because it makes you think that something unpleasant is going to happen.

복습 **aftermath** [ǽftərmæθ] n. (전쟁·사고 등의) 여파, 후유증
The aftermath of an important event, especially a harmful one, is the situation that results from it.

humongous [hjuːmʌ́ŋgəs] a. 거대한
If you describe something or someone as humongous, you are emphasizing that they are very large or important.

복습 **shimmer** [ʃímər] v. 희미하게 빛나다; n. 희미한 빛
If something shimmers, it shines with a faint, unsteady light or has an unclear, unsteady appearance.

★ **vicious** [víʃəs] a. 사나운, 공격적인; 잔인한, 포악한 (viciously ad. 맹렬하게)
If someone behaves viciously, they act in a violent and cruel manner.

복습 **horn** [hɔːrn] n. (동물의) 뿔; (차량의) 경적 (horned a. 뿔이 있는)
A horned animal or object has hard pointed things that grow from its head.

clamber [klǽmbər] v. 기어오르다, 기어가다
If you clamber somewhere, you climb there with difficulty, usually using your hands as well as your feet.

복습 **chaos** [kéias] n. 혼란; 혼돈
Chaos is a state of complete disorder and confusion.

복습 **route** [ruːt] n. 길, 경로; 방법; v. 보내다, 전송하다
A route is a way from one place to another.

복습 **topple** [tapl] v. 넘어지다; 넘어뜨리다; 실각시키다
If someone or something topples somewhere or if you topple them, they become unsteady or unstable and fall over.

복습 **snag** [snæg] v. 잡아채다, 낚아채다; (날카롭거나 튀어나온 것에) 걸리다; n. 날카로운 것; 문제
If you snag something, you succeed in getting them quickly, often before other people.

fray [frei] n. 소동, 난투; 경쟁; v. 닳게 하다; 소모시키다
The fray is an exciting or challenging activity, situation, or argument that you are involved in.

skid [skid] v. 미끄러지다; n. (차량의) 미끄러짐
When a person or object skids while moving, they slide without rotating.

halt [hɔːlt] n. 멈춤, 중단; v. 멈추다, 서다; 중단시키다
A halt refers to a temporary or permanent stop.

spin [spin] v. (spun-spun) 돌아서다; (빙빙) 돌다, 돌리다; n. 회전
If something spins or if you spin it, it turns quickly around a central point.

heap [hiːp] n. 더미, 무더기; 많음; v. 수북이 담다; (아무렇게나) 쌓다
A heap of things is a pile of them, especially a pile arranged in a rather untidy way.

loom [luːm] v. 어렴풋이 나타나다, 흐릿하게 보이다; 불쑥 나타나다; n. 베틀
If something looms over you, it appears as a large or unclear shape, often in a frightening way.

despair [dispɛ́ər] n. 절망; v. 절망하다, 체념하다
Despair is the feeling that everything is wrong and that nothing will improve.

crush [krʌʃ] v. 으스러뜨리다; 밀어 넣다; n. 홀딱 반함
To crush something means to press it very hard so that its shape is destroyed or so that it breaks into pieces.

rookie [rúki] n. 신참, 초보자; (스포츠 팀의) 신인 선수
A rookie is someone who has just started doing a job and does not have much experience, especially someone who has just joined the army or police force.

cower [káuər] v. (겁을 먹고) 몸을 웅크리다
If you cower, you move your body down and away from someone or something because you are frightened.

brace [breis] v. (스스로) 대비를 하다; (몸에) 단단히 힘을 주다; n. 버팀대; 치아 교정기
If you brace yourself for something unpleasant or difficult, you prepare yourself for it.

march [maːrʧ] v. (단호한 태도로 급히) 걸어가다; 행진하다; n. 행군, 행진; 3월
If you say that someone marches somewhere, you mean that they walk there quickly and in a determined way, for example because they are angry.

advance [ædvǽns] v. (공격하기 위해) 다가가다; (지식·기술 등이) 증진되다; n. 진전, 발전; 전진
To advance means to move forward, often in order to attack someone.

clarity [klǽrəti] **n.** 명확성; 명료성; 선명도
Clarity refers to clearness or lucidity as to perception or understanding.

urgent [ə́:rdʒənt] **a.** 다급한; 긴급한, 시급한 (urgently **ad.** 다급하게)
If you speak urgently, you show that you are anxious for people to notice something or to do something.

leap [li:p] **v.** 뛰다, 뛰어오르다; (서둘러) ~하다; **n.** 높이뛰기, 도약; 급증
If you leap somewhere, you move there suddenly and quickly.

★ **canyon** [kǽnjən] **n.** 협곡
A canyon is a long, narrow valley with very steep sides.

★ **steep** [sti:p] **a.** 가파른, 비탈진; 급격한; 터무니없는
A steep slope rises at a very sharp angle and is difficult to go up.

embankment [imbǽŋkmənt] **n.** 경사면; 둑, 제방
An embankment is a thick wall of earth that is built to carry a road or railway over an area of low ground, or to prevent water from a river or the sea from flooding the area.

dart [da:rt] **v.** 쏜살같이 움직이다; 흘깃 쳐다보다; **n.** 쏜살같이 달림; (작은) 화살
If a person or animal darts somewhere, they move there suddenly and quickly.

curve [kə:rv] **v.** 곡선으로 나아가다, 곡선을 이루다; **n.** 커브, 곡선
If something curves, it moves in a smooth, gradually bending line.

bend [bend] **n.** 굽은 곳; **v.** (몸·머리를) 굽히다, 숙이다; 구부리다
A bend in a road, pipe, or other long thin object is a curve or angle in it.

in one's tracks idiom 그 자리에서, 즉각, 당장
If someone stops in their tracks, they stop doing something suddenly or immediately.

pivot [pívət] **v.** 회전하다, 선회하다
If someone or something pivots, they change direction.

crevice [krévis] **n.** (바위나 담에 생긴) 틈
A crevice is a narrow crack or gap, especially in a rock.

smash [smæʃ] **v.** 박살내다; (세게) 부딪치다; 부서지다; **n.** 박살내기; 요란한 소리
If you smash something or if it smashes, it breaks into many pieces, for example when it is hit or dropped.

★ **flee** [fli:] **v.** 달아나다, 도망치다
If you flee from something or someone, or flee a person or thing, you escape from them.

^{복습} **storage** [stɔ́ːridʒ] **n.** 저장고, 보관소; 저장
A storage is a space or area reserved for storing.

‡ **passage** [pǽsidʒ] **n.** 통로, 복도; 통행, 통과
A passage is a long narrow space with walls or fences on both sides, which connects one place or room with another.

^{복습} **row** [rou] **n.** 열, 줄; 노 젓기; **v.** 노를 젓다
A row of things or people is a number of them arranged in a line.

dead end [ded énd] **n.** 막다른 길; 막다른 지경
If a street is a dead end, there is no way out at one end of it.

^{복습} **whirl** [hwəːrl] **v.** 빙그르르 돌다; (마음·생각 등이) 혼란스럽다; **n.** 빙빙 돌기
If something or someone whirls around or if you whirl them around, they move around or turn around in circles.

^{복습} **mechanical** [məkǽnikəl] **a.** 기계와 관련된; (행동이) 기계적인
Mechanical means relating to machines and engines and the way they work.

^{복습} **pant** [pænt] **v.** (숨을) 헐떡이다; **n.** 헐떡거림
If you pant, you breathe quickly and loudly with your mouth open, because you have been doing something energetic.

retract [ritrǽkt] **v.** (속으로) 들어가다; 철회하다, 취소하다
When a part of a machine or a part of a person's body retracts or is retracted, it moves inward or becomes shorter.

^{복습} **replace** [ripléis] **v.** 교체하다; 대신하다, 대체하다
If you replace something that is broken, damaged, or lost, you get a new one to use instead.

^{복습} **boom** [buːm] **n.** 쾅 (하는 소리); **v.** 쾅 하는 소리를 내다; 굵은 목소리로 말하다
A boom refers to a loud, deep sound that lasts for several seconds.

^{복습} **chest** [tʃest] **n.** 가슴, 흉부; 상자, 궤
Your chest is the top part of the front of your body where your ribs, lungs, and heart are.

^{복습} **reveal** [rivíːl] **v.** (보이지 않던 것을) 드러내 보이다; (비밀 등을) 밝히다
If you reveal something that has been out of sight, you uncover it so that people can see it.

^{복습} **violate** [váiəlèit] **v.** 위반하다; 침해하다; 훼손하다 (violation n. 위반, 위배)
A violation involves breaking an agreement, law, or promise.

bound [baund] v. 껑충껑충 달리다; a. ~할 가능성이 큰
If a person or animal bounds in a particular direction, they move quickly with large steps or jumps.

ravine [rəvíːn] n. (좁고 험한) 산골짜기, 협곡
A ravine is a very deep narrow valley with steep sides.

ledge [ledʒ] n. 절벽에서 튀어나온 바위; (튀어나온) 선반
A ledge is a piece of rock on the side of a cliff or mountain, which is in the shape of a narrow shelf.

hillside [hílsàid] n. (산·언덕의) 비탈
A hillside is the sloping side of a hill.

pinpoint [pínpɔint] n. 아주 작은 지점; 뾰족한 것; 핀 끝; v. 정확하게 지적하다
A pinpoint refers to a tiny spot or sharp point.

legion [líːdʒən] n. 군대, 군단; 다수, 많은 수; a. (수가) 아주 많은
A legion is a large group of soldiers who form one section of an army.

enemy [énəmi] n. 적; 장애물
If someone is your enemy, they hate you or want to harm you.

imminent [ímənənt] a. 금방이라도 닥칠 듯한, 목전의, 임박한
If you say that something is imminent, especially something unpleasant, you mean it is almost certain to happen very soon.

race [reis] v. 쏜살같이 가다; 경주하다; (머리·심장 등이) 바쁘게 돌아가다; n. 경주; 인종, 종족
If you race somewhere, you go there as quickly as possible.

launch [lɔːntʃ] n. 발사; 시작; 개시; v. 던지다; 발사하다; 맹렬히 덤비다
A launch refers to the action of sending a rocket, missile, or satellite into the air or into space.

terror [térər] n. 두려움, 공포; 공포의 대상
Terror is very great fear.

comingle [kəmíŋgl] v. 혼합하다
To comingle is to mix or be mixed.

patrol [pətróul] n. 순찰대; 순찰; v. 순찰을 돌다
A patrol is a group of soldiers or vehicles that are moving around an area in order to make sure that there is no trouble there.

barrage [bərá:ʒ] n. 일제 엄호 사격; (질문 등의) 세례
A barrage is continuous firing on an area with large guns and tanks.

복습 **vessel** [vésəl] n. (대형) 선박, 배; 그릇, 용기
A vessel is a ship or large boat.

복습 **be better off** idiom (상태가) 더 낫다; 더 부자이다
If you say someone is better off, you mean that they are or would be happier or more satisfied if they were in a particular position or did a particular thing.

banter [bǽntər] v. (가볍게) 농담하다; n. 농담, 놀림
If you banter with someone, you tease them or joke with them in an amusing, friendly way.

★ **install** [instɔ́:l] v. (장비·가구를) 설치하다
If you install a piece of equipment, you fit it or put it somewhere so that it is ready to be used.

복습 **coil** [kɔil] n. 전선; 고리; v. (고리 모양으로) 감다, 휘감다
A coil is a thick spiral of wire through which an electrical current passes.

복습 **desperate** [déspərət] a. 필사적인; 자포자기의, 절망적인 (desperately ad. 필사적으로)
If you behave desperately, it shows that you are in such a bad situation that you are willing to try anything to change it.

복습 **pod** [pad] n. (우주선·선박의 본체에서) 분리 가능한 부분; 유선형 공간; (콩이 들어 있는) 꼬투리
A pod is a detachable or self-contained unit on an aircraft, spacecraft, vehicle, or vessel, having a particular function.

★ **capability** [kèipəbíləti] n. 능력, 역량
If you have the capability or the capabilities to do something, you have the ability or the qualities that are necessary to do it.

복습 **punch** [pʌnʧ] v. (자판·번호판 등을) 치다; 주먹으로 치다; n. 주먹으로 한 대 침
If you punch something such as the buttons on a keyboard, you touch them give the machine a command to do something.

★ **zip** [zip] v. 쌩 하고 가다; 지퍼를 잠그다; n. 지퍼
If you say that something or someone zips somewhere, you mean that they move there very quickly.

복습 **dodge** [dadʒ] v. 피하다, 재빨리 움직이다; 기피하다; n. 몸을 홱 피함
If you dodge, you move suddenly, often to avoid being hit, caught, or seen.

munition [mjuːníʃən] n. 군사 물품, 군수품
Munitions refer to materials used in war, such as weapons.

spiky [spáiki] a. 뾰족뾰족한, 끝이 뾰족한
Something that is spiky has one or more sharp points.

skeptical [sképtikəl] a. 의심 많은, 회의적인 (skeptically ad. 회의적으로)
If you say something skeptically, it shows that you have doubts about the thing or situation concerned.

hoist [hɔist] v. 들어 올리다, 끌어올리다; n. 끌어올리기
If you hoist something heavy somewhere, you lift it or pull it up there.

satisfy [sǽtisfài] v. 만족시키다; 충족시키다; 납득시키다 (satisfaction n. 만족)
Satisfaction is the pleasure that you feel when you do something or get something that you wanted or needed to do or get.

firework [fáiərwəːrk] n. (pl.) 불꽃놀이; 폭죽
You use fireworks to refer to an occasion on which fireworks are lit to entertain people.

transport [trænspɔ́ːrt] n. 수송; 운송 수단; v. 수송하다; 실어 나르다
Transport is the activity of taking goods or people from one place to another.

disc [disk] n. 동글납작한 판, 원반; 디스크
A disc is a flat, circular shape or object.

impact [ímpækt] n. 충돌, 충격; (강력한) 영향; v. 충돌하다; 영향을 주다
An impact is the action of one object hitting another, or the force with which one object hits another.

vanish [vǽniʃ] v. 사라지다, 없어지다; 모습을 감추다 (vanish into thin air idiom 흔적도 없이 사라지다)
To vanish into thin air is to disappear completely.

retaliate [ritǽlièit] v. 대꾸하다, 응수하다; 보복하다, 앙갚음하다
If you retaliate when someone harms or annoys you, you do something which harms or annoys them in return.

swarm [swɔːrm] v. 많이 모여들다; 무리를 지어 다니다; n. (곤충의) 떼, 무리; 군중
When animals or machines swarm, they move or fly in a large group.

lava [láːvə] n. 용암
Lava is the very hot liquid rock that comes out of a volcano.

pit [pit] n. (크고 깊은) 구덩이; (신체의) 우묵한 곳; v. 자국을 남기다, 구멍을 남기다
A pit is a large hole that is dug in the ground.

^복_습 **inch** [intʃ] **n.** 조금, 약간; **v.** 조금씩 움직이다 (every inch **idiom** 전부 다, 속속들이)
If you talk about every inch of an area, you are emphasizing that you mean the whole of it.

^복_습 **clip** [klip] **v.** 스치다, 부딪치다; 자르다, 깎다; 핀으로 고정하다; **n.** 핀, 클립
If something clips something else, it hits it accidentally at an angle before moving off in a different direction.

★ **pursue** [pərsúː] **v.** 뒤쫓다, 추적하다; 추구하다
If you pursue a person, vehicle, or animal, you follow them, usually in order to catch them.

★ **blaze** [bleiz] **v.** 활활 타다; 눈부시게 빛나다; **n.** 불길, 활활 타는 불; 휘황찬란한 빛
When a fire blazes, it burns strongly and brightly.

★ **suspect** [səspékt] **v.** 의심하다; 수상쩍어하다; **n.** 용의자 (unsuspecting **a.** 의심하지 않는)
You can use unsuspecting to describe someone who is not at all aware of something that is happening or going to happen.

★ **molten** [móultən] **a.** 녹은, 용해된
Molten rock, metal, or glass has been heated to a very high temperature and has become a hot, thick liquid.

^복_습 **terrain** [təréin] **n.** 지역, 지형
Terrain is used to refer to an area of land or a type of land when you are considering its physical features.

zoom [zuːm] **v.** 쌩 하고 가다; 급등하다; **n.** (빠르게) 쌩 하고 지나가는 소리
If you zoom somewhere, you go there very quickly.

close in idiom 접근하다
To close in someone or close in on someone means to move nearer to them, especially in order to surround them and stop them from escaping.

evade [ivéid] **v.** 피하다, 모면하다; 회피하다
If you evade someone or something, you move so that you can avoid meeting them or avoid being touched or hit.

^복_습 **slap** [slæp] **v.** 털썩 놓다; (손바닥으로) 철썩 때리다; **n.** 철썩 때리기, 치기
If you slap something onto a surface, you put it there quickly, roughly, or carelessly.

^복_습 **swift** [swift] **a.** 신속한, 재빠른 (swiftly **ad.** 신속하게)
When someone or something moves swiftly, they move very quickly or without delay.

★ **fasten** [fæsn] v. 매다, 채우다; 고정시키다; (단단히) 잠그다
When you fasten something, you close it by means of buttons or a strap, or some other device.

복습 **sail** [seil] v. 미끄러지듯 나아가다; 항해하다; n. 돛
If a person or object sails somewhere, they move there smoothly and fairly quickly.

복습 **stable** [steibl] a. 안정된, 안정적인; 차분한; n. 마구간
If an object is stable, it is firmly fixed in position and is not likely to move or fall.

★ **transfer** [trænsfə́:r] v. 이동하다, 옮기다; (병을) 옮기다; n. 이동
If you transfer something or someone from one place to another, or they transfer from one place to another, they go from the first place to the second.

복습 **simulate** [símjulèit] v. 모의실험하다; 가장하다 (simulator n. 모의실험 장치)
A simulator is a device which artificially creates the effect of being in conditions of some kind.

복습 **swerve** [swə:rv] v. (갑자기) 방향을 바꾸다
If a vehicle or other moving thing swerves or if you swerve it, it suddenly changes direction, often in order to avoid hitting something.

복습 **back and forth** idiom 여기저기로, 왔다갔다; 앞뒤로; 좌우로
If you move something back and forth, you repeatedly move it in one direction and then in the opposite direction.

oscillate [ásəlèit] v. (두 지점 사이를) 왔다갔다 하다; 진동하다
If an object oscillates, it moves repeatedly from one position to another and back again.

복습 **outstretch** [àutstrétʃ] v. 펴다, 뻗다, 확장하다 (outstretched a. 죽 뻗은)
If a part of the body of a person or animal is outstretched, it is stretched out as far as possible.

scope [skoup] n. 관찰 기기; 범위, 여지; v. 샅샅이 살피다
A scope is an instrument that allows you to look at or examine something carefully.

복습 **gauge** [geidʒ] n. 게이지, 측정기; 치수; 기준; v. 판단하다, 알아내다; 측정하다; 추정하다
A gauge is a device that measures the amount or quantity of something and shows the amount measured.

★ **dash** [dæʃ] n. 계기판; 서두름, 질주; v. 서둘러 가다
The dash of a car is its dashboard, which is the panel facing the driver's seat where most of the instruments and switches are.

^복_습 **eject** [idʒékt] v. 방출하다; 탈출하다; 쫓아내다; 튀어나오게 하다
To eject something means to remove it or push it out forcefully.

^복_습 **sicken** [síkən] v. 메스꺼워지다, 병나다 (sickening a. 메스꺼운)
You describe something as sickening when it gives you feelings of horror or disgust, or makes you feel sick in your stomach.

unceremonious [ʌnserəmóuniəs] a. 예의를 차리지 않는; 무례한, 버릇없는
(unceremoniously ad. 인정사정없이)
If something takes place unceremoniously, it happens in an informal or abrupt way.

^복_습 **dashboard** [dǽʃbɔːrd] n. (자동차·비행기 등의) 계기판
The dashboard in a vehicle is the panel facing the driver's seat where most of the instruments and switches are.

^복_습 **flash** [flæʃ] v. 휙 나타나다; 불현듯 들다; 번쩍이다; n. 번쩍임; (감정이나 생각이) 갑자기 떠오름
If a picture or message flashes up on a screen, or if you flash it onto a screen, it is displayed there briefly or suddenly, and often repeatedly.

bear down idiom 돌진하다; 격파하다; 전력을 다하다
To bear down on someone means to move quickly toward them in a threatening way.

^복_습 **grab** [græb] v. (와락·단단히) 붙잡다; 급히 ~하다; n. 와락 잡아채려고 함
If you grab something, you take it or pick it up suddenly and roughly.

^복_습 **snatch** [snætʃ] v. 와락 붙잡다, 잡아채다; 간신히 얻다; n. 잡아 뺏음, 강탈; 조각
If you snatch something or snatch at something, you take it or pull it away quickly.

^복_습 **groan** [groun] v. (고통·짜증으로) 신음 소리를 내다, 끙끙거리다; n. 신음, 끙 하는 소리
If you groan, you make a long, low sound because you are in pain, or because you are upset or unhappy about something.

✦ **defeat** [difíːt] v. 좌절시키다; 물리치다; 이해가 안 되다; n. 패배 (defeated a. 좌절한)
When someone is defeated, they show signs of discouragement.

crestfallen [kréstfɔ̀ːlən] a. 풀이 죽은, 맥 빠진, 기운 없는
If you look crestfallen, you look sad and disappointed about something.

^복_습 **vast** [væst] a. 어마어마한, 방대한, 막대한
Something that is vast is extremely large.

wasteland [wéistlænd] n. 황무지, 불모지
A wasteland is an area of land on which not much can grow or which has been spoiled in some way.

gut [gʌt] n. 배; 소화관; 직감; v. 내부를 파괴하다
You can refer to someone's stomach as their gut.

let down idiom ~의 기대를 저버리다, ~을 실망시키다
If you let someone down, you disappoint them by failing to do what you agreed to do or were expected to do.

복습 **volunteer** [vàləntíər] n. 자원해서 하는 사람; 자원 봉사자; v. 자원하다; 자진해서 말하다
A volunteer is someone who offers to do a particular task or job without being forced to do it.

culminate [kʌ́lmənèit] v. (~으로) 끝이 나다 (culmination n. 정점, 최고조)
Something, especially something important, that is the culmination of an activity, process, or series of events happens at the end of it.

★ **dedicate** [dédikèit] v. (시간·노력을) 바치다; 헌신하다; (건물·기념물 등을) 봉헌하다
If someone has dedicated themselves to something, they have decided to give a lot of time and effort to it because they think that it is important.

복습 **frighten** [fraitn] v. 겁먹게 하다, 놀라게 하다 (frightened a. 겁먹은, 무서워하는)
If you are frightened, you are anxious or afraid, often because of something that has just happened or that you think may happen.

복습 **plod** [plad] v. 터벅터벅 걷다; 꾸준히 일하다
If someone plods, they walk slowly and heavily.

billow [bílou] v. (연기·구름 등이) 피어오르다; 부풀어 오르다; n. 자욱하게 피어오르는 것
When smoke or dust billows, it moves slowly upward or across the sky.

heartbroken [háːrtbròukən] a. 비통해 하는
Someone who is heartbroken is very sad and emotionally upset.

★ **cloak** [klouk] v. ~에게 외투를 입히다; 가리다; n. 망토
To cloak something is to cover it as if with a cloak.

★ **fiery** [fáiəri] a. 불타는 듯한; (분노가) 맹렬한; 불의
If you describe something as fiery, you mean that it is burning strongly or contains fire.

‡ **struggle** [strʌgl] v. 몸부림치다; 애쓰다; 힘겹게 나아가다; n. 몸부림; 투쟁, 분투
If you struggle when you are being held, you twist, kick, and move violently in order to get free.

13 & 14

1. What did Zurg say he wanted to do?

A. Make copies of the fuel cell

B. Build a larger robot army

C. Take over the planet of T'Kani Prime

D. Help Buzz finish the mission

2. Why was Buzz uneasy about going back in time?

A. It was dangerous for him.

B. It would take a lot of effort.

C. It was not likely to work.

D. It would erase some people.

3. **Why couldn't Sox track Buzz from the ship?**
   A. Buzz had some broken equipment.
   B. Sox was not close enough to Buzz.
   C. Buzz had turned off his suit.
   D. Sox needed the crystal.

4. **What did Izzy tell the team to do when she left the transport room?**
   A. Plan a new operation
   B. Try to repair the door
   C. Protect the Armadillo ship
   D. Look for Buzz with her

5. **Why did Buzz use the autopilot?**
   A. He was too tired from fighting with Zurg.
   B. He was having trouble flying while injured.
   C. He did not know how to use the technology.
   D. He was told by Star Command that he should use it.

Check Your Reading Speed
1분에 몇 단어를 읽는지 리딩 속도를 측정해 보세요.

$$\frac{1{,}539 \text{ words}}{\text{reading time ( ) sec}} \times 60 = (\quad) \text{ WPM}$$

Build Your Vocabulary

hum [hʌm] n. 웅성거리는 소리; v. 웅웅거리다; (노래를) 흥얼거리다
Hum refers to a low and continuous murmuring sound.

odd [ad] a. 이상한, 특이한; 홀수의 (oddly ad. 이상하게)
If something takes place oddly, it happens in a strange or unusual way.

serene [sərí:n] a. 고요한, 평화로운, 조용한
Someone or something that is serene is calm and quiet.

pile [pail] n. 무더기, 더미; 쌓아 놓은 것; v. 쌓다; (차곡차곡) 포개다; 우르르 가다
A pile of things is a mass of them that is high in the middle and has sloping sides.

heap [hi:p] n. 더미, 무더기; 많음; v. 수북이 담다; (아무렇게나) 쌓다
A heap of things is a pile of them, especially a pile arranged in a rather untidy way.

teleport [téləpɔ:rt] v. (공상 과학 소설에서) 순간 이동시키다 (teleportation n. 순간 이동)
In science fiction, teleportation refers to the process in which someone or something moves across a distance instantaneously.

clutch [klʌtʃ] n. 움켜쥠; v. (꽉) 움켜잡다
If someone is in another person's clutches, that person has captured them or has power over them.

strain [strein] v. 안간힘을 쓰다; 무리하게 사용하다; 한계에 이르게 하다; n. 부담; 압박
If you strain to do something, you make a great effort to do it when it is difficult to do.

wrist [rist] n. 손목, 팔목
Your wrist is the part of your body between your hand and your arm which bends when you move your hand.

wriggle [rigl] v. 꿈틀거리며 가다; (몸을) 꿈틀거리다; n. 꿈틀거리기
If you wriggle somewhere, for example through a small gap, you move there by twisting and turning your body.

^복_습 **grasp** [græsp] n. 움켜잡기; 통제; 이해; v. 꽉 잡다; 완전히 이해하다, 파악하다
A grasp is a very firm hold or grip.

^복_습 **absorb** [æbsɔ́:rb] v. 흡수하다; (관심을) 빼앗다
If something absorbs a force or shock, it reduces its effect.

^복_습 **blast** [blæst] n. 폭발; (한 줄기의) 강한 바람; v. 폭발시키다, 폭파하다; 확 뿌리다; 발사하다
A blast is a big explosion, especially one caused by a bomb.

throaty [θróuti] a. 목이 쉰 듯한
A throaty voice or laugh is low and rather rough.

^복_습 **rumble** [rʌmbl] v. 웅웅거리는 소리를 내다; 덜커덩거리며 나아가다; n. 웅웅거리는 소리
If something rumbles, it makes a low, continuous noise.

^복_습 **metallic** [mətǽlik] a. 금속의, 금속성의
Metallic means consisting entirely or partly of metal.

★ **chamber** [ʧéimbər] n. (특정한 용도를 위한) 방; 회의실; (지하의) 공간
A chamber is a room designed and equipped for a particular purpose.

^복_습 **demand** [dimǽnd] v. 강력히 묻다, 따지다; 요구하다; n. 요구; 수요
If you demand something such as information or action, you ask for it in a very forceful way.

make sense idiom 이해가 되다; 타당하다; 이해하기 쉽다
If something makes sense, you can understand it.

in due time idiom (언젠가) 때가 되면, 머지않아
You use the expression 'in due time' to say 'eventually' or 'at the right time.'

⚡ **track** [træk] v. 뒤쫓다; 추적하다; n. 길; 경주로, 트랙; 자국
To track someone or something means to follow their movements by means of a special device, such as a satellite or radar.

★ **menace** [ménis] v. 위협하다; n. 위험한 존재; 위협, 협박 (menacing a. 위협적인)
If someone or something looks menacing, they give you a feeling that they are likely to cause you harm or put you in danger.

★ **foe** [fou] n. 적, 원수
Someone's foe is their enemy.

^복_습 **echo** [ékou] v. 그대로 따라 하다; (소리가) 울리다, 메아리치다; n. 반복; (소리의) 울림, 메아리
If you echo someone's words, you repeat them or express agreement with their attitude or opinion.

take aback idiom 허를 찌르다, 깜짝 놀라게 하다
If you are taken aback by something, you are surprised or shocked by it and you cannot respond at once.

‡ **machinery** [məʃíːnəri] n. 기계, 기계류; 기계 부품들; 조직, 기구
You can use machinery to refer to machines in general, or machines that are used in a factory or on a farm.

advance [ædvǽns] v. (지식·기술 등이) 증진되다; (공격하기 위해) 다가가다; n. 진전, 발전; 전진 (advanced a. 발전된)
An advanced system, method, or design is modern and has been developed from an earlier version of the same thing.

crew [kruː] n. (함께 일을 하는) 팀, 조; (배·항공기의) 승무원; v. 승무원을 하다
A crew is a group of people with special technical skills who work together on a task or project.

pause [pɔːz] v. (말·일을 하다가) 잠시 멈추다; 정지시키다; n. (말·행동 등의) 멈춤
If you pause while you are doing something, you stop for a short period and then continue.

align [əláin] v. 나란히 만들다, 일직선으로 하다; 조정하다
If two things are aligned, they are the same as or similar to each other.

judgment [dʒʌ́dʒmənt] n. 판단력; 재판, 심판; 판단, 평가
Judgment is the ability to make sensible guesses about a situation or sensible decisions about what to do.

trail off idiom (목소리가) 차츰 잦아들다
If someone's speech trails off, it gradually becomes quieter and then stops.

process [práses] v. 처리하다; 가공하다; n. 과정, 절차; 공정
To process something is to handle it.

★ **dawn** [dɔːn] v. 분명해지다; 밝다; n. 새벽, 여명
If a fact or idea dawns on you, you realize it.

glow [glou] v. 빛나다, 타다; (얼굴이) 상기되다; n. (은은한) 불빛; 홍조
If something glows, it produces a dull, steady light.

perimeter [pərímitər] n. (어떤 구역의) 주위, 주변; 방어선
The perimeter of an area of land is the whole of its outer edge or boundary.

★ **dim** [dim] a. (빛이) 어둑한; (형체가) 흐릿한; v. 어둑해지다 (dimly ad. 어둑하게)
If light shines dimly somewhere, the place is not bright.

wear out idiom 소진하다; 낡아서 떨어지다; 지치다
When you wear something out, it is used so much that it becomes thin or weak and unable to be used anymore.

realize [ríːəlàiz] v. 깨닫다, 알아차리다; 실현하다, 달성하다
If you realize that something is true, you become aware of that fact or understand it.

★ **setup** [sétʌp] n. (기계 등의) 구성, 설정; (조직 등의) 구조; (실험 등의) 장비
A particular setup is a particular system or way of organizing something.

★ **vague** [veig] a. 어렴풋한, 희미한; 모호한, 애매한 (vaguely ad. 어렴풋이)
Vaguely means to some degree but not to a very large degree.

intuitive [intjúːətiv] a. 직감에 의한; 이해하기 쉬운 (intuitively ad. 직감적으로)
If you feel intuitively about something, you feel that it is true although you have no evidence or proof of it.

insist [insíst] v. 고집하다, 주장하다, 우기다
If you insist that something is the case, you say so very firmly and refuse to say otherwise, even though other people do not believe you.

stable [steibl] a. 안정된, 안정적인; 차분한; n. 마구간
If something is stable, it is not likely to change or come to an end suddenly.

flip [flip] v. 휙 젖히다, 젖혀지다; 홱 뒤집다, 뒤집히다; 툭 던지다; n. 회전; 툭 던지기
If something flips, or if you flip it, it moves or is moved with a quick sudden movement into a different position.

unison [júːnisn] n. 조화, 화합, 일치 (in unison idiom 일제히)
If two or more people do something in unison, they do it together at the same time.

swap [swap] v. 교환하다; (다른 것으로) 바꾸다; n. 바꾸기, 교환
If you swap one thing for another, you remove the first thing and replace it with the second, or you stop doing the first thing and start doing the second.

reminisce [rèmənís] v. 추억에 잠기다, 추억담을 나누다
If you reminisce about something from your past, you write or talk about it, often with pleasure.

fond [fand] a. 다정한, 애정 어린; 좋아하는 (fondly ad. 애정을 담아)
If you talk about someone fondly, you show affection for them.

midair [midέər] n. 공중, 상공
If something happens in midair, it happens in the air, rather than on the ground.

복습 **reflect** [riflékt] v. 반사하다; (상을) 비추다; 깊이 생각하다
When light, heat, or other rays reflect off a surface or when a surface reflects them, they are sent back from the surface and do not pass through it.

복습 **notice** [nóutis] v. 알아채다, 인지하다; 주의하다; n. 신경 씀, 주목, 알아챔
If you notice something or someone, you become aware of them.

복습 **toss** [tɔːs] v. (가볍게) 던지다; (고개를) 홱 쳐들다; n. 던지기
If you toss something somewhere, you throw it there lightly, often in a rather careless way.

복습 **furrow** [fə́ːrou] v. (미간을) 찡그리다; (밭에) 고랑을 만들다; n. 깊은 주름; 고랑
If someone furrows their brow or forehead or if it furrows, deep folds appear in it because the person is annoyed, unhappy, or confused.

복습 **brow** [brau] n. 이마; 눈썹
Your brow is your forehead.

★ **erase** [iréis] v. (완전히) 지우다; (지우개 등으로) 지우다
If you erase something, you get rid of them so that they have gone completely and no longer exist.

복습 **spit** [spit] v. (spat/spit-spat/spit) (말을) 내뱉다; (침·음식 등을) 뱉다; n. 침; (침 등을) 뱉기
If someone spits an insult or comment, they say it in a forceful way.

★ **haunt** [hɔːnt] v. (생각이) 계속 떠오르다; (오랫동안) 괴롭히다, 문제가 되다; 귀신이 나타나다
(haunted a. 사로잡힌)
If you are haunted by something, you are preoccupied, as with an emotion, memory, or idea.

복습 **let go of** idiom ~을 잊어버리다; ~을 포기하다; ~에서 손을 놓다
If you let go of something, you stop focusing or fixating on them in your mind.

복습 **renew** [rinjúː] v. (젊음·힘 등을) 되찾다; 재개하다; 갱신하다
When something is renewed, it is happening again after a pause, especially with more vigor, energy or enthusiasm than before.

복습 **square** [skwɛər] v. 똑바로 펴다; 네모지게 만들다; a. 정사각형 모양의; 직각의; ad. 똑바로
If you square your shoulders, you stand straight and push them back, usually to show your determination.

forlorn [fərlɔ́ːrn] a. 고독한, 쓸쓸한; 버려진, 버림받은 (forlornly ad. 쓸쓸하게)
If someone behaves forlornly, they act in a way that is alone and unhappy.

get in over one's head idiom 감당할 수 없는 일을 벌이다
If you get in over your head, you become deeply involved in a situation which is too
difficult for you to deal with.

snap [snæp] v. (화난 목소리로) 딱딱거리다; 탁 소리를 내다; 빠르게 움직이다; n. 탁 하는 소리
If someone snaps at you, they speak to you in a sharp, unfriendly way.

strand [strænd] v. 오도 가도 못 하게 하다, 발을 묶다; n. 가닥, 꼰 줄
If you are stranded, you are prevented from leaving a place, for example because of
bad weather.

bicker [bíkər] v. (사소한 일로) 다투다
When people bicker, they argue or quarrel about unimportant things.

let down idiom ~의 기대를 저버리다, ~을 실망시키다
If you let someone down, you disappoint them by failing to do what you agreed to do
or were expected to do.

★ **capture** [kǽpʃ*ə*r] v. 포로로 잡다; 사로잡다; 붙잡다; n. 생포; 구금, 억류
If you capture someone or something, you catch them, especially in a war.

frustrate [frʌ́streit] v. 불만스럽게 하다, 좌절감을 주다; 방해하다
(frustrated a. 불만스러워하는, 좌절감을 느끼는)
If you feel frustrated, you are disappointed or dissatisfied.

rip [rip] v. (재빨리·거칠게) 뜯어 내다; (갑자기) 찢다, 찢어지다; n. (길게) 찢어진 곳
If you rip something away, you remove it quickly and forcefully.

pad [pæd] v. 소리 안 나게 걷다; 완충재를 대다; n. 패드; 보호대
When someone pads somewhere, they walk there with steps that are fairly quick, light,
and quiet.

sigh [sai] v. 한숨을 쉬다, 한숨짓다; 탄식하듯 말하다; n. 한숨
When you sigh, you let out a deep breath, as a way of expressing feelings such as
disappointment, tiredness, or pleasure.

★ **endure** [indjúər] v. 참다, 견디다, 인내하다
If you endure a painful or difficult situation, you experience it and do not avoid it or
give up, usually because you cannot.

blank [blæŋk] a. 멍한, 무표정한; 빈; n. 빈칸, 여백; v. (갑자기) 멍해지다 (blankly ad. 멍하니)
When you act blankly, your face shows no feeling, understanding, or interest.

^복_습 **gasp** [gæsp] v. 헉 하고 숨을 쉬다; 숨을 제대로 못 쉬다; n. 헉 하는 소리를 냄
When you gasp, you take a short quick breath through your mouth, especially when you are surprised, shocked, or in pain.

★ **verbal** [vɔ́:rbəl] a. 말로 하는, 구두로 된; 언어의
You use verbal to indicate that something is expressed in speech rather than in writing or action.

tirade [táireid] n. 장황한 비난
A tirade is a long angry speech in which someone criticizes a person or thing.

^복_습 **clamber** [klǽmbər] v. 기어오르다, 기어가다
If you clamber somewhere, you climb there with difficulty, usually using your hands as well as your feet.

★ **fuel** [fjú:əl] v. (감정 등을) 부채질하다; 연료를 공급하다; n. 연료
To fuel something means to make it become more intense.

^복_습 **lean** [li:n] v. 기울이다, (몸을) 숙이다; ~에 기대다; a. 호리호리한
When you lean in a particular direction, you bend your body in that direction.

^복_습 **slam** [slæm] v. 세게 치다, 놓다; 쾅 닫다, 닫히다; n. 쾅 하고 닫기; 쾅 하는 소리
If you slam something, you strike or beat it with force and noise.

^복_습 **fist** [fist] n. 주먹
Your hand is referred to as your fist when you have bent your fingers in toward the palm in order to hit someone, to make an angry gesture, or to hold something.

Check Your Reading Speed

1분에 몇 단어를 읽는지 리딩 속도를 측정해 보세요.

$$\frac{1{,}017 \text{ words}}{\text{reading time ( ) sec}} \times 60 = (\quad) \text{ WPM}$$

Build Your Vocabulary

^복_습 **resist** [rizíst] v. 저항하다; 참다, 견디다; 굴하지 않다
If you resist someone or resist an attack by them, you fight back against them.

★ **restrain** [ristréin] v. 저지하다; (감정 등을) 억누르다
If you restrain someone, you stop them from doing what they intended or wanted to do, usually by using your physical strength.

^복_습 **erase** [iréis] v. (완전히) 지우다; (지우개 등으로) 지우다
If you erase something, you get rid of them so that they have gone completely and no longer exist.

^복_습 **flash** [flæʃ] v. 번쩍이다; 불현듯 들다; 휙 나타나다; n. (감정이나 생각이) 갑자기 떠오름; 번쩍임
If someone's eyes flash, they suddenly show a strong emotion, especially anger.

^복_습 **stride** [straid] v. (strode-stridden) 성큼성큼 걷다; n. 걸음; 걸음걸이
If you stride somewhere, you walk there with quick, long steps.

^복_습 **exclaim** [ikskléim] v. 소리치다, 외치다
If you exclaim, you cry out suddenly in surprise, strong emotion, or pain.

^복_습 **topple** [tapl] v. 넘어지다; 넘어뜨리다; 실각시키다
If someone or something topples somewhere or if you topple them, they become unsteady or unstable and fall over.

^복_습 **foe** [fou] n. 적, 원수
Someone's foe is their enemy.

^복_습 **crash** [kræʃ] v. 부딪치다; 추락하다; 충돌하다; 굉음을 내다; n. 요란한 소리; (자동차·항공기) 사고
If something crashes somewhere, it moves and hits something else violently, making a loud noise.

panel [pænl] n. 계기판; 판; 패널, 자문단
A control panel or instrument panel is a board or surface which contains switches and
controls to operate a machine or piece of equipment.

spring [spriŋ] v. (sprang-sprung) 휙 움직이다; 튀다; 갑자기 ~하다; n. 생기, 활기; 봄; 샘
If something springs in a particular direction, it moves suddenly and quickly.

sprint [sprint] v. (짧은 거리를) 전력 질주하다; n. 전력 질주; 단거리 경기
If you sprint, you run or ride as fast as you can over a short distance.

operate [ápərèit] v. 작전을 벌이다; 조작하다; 작동하다; 작업하다; 수술하다 (operation n. 작전)
An operation is a highly organized activity that involves many people doing different
things.

blow up idiom 폭파하다, 터뜨리다
If someone blows something up or if it blows up, it is destroyed by an explosion.

unlikely [ʌnláikli] a. 예상 밖의; 있음직하지 않은
An unlikely place, person, or thing is strange and not what you would expect.

quartet [kwɔːrtét] n. 4인조, 4개 세트; 사중주단; 사중주곡
A quartet of people or things is a group or set of four people or things.

blind [blaind] v. (잠시) 앞이 안 보이게 하다; 눈이 멀게 하다; a. 눈이 먼; 눈치 채지 못하는
(blinding a. 눈이 부신)
A blinding light is extremely bright.

teleport [téləpɔːrt] v. (공상 과학 소설에서) 순간 이동시키다
In science fiction, if someone or something teleports, they move across a distance
instantaneously.

unison [júːnisn] n. 조화, 화합, 일치 (in unison idiom 일제히)
If two or more people do something in unison, they do it together at the same time.

ranger [réindʒər] n. 경비 대원; 기습 공격대원
A ranger is an armed guard who patrols a region.

seal [siːl] v. 봉쇄하다; 봉인하다; 확정짓다; n. 도장; [동물] 바다표범
If one object or area is sealed off from another, there is a physical barrier between
them, so that nothing can pass between them.

inspire [inspáiər] v. 고무하다; 영감을 주다; (감정 등을) 불어넣다
If someone or something inspires you to do something new or unusual, they make you
want to do it.

track [træk] v. 추적하다; 뒤쫓다; n. 길; 경주로, 트랙; 자국
If you track animals or people, you try to follow them by looking for their signs.

confirm [kənfɔ́:rm] v. 확인해 주다, 사실임을 보여주다; 더 분명히 해 주다
If you confirm something that has been stated or suggested, you say that it is true because you know about it.

shortcut [ʃɔ́:rtkʌ̀t] n. 지름길; 손쉬운 방법
A shortcut is a quicker way of getting somewhere than the usual route.

slap [slæp] v. 털썩 놓다; (손바닥으로) 철썩 때리다; n. 철썩 때리기, 치기
If you slap something onto a surface, you put it there quickly, roughly, or carelessly.

slip [slip] v. 슬며시 가다; (말이) 무심코 나오다; 미끄러지다; n. 미끄러짐; (작은) 실수
If you slip somewhere, you go there quickly and quietly.

stealthy [stélθi] a. 살며시 하는, 잠행하는 (stealthily ad. 몰래, 은밀히)
If you do something stealthily, you do it quietly and carefully so that no one will notice what you are doing.

corridor [kɔ́:ridər] n. 복도; 통로
A corridor is a long passage in a building or train, with doors and rooms on one or both sides.

home in on idiom ~을 향해 곧장 나아가다; 전념하다
To home in on someone or something is to find and move directly toward them.

observatory [əbzɔ́:rvətɔ̀:ri] n. 천문대, 전망대; 관측소
An observatory is a building with a large telescope from which scientists study things such as the planets by watching them.

glimpse [glimps] n. 잠깐 봄; 짧은 경험; v. 언뜻 보다; 깨닫다, 이해하다
If you get a glimpse of someone or something, you see them very briefly and not very well.

vast [væst] a. 어마어마한, 방대한, 막대한 (vastness n. 방대함)
Vastness refers to a very great extent or size.

gulp [gʌlp] v. 침을 꿀떡 삼키다; (숨을) 깊이 들이마시다; n. 꿀꺽 마시기
If you gulp, you swallow air, often making a noise in your throat as you do so, because you are nervous or excited.

knot [nat] n. (긴장·화 등으로) 뻣뻣한 느낌; 매듭; v. 매듭을 묶다
If you feel a knot in your stomach, you get an uncomfortable tight feeling in your stomach, usually because you are afraid or excited.

throw up idiom 토하다
If you throw up, you bring food you have eaten back out of your mouth.

keep it together idiom 마음을 진정시키다; 생각을 정리하다
If you try to keep it together, you manage to control your feelings in a difficult situation.

whisper [hwíspər] v. 속삭이다, 소곤거리다; n. 속삭임, 소곤거리는 소리
When you whisper, you say something very quietly, using your breath rather than your throat, so that only one person can hear you.

trigger [trígə:r] v. 촉발시키다; n. 폭파 장치; (총의) 방아쇠
To trigger a bomb or system means to cause it to work.

security [sikjúərəti] n. 보안, 경비; (미래를 위한) 보장; 안도감, 안심
Security refers to all the measures that are taken to protect a place, or to ensure that only people with permission enter it or leave it.

thunder [θʌ́ndər] v. 우르릉거리며 질주하다; 우르릉거리다; 천둥이 치다; n. 천둥, 우레
If something or someone thunders somewhere, they move there quickly and with a lot of noise.

slide [slaid] v. (slid-slid/slidden) 미끄러지다; 미끄러지듯이 움직이다; n. 떨어짐; 미끄러짐
When something slides somewhere or when you slide it there, it moves there smoothly over or against something.

resound [rizáund] v. (소리가 가득) 울리다 (resounding a. 울려 퍼지는)
A resounding sound is loud and clear.

pound [paund] v. (요란한 소리로 여러 차례) 두드리다; (가슴이) 쿵쿵 뛰다; 쿵쾅거리며 걷다
If you pound something or pound on it, you hit it with great force, usually loudly and repeatedly.

begrudging [bigrʌ́dʒiŋ] a. 내키지 않는, 떨떠름한 (begrudgingly ad. 마지못해)
If you do something begrudgingly, you do it unwillingly.

gaze [geiz] n. 응시, (눈여겨보는) 시선; v. (가만히) 응시하다, 바라보다
You can talk about someone's gaze as a way of describing how they are looking at something, especially when they are looking steadily at it.

rhythmic [ríðmik] a. 주기적인; 리드미컬한; (rhythmically ad. 주기적으로; 리드미컬하게)
If something moves rhythmically, its movements are repeated at regular intervals, forming a regular pattern or beat.

barrier [bǽriər] n. 장벽; 장애물; 한계
A barrier is something such as a fence or wall that is put in place to prevent people from moving easily from one area to another.

^복_습 **immense** [iméns] a. 엄청난, 어마어마한
If you describe something as immense, you mean that it is extremely large or great.

void [vɔid] n. (커다란) 빈 공간; 공허감; a. ~이 전혀 없는; 텅 빈
You can describe a large or frightening space as a void.

* **portion** [pɔ́:rʃən] n. 부분, 일부; 1인분; 몫; v. 나누다
A portion of something is a part of it.

jut [dʒʌt] v. 돌출하다, 튀어나오다; 내밀다
If something juts out, it sticks out above or beyond a surface.

^복_습 **press** [pres] v. (무엇에) 바짝 대다; 꾹 밀어 넣다; 누르다; n. 언론
If you press something somewhere, you push it firmly against something else.

^복_습 **make sense** idiom 이해가 되다; 타당하다; 이해하기 쉽다
If something makes sense, you can understand it.

^복_습 **command** [kəmǽnd] n. 지휘; 명령; 사령부; v. 명령하다; 지휘하다
If someone has command of a situation, they have control of it because they have, or seem to have, power or authority.

^복_습 **console** [kánsoul] n. 제어반, 계기반; v. 위로하다, 위안을 주다
A console is a panel with a number of switches or knobs that is used to operate a machine.

^복_습 **frustrate** [frʌ́streit] v. 불만스럽게 하다, 좌절감을 주다; 방해하다
(frustrated a. 불만스러워하는, 좌절감을 느끼는)
If you feel frustrated, you are disappointed or dissatisfied.

^복_습 **pilot** [páilət] n. 조종사, 비행사; v. 조종하다 (autopilot n. (항공기·배의) 자동 조종 장치)
An autopilot is a device in an aircraft or a ship that keeps it on a fixed course without the need for a person to control it.

^복_습 **odds** [adz] n. 가능성; 역경, 곤란
You refer to how likely something is to happen as the odds that it will happen.

^복_습 **instruct** [instrʌ́kt] v. 지시하다; 가르치다; (정보를) 알려 주다
If you instruct someone to do something, you formally tell them to do it.

^복_습 **initiate** [iníʃièit] v. 개시되게 하다, 착수시키다; 가입시키다; n. 가입자
If you initiate something, you start it or cause it to happen.

self-destruct [self-distrʌ́kt] a. 자폭하는; v. (기계 등이) 저절로 폭파되다, 못 쓰게 되다
A self-destruct process involves an automatic explosion or disintegration as a result of pre-programming.

sequence [síːkwəns] n. 순서, 차례; (일련의) 연속적인 사건들
A particular sequence is a particular order in which things happen or are arranged.

countdown [káuntdaun] n. 카운트다운; (중요한 행사의) 초읽기
A countdown is the counting aloud of numbers in reverse order before something happens, especially before a spacecraft is launched.

chokehold [tʃóukhoùld] n. 목 조르기
A chokehold is the act of holding someone tightly around the neck.

bellow [bélou] v. (우렁찬 소리로) 고함치다; 크게 울리다; n. 울부짖는 소리; 고함소리
If someone bellows, they shout angrily in a loud, deep voice.

fling [fliŋ] v. (flung-flung) (거칠게) 내던지다, 내팽개치다; (몸이나 신체를) 내밀다; n. (한바탕) 실컷 즐기기
If you fling something somewhere, you throw it there using a lot of force.

★ throb [θrab] v. (몸이) 욱신거리다, 지끈거리다; 고동치다, 울리다; n. 욱신거림; 진동
If part of your body throbs, you feel a series of strong and usually painful beats there.

impact [ímpækt] n. 충돌, 충격; (강력한) 영향; v. 충돌하다; 영향을 주다
An impact is the action of one object hitting another, or the force with which one object hits another.

hover [hʌ́vər] v. (허공을) 맴돌다; 서성이다; 주저하다; n. 공중을 떠다님
To hover means to stay in the same position in the air without moving forward or backward.

daze [deiz] v. 멍하게 하다; 눈부시게 하다; n. 멍한 상태; 눈이 부심 (dazed a. 멍한)
If someone is dazed, they are confused and unable to think clearly, often because of shock or a blow to the head.

accidental [æksədéntl] a. 우연한, 돌발적인 (accidentally ad. 우연히, 뜻하지 않게)
If an event takes place accidentally, it happens by chance or as the result of an accident, and is not deliberately intended.

sight [sait] n. 보기, 봄; 시야; 광경, 모습; v. 갑자기 보다 (catch sight of idiom ~을 흘끗 보다)
If you catch sight of someone, you suddenly see them, often briefly.

menace [ménis] v. 위협하다; n. 위험한 존재; 위협, 협박 (menacing a. 위협적인)
If someone or something looks menacing, they give you a feeling that they are likely to cause you harm or put you in danger.

chuckle [tʃʌkl] v. 킬킬 웃다, 빙그레 웃다, 싱긋 웃다; n. 킬킬거림, 빙그레 웃기
To chuckle is to laugh softly or amusedly, usually with satisfaction.

^복_습 **yell** [jel] v. 고함치다, 소리 지르다; n. 고함, 외침
If you yell, you shout loudly, usually because you are excited, angry, or in pain.

woozy [wúːzi] a. (정신이) 멍한, (머리가) 띵한
If you feel woozy, you feel rather weak and unsteady and cannot think clearly.

^복_습 **explode** [iksplóud] v. 폭발하다; 갑자기 ~하다; (강한 감정을) 터뜨리다
If an object such as a bomb explodes or if someone or something explodes it, it bursts
loudly and with great force, often causing damage or injury.

^복_습 **opposite** [ápəzit] a. (정)반대의; 건너편의; 맞은편의; n. 반대
Opposite means situated or being on the other side or at each side of something
between.

^복_습 **flicker** [flíkər] v. (불·빛 등이) 깜박거리다; 움직거리다; n. (빛의) 깜박거림; 움직거림
If a light or flame flickers, it shines unsteadily.

^복_습 **vision** [víʒən] n. 시야; 환상, 상상; 환영
Your vision is everything that you can see from a particular place or position.

^복_습 **dim** [dim] v. 어두워지다; a. (빛이) 어두운; (형체가) 흐릿한
If your eyes dim or are dimmed by something, they become weaker or unable to see
clearly.

^복_습 **listless** [lístlis] a. 무기력한, 열의가 없는 (listlessly ad. 무력하게)
If someone behaves listlessly, they act in a way that has no energy or enthusiasm.

^복_습 **blink** [bliŋk] v. 눈을 깜박이다; (불빛이) 깜박거리다; n. 눈을 깜박거림
When you blink or when you blink your eyes, you shut your eyes and very quickly
open them again.

^복_습 **stupor** [stjúːpər] n. 멍함, 황홀함; 무감각; 인사불성
Someone who is in a stupor is unable to think or act normally because they are not
completely conscious.

^복_습 **distant** [dístənt] a. 먼, (멀리) 떨어져 있는; 다정하지 않은
Distant means very far away.

cobweb [kábwèb] n. (머리의) 혼란; 거미줄
Cobweb refers to the state of being confused or muddled.

^복_습 **squint** [skwint] v. 눈을 가늘게 뜨고 보다; 사시이다; n. 잠깐 봄; 사시
If you squint at something, you look at it with your eyes partly closed.

15 & 16

1. How did Sox suggest getting to the bridge?

A. By sneaking onto a different ship

B. By going through the air lock into space

C. By climbing on top of the ship

D. By sending a signal to Buzz

2. What did Izzy do once she could be seen on the bridge?

A. She ran away from Zurg.

B. She threw a wrist blaster to Buzz.

C. She tried to hit the antigravity button.

D. She fired at Zurg.

3. What did Buzz hit with his laser after he ejected from the ship?

   A. The crystal

   B. Zurg

   C. The Armadillo

   D. Zurg's ship

4. What was Buzz's new mission?

   A. To shut Zurg down

   B. To find a new ship

   C. To save his friends

   D. To make more fuel

5. What was used to open the air brake cover?

   A. A laser

   B. A hair clip

   C. A screwdriver

   D. Mo's pen

Check Your Reading Speed
1분에 몇 단어를 읽는지 리딩 속도를 측정해 보세요.

$$\frac{975 \text{ words}}{\text{reading time ( ) sec}} \times 60 = (\quad) \text{ WPM}$$

Build Your Vocabulary

observatory [əbzɔ́ːrvətɔ̀ːri] n. 천문대, 전망대; 관측소
An observatory is a building with a large telescope from which scientists study things such as the planets by watching them.

desperate [déspərət] a. 필사적인; 자포자기의, 절망적인 (desperately ad. 필사적으로)
If you behave desperately, it shows that you are in such a bad situation that you are willing to try anything to change it.

scan [skæn] v. (유심히) 살피다; 훑어보다; 정밀 촬영하다; 스캔하다; n. 정밀 검사
When you scan a place or group of people, you look at it carefully, usually because you are looking for something or someone.

indicate [índikèit] v. (손가락이나 고갯짓으로) 가리키다; 보여 주다; (계기가) 가리키다
If you indicate something to someone, you show them where it is, especially by pointing to it.

chest [ʧest] n. 가슴, 흉부; 상자, 궤
Your chest is the top part of the front of your body where your ribs, lungs, and heart are.

seize up idiom (신체 부위가) 잘 움직이지 않다; (기계가) 작동하지 않다
If a part of your body seizes up, it suddenly stops working, because you have strained it or because you are getting old.

stare [stɛər] v. 빤히 쳐다보다, 응시하다; n. 빤히 쳐다보기, 응시
If you stare at someone or something, you look at them for a long time.

identical [aidéntikəl] a. 동일한, 꼭 같은
Things that are identical are exactly the same.

theoretical [θìːərétikəl] a. 이론상의, 이론적인 (theoretically ad. 이론상으로는)
You use theoretically to say that although something is supposed to be true or to happen in the way stated, it may not in fact be true or happen in that way.

LIGHTYEAR

★ **drift** [drift] v. (물·공기에) 떠가다; ~하게 되다; n. 표류; 흐름
When something drifts somewhere, it is carried there by the movement of wind or water.

복습 **float** [flout] v. (물 위나 공중에서) 떠가다; (물에) 뜨다; n. 부표
Something that floats in or through the air hangs in it or moves slowly and gently through it.

★ **limp** [limp] a. 기운이 없는, 축 처진; v. 다리를 절다, 절뚝거리다; n. 절뚝거림
(limply ad. 축 처진 채로)
If someone moves limply, their body has no strength and is not moving, for example because they are asleep or unconscious.

복습 **run out of** idiom ~이 없어지다; ~을 다 써버리다
If you run out of something like money or time, you have used up all of it.

복습 **rhythmic** [ríðmik] a. 주기적인; 리드미컬한
A rhythmic movement or sound is repeated at regular intervals, forming a regular pattern or beat.

복습 **shield** [ʃiːld] n. 보호 장치; 방패; v. 보호하다, 가리다
Something or someone which is a shield against a particular danger or risk provides protection from it.

복습 **release** [rilíːs] n. 해제; 방출; 풀어 줌; 공개; v. 석방하다, 놓아 주다; 풀다; (감정을) 발산하다
A release refers to an act or device that causes gas, heat, or a substance to leave its container.

복습 **stretch** [streʧ] v. 뻗어 있다; (팔·다리를) 뻗다; 이어지다, 계속되다; 늘어나다; n. (길게) 뻗은 구간
Something that stretches over an area or distance covers or exists in the whole of that area or distance.

★ **infinite** [ínfənət] a. 한계가 없는, 무한한; (수량이) 무한한
Something that is infinite has no limit, end, or edge.

abyss [əbís] n. 심연, 깊은 구렁
An abyss is a very deep hole in the ground.

복습 **grab** [græb] v. (와락·단단히) 붙잡다; 급히 ~하다; n. 와락 잡아채려고 함
If you grab something, you take it or pick it up suddenly and roughly.

★ **endless** [éndlis] a. 끝없는; 무한한, 한없는
If you say that something is endless, you mean that it is very large or lasts for a very long time, and it seems as if it will never stop.

^{복습} **instruct** [instrʌ́kt] v. 지시하다; 가르치다; (정보를) 알려 주다
If you instruct someone to do something, you formally tell them to do it.

^{복습} **greet** [griːt] v. (눈·귀에) 들어오다; 환영하다; 인사하다; 반응을 보이다
If you are greeted by a sight, sound, or smell, it is the first thing that you notice.

^{복습} **void** [vɔid] n. (커다란) 빈 공간; 공허감; a. ~이 전혀 없는; 텅 빈
You can describe a large or frightening space as a void.

^{복습} **suck** [sʌk] v. (특정한 방향으로) 빨아들이다; 빨아 먹다; n. 빨기, 빨아 먹기
If something sucks a liquid, gas, or object in a particular direction, it draws it there with a powerful force.

^{복습} **gulp** [gʌlp] v. 침을 꿀떡 삼키다; (숨을) 깊이 들이마시다; n. 꿀꺽 마시기
If you gulp, you swallow air, often making a noise in your throat as you do so, because you are nervous or excited.

★ **fiber** [fáibər] n. 섬유; (식품의) 섬유질 (every fiber of one's being idiom 온몸)
If you do something with every fiber of your being, you do so with all of your effort or desire.

^{복습} **force** [fɔːrs] v. ~을 강요하다; 억지로 ~하다; n. 힘; 영향력; 세력
If someone forces you to do something, they make you do it even though you do not want to, for example by threatening you.

^{복습} **regain** [rigéin] v. 되찾다, 회복하다; 되돌아오다
If you regain something that you have lost, you get it back again.

leverage [lévəridʒ] n. 지렛대의 힘; 지렛대 사용; 영향력
Leverage is the force that is applied to an object when something such as a lever is used.

^{복습} **propel** [prəpél] v. 나아가게 하다; 몰고 가다
To propel something in a particular direction means to cause it to move in that direction.

^{복습} **countdown** [káuntdaun] n. 카운트다운; (중요한 행사의) 초읽기
A countdown is the counting aloud of numbers in reverse order before something happens, especially before a spacecraft is launched.

^{복습} **twist** [twist] v. 비틀다; 돌리다; 구부리다; 왜곡하다; n. 변형; 돌리기; 굽이
If you twist something, especially a part of your body, or if it twists, it moves into an unusual, uncomfortable, or bent position, for example because of being hit or pushed.

unexpected [ʌnikspéktid] a. 예기치 않은, 예상 밖의
If an event or someone's behavior is unexpected, it surprises you because you did not
think that it was likely to happen.

lurch [ləːrʧ] n. 요동침; 휘청함; v. (갑자기) 휘청하다, 휘청거리다; (공포·흥분으로) 떨리다
A lurch is a sudden feeling of being excited or upset.

slam [slæm] v. 세게 치다, 놓다; 쾅 닫다, 닫히다; n. 쾅 하고 닫기; 쾅 하는 소리
If one thing slams into or against another, it crashes into it with great force.

skid [skid] v. 미끄러지다; n. (차량의) 미끄러짐
When a person or object skids while moving, they slide without rotating.

triumphant [traiʌmfənt] a. 의기양양한; 크게 성공한, 큰 승리를 거둔
(triumphantly ad. 의기양양하게)
Someone who acts triumphantly is very happy about a victory or success.

★ **artificial** [àːrtəfíʃəl] a. 인공의; 인위적인; 거짓된, 꾸민
Artificial objects, materials, or processes do not occur naturally and are created by
human beings, for example using science or technology.

reinstate [rìːinstéit] v. 회복시키다; 복귀시키다
To reinstate a law, facility, or practice means to start having it again.

chime [ʧaim] v. (노래하듯) 말하다; (종이나 시계가) 울리다; n. 차임, 종
To chime is to speak or recite in a musical or rhythmic manner.

★ **manual** [mǽnjuəl] a. 수동의; 손으로 하는, 육체노동의; n. 설명서
Manual means operated by hand, rather than by electricity or a motor.

override [ouvərráid] n. (자동 기기의) 보조 수동 장치; v. 중단시키다
An override is a system or device for changing or canceling an automatic function.

activate [ǽktəvèit] v. 작동시키다; 활성화시키다
If a device or process is activated, something causes it to start working.

chuckle [ʧʌkl] v. 킬킬 웃다, 빙그레 웃다, 싱긋 웃다; n. 킬킬거림, 빙그레 웃기
To chuckle is to laugh softly or amusedly, usually with satisfaction.

self-destruct [self-distrʌkt] a. 자폭하는; v. (기계 등이) 저절로 폭파되다, 못 쓰게 되다
A self-destruct process involves an automatic explosion or disintegration as a result
of pre-programming.

whip [hwip] v. 격렬하게 움직이다; 휙 빼내다; n. 채찍
If something or someone whips somewhere, they move there or go there very quickly.

confuse [kənfjúːz] v. (사람을) 혼란시키다; 혼동하다 (confusion n. 혼란)
Confusion is a situation in which everything is in disorder, especially because there are lots of things happening at the same time.

extend [iksténd] v. (신체 부위를) 뻗다; 뻗어 있다; (거리·기간을) 포괄하다
To extend is to stretch forth an arm or other body parts.

snare [snέər] v. 덫으로 잡다, 유혹하다; n. 덫, 올가미, 유혹
If someone is snared, they are caught in a trap.

squeeze [skwiːz] n. 꼭 쥐기; 꼭 껴안기; v. 꼭 껴안다; 꼭 쥐다, 짜다; 비집고 들어가다
A squeeze is the act or an instance of gripping or pressing firmly.

inexplicable [inéksplikəbl] a. 설명할 수 없는, 불가사의한
If something is inexplicable, you cannot explain why it happens or why it is true.

figure [fígjər] n. (멀리서 흐릿하게 보이는) 사람; 수치; (중요한) 인물; v. 생각하다; 중요하다
You describe someone as a figure when you cannot see them clearly.

materialize [mətíəriəlàiz] v. (갑자기) 나타나다; (예상·계획대로) 실현되다
If a person or thing materializes, they suddenly appear, after they have been invisible or in another place.

out of thin air idiom 난데없이
If someone or something appears out of thin air, they appear suddenly and mysteriously.

disbelief [dìsbilíːf] n. 믿기지 않음, 불신감
Disbelief is not believing that something is true or real.

visible [vízəbl] a. (눈에) 보이는, 알아볼 수 있는; 뚜렷한
If something is visible, it can be seen.

stealth [stelθ] n. 살며시 함, 몰래 함, 잠행
If you use stealth when you do something, you do it quietly and carefully so that no one will notice what you are doing.

gasp [gæsp] v. 헉 하고 숨을 쉬다; 숨을 제대로 못 쉬다; n. 헉 하는 소리를 냄
When you gasp, you take a short quick breath through your mouth, especially when you are surprised, shocked, or in pain.

snatch [snætʃ] v. 와락 붙잡다, 잡아채다; 간신히 얻다; n. 잡아 뺏음, 강탈; 조각
If you snatch something or snatch at something, you take it or pull it away quickly.

grip [grip] v. 움켜잡다; (마음·흥미·시선을) 끌다; n. 꽉 붙잡음, 움켜쥠; 통제, 지배
If you grip something, you take hold of it with your hand and continue to hold it firmly.

* **cord** [kɔːrd] n. 전선; 끈, 줄
Cord is wire covered in rubber or plastic which connects electrical equipment to an electricity supply.

* **spray** [sprei] n. 물보라; 뿌리기; 분무기; v. 뿌리다; (작은 것을 아주 많이) 뿌리다
Sprays are a lot of small things that are scattered somewhere with a lot of force.

복습 **spark** [spaːrk] n. 불꽃, 불똥; 아주 조금; (전류의) 스파크; v. 촉발시키다; 불꽃을 일으키다
A spark is a tiny bright piece of burning material that flies up from something that is burning.

복습 **sever** [sévər] v. 끊어지다, 갈라지다; 자르다, 절단하다; (관계·연락을) 끊다, 단절하다
To sever something means to cut completely through it or to cut it completely off.

복습 **recoil** [rikɔ́il] n. 반동; v. 반동이 생기다; 움찔하다, 흠칫 놀라다
Recoil refers to an action of springing back to the starting point, as in consequence of force of impact.

* **reel** [riːl] v. 비틀거리다; (마음이) 어지럽다; n. (실·필름 등을 감는) 틀
If someone reels, they move about in an unsteady way as if they are going to fall.

somersault [sʌ́mərsɔ̀ːlt] v. 공중제비를 하다; n. 공중제비, 재주넘기
If someone or something somersaults, they turn over completely in the air.

* **cradle** [kreidl] v. 부드럽게 안다; n. 요람, 아기 침대; 발상지
If you cradle someone or something in your arms or hands, you hold them carefully and gently.

복습 **blow up** idiom 폭파하다, 터뜨리다
If someone blows something up or if it blows up, it is destroyed by an explosion.

복습 **transport** [trænspɔ́ːrt] n. 수송; 운송 수단; v. 수송하다; 실어 나르다
Transport is the activity of taking goods or people from one place to another.

복습 **disc** [disk] n. 둥글납작한 판, 원반; 디스크
A disc is a flat, circular shape or object.

* **surge** [səːrdʒ] n. (감정이) 치밀어 오름; (갑자기) 밀려듦; v. (감정이) 휩싸다; (재빨리) 밀려들다
If you feel a surge of a particular emotion or feeling, you experience it suddenly and powerfully.

복습 **nod** [nad] n. (고개를) 끄덕임; v. (고개를) 끄덕이다, 까딱하다
A nod is a quick down-and-up movement of the head, as in assent or command.

* resume [rizú:m] v. 재개하다; 자기 위치로 돌아가다
If you resume an activity or if it resumes, it begins again.

monolith [mánəliθ] n. 거대한 돌 기둥; 거대한 단일 조직
A monolith is a very large, upright piece of stone, especially one that was put in place in ancient times.

livid [lívid] a. 몹시 화가 난, 격노한; 검푸른, 시퍼런
Someone who is livid is extremely angry.

복습 **bellow** [bélou] v. (우렁찬 소리로) 고함치다; 크게 울리다; n. 울부짖는 소리; 고함소리
If someone bellows, they shout angrily in a loud, deep voice.

‡‡ **intend** [inténd] v. 의도하다, 작정하다; 의미하다, 뜻하다
If you intend to do something, you have decided or planned to do it.

복습 **shut down** idiom (기계를) 정지시키다; (공장·가게의) 문을 닫다
If a business or a large piece of equipment shuts down or someone shuts it down, it stops operating.

복습 **lava** [lá:və] n. 용암
Lava is the very hot liquid rock that comes out of a volcano.

복습 **peer** [piər] v. 유심히 보다, 눈여겨보다; n. 또래
If you peer at something, you look at it very hard, usually because it is difficult to see clearly.

복습 **panel** [pænl] n. 계기판; 판; 패널, 자문단
A panel is a board or surface which contains switches and controls to operate a machine or piece of equipment.

‡ **ruin** [rú:in] v. 엉망으로 만들다; 폐허로 만들다; n. 붕괴, 몰락; 파멸
If something is ruined, it has been very badly damaged or has gradually fallen down.

* **roar** [rɔ:r] v. 고함치다; 으르렁거리다; 굉음을 내며 질주하다; n. 함성; 으르렁거림
If someone roars, they shout something in a very loud voice.

복습 **witness** [wítnis] v. (사건·사고를) 목격하다; 증명하다; n. 목격자; 증인
If you witness something, you see it happen.

wrath [ræθ] n. (극도의) 분노, 노여움
Wrath means extreme anger.

Check Your Reading Speed
1분에 몇 단어를 읽는지 리딩 속도를 측정해 보세요.

$$\frac{1{,}846 \text{ words}}{\text{reading time ( ) sec}} \times 60 = (\quad) \text{ WPM}$$

Build Your Vocabulary

exclaim [ikskléim] v. 소리치다, 외치다
If you exclaim, you cry out suddenly in surprise, strong emotion, or pain.

transport [trænspɔ́:rt] n. 수송; 운송 수단; v. 수송하다; 실어 나르다
Transport is the activity of taking goods or people from one place to another.

slide [slaid] v. (slid-slid/slidden) 미끄러지다; 미끄러지듯이 움직이다; n. 떨어짐; 미끄러짐
When something slides somewhere or when you slide it there, it moves there smoothly over or against something.

pile [pail] n. 무더기, 더미; 쌓아 놓은 것; v. 쌓다; (차곡차곡) 포개다; 우르르 가다
A pile of things is a mass of them that is high in the middle and has sloping sides.

wreck [rek] v. 망가뜨리다, 파괴하다; n. 충돌; 난파선; 사고 잔해 (wreckage n. 잔해)
When something such as a plane, car, or building has been destroyed, you can refer to what remains as the wreckage.

seal [si:l] v. 봉쇄하다; 봉인하다; 확정짓다; n. 도장; [동물] 바다표범
If someone in authority seals an area, they stop people entering or passing through it, for example by placing barriers in the way.

trigger [trígə:r] v. 촉발시키다; n. 폭파 장치; (총의) 방아쇠
To trigger a bomb or system means to cause it to work.

hurried [hə́:rid] a. 서둘러 하는 (hurriedly ad. 황급히, 다급하게)
If an action is done hurriedly, it is done quickly, because there is not much time in which to do it.

boom [bu:m] n. 쾅 (하는 소리); v. 쾅 하는 소리를 내다; 굵은 목소리로 말하다
A boom refers to a loud, deep sound that lasts for several seconds.

★ **urge** [ə:rdʒ] v. 재촉하다; 충고하다, 설득하려 하다; n. (강한) 욕구, 충동
If you urge someone somewhere, you make them move in a particular direction by pushing or forcing them.

복습 **clamber** [klǽmbər] v. 기어오르다, 기어가다
If you clamber somewhere, you climb there with difficulty, usually using your hands as well as your feet.

복습 **hasty** [héisti] a. 서두른; 성급한 (hastily ad. 급히, 서둘러서)
If someone acts hastily, their movement or statement is sudden, and often done in reaction to something that has just happened.

복습 **insert** [insə́:rt] v. 끼우다, 넣다; n. 부속품; 삽입 광고
If you insert an object into something, you put the object inside it.

복습 **self-destruct** [self-distrʌ́kt] a. 자폭하는; v. (기계 등이) 저절로 폭파되다, 못 쓰게 되다
A self-destruct process involves an automatic explosion or disintegration as a result of pre-programming.

복습 **explode** [iksplóud] v. 폭발하다; 갑자기 ~하다; (강한 감정을) 터뜨리다 (explosion n. 폭발)
An explosion is a sudden, violent burst of energy, for example one caused by a bomb.

복습 **vessel** [vésəl] n. (대형) 선박, 배; 그릇, 용기
A vessel is a ship or large boat.

list [list] v. 기울다, 비스듬해지다; n. 기울기, 경사
In sailing, if something, especially a ship, lists, it leans over to one side.

복습 **grip** [grip] n. 꽉 붙잡음, 움켜쥠; 통제, 지배; v. 움켜잡다; (마음·흥미·시선을) 끌다
A grip is a firm, strong hold on something.

★ **cargo** [káːrgou] n. (선박·비행기의) 화물
The cargo of a ship or plane is the goods that it is carrying.

복습 **bay** [bei] n. 구역, 구간; 만(灣)
A bay is a partly enclosed area, inside or outside a building, that is used for a particular purpose.

복습 **grab** [græb] v. (와락·단단히) 붙잡다; 급히 ~하다; n. 와락 잡아채려고 함
If you grab something, you take it or pick it up suddenly and roughly.

복습 **force** [fɔ:rs] n. 힘; 영향력; 세력; v. 억지로 ~하다; ~을 강요하다
Force is the power or strength which something has.

^복_습 **tumble** [tʌmbl] **v.** 허겁지겁 나오다; 굴러떨어지다; 폭삭 무너지다; **n.** (갑자기) 굴러떨어짐; 폭락
If someone or something tumbles somewhere, they move or fall there in a relaxed or noisy way, or with a lack of control.

^복_습 **void** [vɔid] **n.** (커다란) 빈 공간; 공허감; **a.** ~이 전혀 없는; 텅 빈
You can describe a large or frightening space as a void.

^복_습 **drift** [drift] **v.** (물·공기에) 떠가다; ~하게 되다; **n.** 표류; 흐름
When something drifts somewhere, it is carried there by the movement of wind or water.

^복_습 **blast** [blæst] **n.** 폭발; (한 줄기의) 강한 바람; **v.** 폭발시키다, 폭파하다; 확 뿌리다; 발사하다
A blast is a big explosion, especially one caused by a bomb.

^복_습 **hurtle** [həːrtl] **v.** 돌진하다
If someone or something hurtles somewhere, they move there very quickly, often in a rough or violent way.

^복_습 **collide** [kəláid] **v.** 부딪치다, 충돌하다; (의견 등이) 상충하다
If two or more moving people or objects collide, they crash into one another.

^복_습 **bounce** [bauns] **v.** 튀다; 깡충깡충 뛰다; **n.** 튐, 튀어 오름; 탄력
When an object such as a ball bounces, it moves upward from a surface or away from it immediately after hitting it.

^복_습 **hull** [hʌl] **n.** (배의) 선체; **v.** (콩 등의) 껍질을 벗기다
The hull of a boat or aircraft is the main body of it.

^복_습 **snag** [snæg] **v.** 잡아채다, 낚아채다; (날카롭거나 튀어나온 것에) 걸리다; **n.** 날카로운 것; 문제
If you snag something, you catch or grab it quickly.

^복_습 **strain** [strein] **v.** 안간힘을 쓰다; 무리하게 사용하다; 한계에 이르게 하다; **n.** 부담; 압박
If you strain to do something, you make a great effort to do it when it is difficult to do.

^복_습 **fiber** [fáibər] **n.** 섬유; (식품의) 섬유질 (with every fiber of one's body **idiom** 온몸으로)
If you do something with every fiber of your body, you do so with all of your effort or desire.

^복_습 **heave** [hiːv] **v.** (무거운 것을) 들어 올리다; (크게 한숨 등을) 내쉬다; **n.** 들어올리기; 들썩거림
If you heave something heavy or difficult to move somewhere, you push, pull, or lift it using a lot of effort.

^복_습 **cling** [kliŋ] **v.** 꼭 붙잡다, 매달리다; 들러붙다; 애착을 갖다
If you cling to someone or something, you hold onto them tightly.

for dear life idiom 필사적으로, 죽을힘을 다해서, 가까스로
If you do something for dear life, you do it with as much effort as possible, usually to avoid danger.

inch [inʧ] n. 조금, 약간; v. 조금씩 움직이다 (inch by inch idiom 조금씩)
If someone or something moves inch by inch, they move very slowly and carefully.

fiery [fáiəri] a. 불타는 듯한; (분노가) 맹렬한; 불의
If you describe something as fiery, you mean that it is burning strongly or contains fire.

debris [dəbríː] n. 파편, 잔해; 쓰레기
Debris is pieces from something that has been destroyed or pieces of rubbish or unwanted material that are spread around.

crash [kræʃ] n. (자동차·항공기) 사고; 요란한 소리; v. 추락하다; 부딪치다; 충돌하다; 굉음을 내다
A crash is an accident in which a moving vehicle hits something and is damaged or destroyed.

sail [seil] v. 미끄러지듯 나아가다; 항해하다; n. 돛
If a person or object sails somewhere, they move there smoothly and fairly quickly.

knock [nak] v. 치다, 부딪치다; (문 등을) 두드리다; n. 부딪침; 문 두드리는 소리
If you knock something, you touch or hit it roughly, especially so that it falls or moves.

pry [prai] v. ~을 지레로 들어 올리다; 엿보다; n. 지레; 엿보기; 탐색
If you pry something open or pry it away from a surface, you force it open or away from a surface.

★ **shove** [ʃʌv] v. 아무렇게나 넣다; (거칠게) 밀치다; n. 힘껏 떠밂
If you shove someone or something, you push them with a quick, violent movement.

hum [hʌm] n. 웅성거리는 소리; v. 웅웅거리다; (노래를) 흥얼거리다
Hum refers to a low and continuous murmuring sound.

cockpit [kákpit] n. (항공기·경주용 자동차 등의) 조종석
In an airplane or racing car, the cockpit is the part where the pilot or driver sits.

whoosh [hwuːʃ] v. (아주 빠르게) 휙 하고 움직이다; n. 쉭 하는 소리
If something whooshes somewhere, it moves there quickly or suddenly.

drench [drenʧ] v. 흠뻑 적시다
To drench something or someone means to make them completely wet.

helpless [hélplis] a. 무력한, 속수무책인
If you are helpless, you do not have the strength or power to do anything useful or to control or protect yourself.

gravity [grǽvəti] n. 중력; 심각성, 중대성; 엄숙함 (gravitational a. 중력의)
Gravitational means relating to or resulting from the force of gravity.

suck [sʌk] v. (특정한 방향으로) 빨아들이다; 빨아 먹다; n. 빨기, 빨아 먹기
If something sucks a liquid, gas, or object in a particular direction, it draws it there with a powerful force.

atmosphere [ǽtməsfiər] n. 대기; 공기; 분위기
A planet's atmosphere is the layer of air or other gases around it.

transfer [trænsfɔ́:r] v. 이동하다, 옮기다; (병을) 옮기다; n. 이동
If you transfer something or someone from one place to another, or they transfer from one place to another, they go from the first place to the second.

plummet [plʌ́mit] v. 곤두박질치다, 급락하다
If someone or something plummets, they fall very fast toward the ground, usually from a great height.

grit [grit] v. 이를 악물다; 이를 갈다; 잔모래를 뿌리다; n. 투지, 기개; 모래
If you grit your teeth, you press your upper and lower teeth tightly together, usually because you are angry about something.

throttle [θratl] n. (자동차 등의 연료) 조절판; v. 목을 조르다
The throttle of a motor vehicle or aircraft is the device, lever, or pedal that controls the quantity of fuel entering the engine and is used to control the vehicle's speed.

pitch [pitʃ] v. 떨어지다, 떨어지게 하다; 힘껏 던지다; n. 경사; 정점, 최고조; 음의 높이
To pitch somewhere means to fall forward suddenly and with a lot of force.

pit [pit] n. (신체의) 우묵한 곳; (크고 깊은) 구덩이; v. 자국을 남기다, 구멍을 남기다
If you have a feeling in the pit of your stomach, you have a tight or sick feeling in your stomach, usually because you are afraid or anxious.

mechanical [məkǽnikəl] a. 기계와 관련된; (행동이) 기계적인
Mechanical means relating to machines and engines and the way they work.

latch [lætʃ] v. 걸쇠를 걸다; n. 걸쇠, 빗장 (latch onto idiom ~을 붙잡다, ~을 꼭 쥐다)
If you latch onto something, you hold tightly to it with your hand or mouth.

rip [rip] v. (재빨리·거칠게) 뜯어 내다; (갑자기) 찢다, 찢어지다; n. (길게) 찢어진 곳
If you rip something away, you remove it quickly and forcefully.

ᵇᵘ **hurl** [hə:rl] v. (거칠게) 던지다; (욕·비난 등을) 퍼붓다
If you hurl something, you throw it violently and with a lot of force.

ᵇᵘ **struggle** [strʌgl] v. 애쓰다; 몸부림치다; 힘겹게 나아가다; n. 몸부림; 투쟁, 분투
If you struggle to do something, you try hard to do it, even though other people or
things may be making it difficult for you to succeed.

⋆ **spiral** [spáiərəl] v. 나선형으로 움직이다, 나선형을 그리다; n. 나선, 나선형; a. 나선형의
If something spirals, it moves in a continuous circle that gets nearer to or further from
its central point as it goes round.

⋆ **wrench** [renʧ] v. 확 비틀다; (가슴을) 쓰라리게 하다; (발목·어깨를) 삐다; n. 확 비틂
If you wrench something that is fixed in a particular position, you pull or twist it
violently, in order to move or remove it.

ᵇᵘ **shut down** idiom (기계를) 정지시키다; (공장·가게의) 문을 닫다
If a business or a large piece of equipment shuts down or someone shuts it down, it
stops operating.

ᵇᵘ **defend** [difénd] v. 방어하다, 수비하다; 옹호하다, 변호하다 (defense n. 방어)
Defense is action that is taken to protect someone or something against attack.

ᵇᵘ **emergency** [imə́:rdʒənsi] n. 비상, 비상 사태
An emergency is an unexpected and difficult or dangerous situation, especially an
accident, which happens suddenly and which requires quick action to deal with it.

‡ **retain** [ritéin] v. 계속 유지하다, 보유하다
To retain something means to continue to have that thing.

residual [rizídʒuəl] a. 남아 있는, 나머지의; n. 잔여물; 나머지, 오차
Residual is used to describe what remains of something when most of it has gone.

ᵇᵘ **glow** [glou] v. 빛나다, 타다; (얼굴이) 상기되다; n. (은은한) 불빛; 홍조
If something glows, it produces a dull, steady light.

ᵇᵘ **eject** [idʒékt] v. 탈출하다; 쫓아내다; 방출하다; 튀어나오게 하다
When a pilot ejects from an aircraft, they leave the aircraft quickly using an ejector
seat, usually because the plane is about to crash.

ᵇᵘ **echo** [ékou] v. (소리가) 울리다, 메아리치다; 그대로 따라 하다; n. (소리의) 울림, 메아리; 반복
If a sound echoes, it is reflected off a surface and can be heard again after the original
sound has stopped.

ᵇᵘ **foe** [fou] n. 적, 원수
Someone's foe is their enemy.

^복_습 **creep** [kriːp] **v.** (crept-crept) 살금살금 움직이다; 서서히 다가가다; 기다; **n.** 너무 싫은 사람
When people or animals creep somewhere, they move quietly and slowly.

^복_습 **practically** [prǽktikəli] **ad.** 사실상, 거의; 현실적으로, 실제로
Practically means almost, but not completely or exactly.

sear [siər] **v.** 그슬다, 표면을 태우다; (강한 통증 등이) 후끈 치밀다, 화끈거리게 하다
To sear something means to burn its surface with a sudden intense heat.

^복_습 **shield** [ʃiːld] **n.** 보호 장치; 방패; **v.** 보호하다, 가리다 (windshield n. (자동차 등의) 방풍 유리)
The windshield of a car or other vehicle is the glass window at the front through which the driver looks.

^복_습 **erase** [iréis] **v.** (완전히) 지우다; (지우개 등으로) 지우다
If you erase something, you get rid of them so that they have gone completely and no longer exist.

^복_습 **strap** [stræp] **v.** 끈으로 묶다; 붕대를 감다; **n.** 끈, 줄, 띠
If you strap something somewhere, you fasten it there with a piece of cloth or other material.

^복_습 **burst** [bəːrst] **v.** (burst-burst) 불쑥 움직이다; 갑자기 ~하다; 터지다; **n.** (갑자기) ~을 함; 파열, 폭발
When a door or lid bursts open, it opens very suddenly and violently because someone pushes it or there is great pressure behind it.

^복_습 **launch** [lɔːntʃ] **v.** 던지다; 발사하다; 맹렬히 덤비다; **n.** 발사; 시작; 개시
To launch something means to throw it forward.

^복_습 **reveal** [rivíːl] **v.** (보이지 않던 것을) 드러내 보이다; (비밀 등을) 밝히다
If you reveal something that has been out of sight, you uncover it so that people can see it.

^복_습 **flip** [flip] **v.** 휙 젖히다; 젖혀지다; 홱 뒤집다, 뒤집히다; 툭 던지다; **n.** 회전; 툭 던지기
If something flips, or if you flip it, it moves or is moved with a quick sudden movement into a different position.

^복_습 **careen** [kəríːn] **v.** 위태롭게 달리다, 흔들리면서 질주하다
To careen somewhere means to rush forward in an uncontrollable way.

^복_습 **wrist** [rist] **n.** 손목, 팔목
Your wrist is the part of your body between your hand and your arm which bends when you move your hand.

^복_습 **clutch** [klʌtʃ] **v.** (꽉) 움켜잡다; **n.** 움켜쥠
If you clutch at something or clutch something, you hold it tightly, usually because you are afraid or anxious.

복습 **blaze** [bleiz] n. 휘황찬란한 빛; 불길, 활활 타는 불; v. 활활 타다; 눈부시게 빛나다
A blaze of something is a very bright show of it.

복습 **witness** [wítnis] v. (사건·사고를) 목격하다; 증명하다; n. 목격자; 증인
If you witness something, you see it happen.

복습 **engulf** [ingʌ́lf] v. 완전히 에워싸다, 휩싸다; (강한 감정 등이) 사로잡다
If one thing engulfs another, it completely covers or hides it, often in a sudden and unexpected way.

복습 **culminate** [kʌ́lmənéit] v. (~으로) 끝이 나다 (culmination n. 정점, 최고조)
Something, especially something important, that is the culmination of an activity, process, or series of events happens at the end of it.

복습 **brilliant** [bríljənt] a. 눈부신; 훌륭한, 멋진; (재능이) 뛰어난
You describe light, or something that reflects light, as brilliant when it shines very brightly.

복습 **engage** [ingéidʒ] v. 사용하다; 약혼시키다; 관계를 맺다; 교전을 벌이다
To engage is to bring a mechanism into operation.

복습 **alert** [əlɔ́:rt] v. (위험 등을) 알리다; a. 기민한; 경계하는; n. 경계 태세
If you alert someone to a situation, especially a dangerous or unpleasant situation, you tell them about it.

doom [du:m] n. 파멸, 비운, 죽음; v. 불행한 운명을 맞게 하다
Doom is a terrible future state or event which you cannot prevent.

복습 **frighten** [fraitn] v. 겁먹게 하다, 놀라게 하다 (frightened a. 겁먹은, 무서워하는)
If you are frightened, you are anxious or afraid, often because of something that has just happened or that you think may happen.

whimper [hwímpər] n. (사람이) 훌쩍거림; (동물이) 낑낑거림; v. 훌쩍이다; 낑낑거리다
A whimper is a soft plaintive whine.

복습 **press** [pres] v. (무엇에) 바짝 대다; 꾹 밀어 넣다; 누르다; n. 언론
If you press something somewhere, you push it firmly against something else.

복습 **descend** [disénd] v. 내려오다, 내려가다; (아래로) 경사지다; 불시에 습격하다 (descent n. 하강)
A descent is a movement from a higher to lower level or position.

복습 **odds** [adz] n. 가능성; 역경, 곤란
You refer to how likely something is to happen as the odds that it will happen.

* slim [slim] **a.** 희박한; 얇은; 날씬한, 호리호리한
A slim chance or possibility is a very small one.

match up to idiom ~에 필적하다; ~에 부응하다
If someone or something does not match up to what was expected, they are smaller, less impressive, or of poorer quality.

might [mait] **n.** (강력한) 힘; 권력; 세력 (with all one's might idiom 전력을 다하여, 힘껏)
If you do something with all your might, you do it using all your strength and energy.

crush [krʌʃ] **v.** 으스러뜨리다; 밀어 넣다; **n.** 홀딱 반함
To crush something means to press it very hard so that its shape is destroyed or so that it breaks into pieces.

pressure [préʃər] **n.** 압박; 압력; 스트레스; **v.** 압력을 가하다; 강요하다
Pressure is force that you produce when you press hard on something.

expectant [ikspéktənt] **a.** 기대하는
If someone is expectant, they are excited because they think something interesting is about to happen.

‡ plain [plein] **a.** 분명한; 솔직한; 평범한; **ad.** 분명히, 완전히; **n.** (pl.) 평원 (plainly ad. 분명하게)
You use plainly to indicate that something is easily seen, noticed, or recognized.

pin [pin] **v.** 두다, 걸다; 꼼짝 못 하게 하다; (핀으로) 고정시키다; **n.** 핀
If you pin your hopes on something or pin your faith on something, you hope very much that it will produce the result you want.

let down idiom ~의 기대를 저버리다, ~을 실망시키다
If you let someone down, you disappoint them by failing to do what you agreed to do or were expected to do.

inexplicable [inéksplikəbl] **a.** 설명할 수 없는, 불가사의한 (inexplicably ad. 뚜렷한 이유 없이)
If something takes place inexplicably, you cannot explain why it happens or why it is true.

steady [stédi] **a.** 흔들림 없는, 안정된; 꾸준한; 차분한, 침착한; **v.** 균형을 잡다, 진정시키다
If an object is steady, it is firm and does not shake or move about.

zoom [zu:m] **v.** 쌩 하고 가다; 급등하다; **n.** (빠르게) 쌩 하고 지나가는 소리
If you zoom somewhere, you go there very quickly.

pop [pap] **v.** 불쑥 나타나다; 불쑥 내놓다; 쏙 넣다; 펑 하는 소리가 나다; **n.** 펑 하는 소리
If someone or something pops, they come suddenly or unexpectedly out of or away from somewhere.

spring [spriŋ] v. (sprang-sprung) 갑자기 ~하다; 휙 움직이다; 튀다; n. 생기, 활기; 봄; 샘
If things or people spring into action or spring to life, they suddenly start being active or suddenly come into existence.

pilot [páilət] n. 조종사, 비행사 (copilot n. 부조종사)
A copilot is the assistant pilot of an airplane, who aids or relieves the pilot.

simulate [símjulèit] v. 모의실험하다; 가장하다 (simulator n. 모의실험 장치)
A simulator is a device which artificially creates the effect of being in conditions of some kind.

hesitant [hézətənt] a. 주저하는, 망설이는, 머뭇거리는 (hesitantly ad. 머뭇거리며)
If someone behaves hesitantly, they do not act quickly or immediately, usually because they are uncertain, embarrassed, or worried.

yank [jæŋk] v. 홱 잡아당기다; n. 홱 잡아당기기
If you yank someone or something somewhere, you pull them there suddenly and with a lot of force.

flap [flæp] n. 덮개; 퍼덕거림; v. 퍼덕거리다; 펄럭거리다
A flap is a piece of material that is attached at one edge of something, which is usually used to cover an opening.

whiz [hwiz] v. 빠르게 지나가다; 윙 하는 소리가 나다; n. 윙 하는 소리
If something whizzes somewhere, it moves there very fast.

grimace [gríməs] v. 얼굴을 찡그리다; n. 찡그린 표정
If you grimace, you twist your face in an ugly way because you are annoyed, disgusted, or in pain.

entry [éntri] n. 입장; 가입; 참가; 입구 (reentry n. (우주선의 지구 궤도) 재진입)
Reentry refers to the moment when a spacecraft comes back into the Earth's atmosphere after being in space.

grateful [gréitfəl] a. 고마워하는, 감사하는
If you are grateful for something that someone has given you or done for you, you have warm, friendly feelings toward them and wish to thank them.

static [stǽtik] n. (수신기의) 잡음; 정전기; a. 고정된; 정지 상태의
If there is static on the radio or television, you hear a series of loud noises which spoils the sound.

dash [dæʃ] n. 계기판; 서두름, 질주; v. 서둘러 가다
The dash of a car is its dashboard, which is the panel facing the driver's seat where most of the instruments and switches are.

^복_습 **realize** [ríːəlàiz] v. 깨닫다, 알아차리다; 실현하다, 달성하다 (realization n. 깨달음)
Realization refers to the process in which you become aware of a certain fact or understand it.

^복_습 **spot** [spat] v. 발견하다, 찾다, 알아채다; n. (작은) 점; (특정한) 곳
If you spot something or someone, you notice them.

^복_습 **bend** [bend] v. (bent-bent) (몸·머리를) 굽히다, 숙이다; 구부리다; n. 굽은 곳
When you bend a part of your body such as your arm or leg, or when it bends, you change its position so that it is no longer straight.

‡ **jam** [dʒæm] v. 움직이지 못하게 되다; 밀어 넣다; n. 잼; 교통 체증; (기계) 고장
When something is jammed, it is stuck or locked.

^복_습 **clip** [klip] n. 핀, 클립; v. 자르다, 깎다; 핀으로 고정하다; 스치다, 부딪치다
A clip is a small device, usually made of metal or plastic, that is specially shaped for holding things together.

★ **wedge** [wedʒ] n. 쐐기; 분열의 원인; v. (좁은 틈 사이에) 끼워 넣다; 고정시키다
A wedge is a piece of metal with a pointed edge which is used for splitting a material such as stone or wood, by being hammered into a crack in the material.

wield [wiːld] v. (무기·도구를) 휘두르다; (권력·권위 등을) 행사하다
If you wield a weapon, tool, or piece of equipment, you carry and use it.

‡ **sword** [sɔːrd] n. 검(劍), 칼
A sword is a weapon with a handle and a long sharp blade.

^복_습 **lean** [liːn] v. 기울이다, (몸을) 숙이다; ~에 기대다; a. 호리호리한
When you lean in a particular direction, you bend your body in that direction.

★ **fury** [fjúəri] n. (격렬한) 분노, 격분; 흥분 상태
Fury is violent or very strong anger.

^복_습 **incredible** [inkrédəbl] a. 믿을 수 없는, 믿기 힘든 (incredibly ad. 믿을 수 없을 정도로)
You use incredibly to emphasize that you like something very much or are impressed by them, because they are extremely or unusually good.

^복_습 **whip** [hwip] v. 격렬하게 움직이다; 휙 빼내다; n. 채찍
If something or someone whips somewhere, they move there or go there very quickly.

^복_습 **race** [reis] v. 쏜살같이 가다; 경주하다; (머리·심장 등이) 바쁘게 돌아가다; n. 경주; 인종, 종족
If you race somewhere, you go there as quickly as possible.

^복_습 **scrape** [skreip] v. (상처가 나도록) 긁다; (무엇을) 긁어내다; 간신히 얻다; n. 긁기
If something scrapes against something else, they rub against it, making a noise or causing slight damage.

^복_습 **massive** [mǽsiv] a. 거대한; 엄청나게 심각한
Something that is massive is very large in size, quantity, or extent.

^복_습 **skid** [skid] v. 미끄러지다; n. (차량의) 미끄러짐
If a vehicle skids, it slides sideways or forward while moving, for example when you are trying to stop it suddenly on a wet road.

^복_습 **pound** [paund] v. (가슴이) 쿵쿵 뛰다; (요란한 소리로 여러 차례) 두드리다; 쿵쾅거리며 걷다
If your heart is pounding, it is beating with an unusually strong and fast rhythm, usually because you are afraid.

⋆ **loop** [lu:p] v. 고리 모양으로 이동하다; 고리 모양을 만들다; n. 고리
If something loops somewhere, it goes there in a circular direction that makes the shape of a loop.

^복_습 **sprint** [sprint] v. (짧은 거리를) 전력 질주하다; n. 전력 질주; 단거리 경기
If you sprint, you run or ride as fast as you can over a short distance.

^복_습 **emerge** [imə́:rdʒ] v. 나오다, 모습을 드러내다; (어려움 등을) 헤쳐 나오다
To emerge means to come out from an enclosed or dark space such as a room or a vehicle, or from a position where you could not be seen.

⋆ **embrace** [imbréis] v. 껴안다, 포옹하다; 받아들이다; n. 포옹
If you embrace someone, you put your arms around them and hold them tightly, usually in order to show your love or affection for them.

⋆ **fierce** [fiərs] a. 극심한, 맹렬한; 사나운, 험악한
Fierce conditions are very intense, great, or strong.

^복_습 **alien** [éiljən] a. 외계의; 생경한; 이질적인; n. 외계인
Alien means coming from another world, such as an outer space.

^복_습 **emotional** [imóuʃənl] a. 감동적인, 감정에 호소하는; 감정의, 정서의
An emotional situation or issue is one that causes people to have strong feelings.

⋆ **cop** [kap] n. 경찰관
A cop is a policeman or policewoman.

^복_습 **rescue** [réskju:] n. 구출, 구조, 구제; v. 구하다, 구출하다
Rescue is help which gets someone out of a dangerous or unpleasant situation.

relieve [rilíːv] v. 안도하다; 해임하다; 덜어 주다, 없애 주다; 완화하다 (relieved a. 안도한)
If you are relieved, you feel happy because something unpleasant has not happened or is no longer happening.

decent [díːsnt] a. 점잖은, 품위 있는; (수준·질이) 괜찮은; 적당한
Decent people are honest and behave in a way that most people approve of.

incarcerate [inkáːrsərèit] v. 감금하다, 투옥하다 (incarceration n. 투옥, 감금)
Incarceration is the legal process in which a person is kept in a prison or other place.

relative [rélətiv] a. 상대적인; 비교적인; 관계가 있는; n. 친척
Relative to something means with reference to it or in comparison with it.

desperate [déspərət] a. 자포자기의, 절망적인; 필사적인 (desperation n. 절망)
Desperation is the feeling that you have when you are in such a bad situation that you will try anything to change it.

aloft [əlɔ́ːft] ad. 위로 높이; 하늘 높이
Something that is aloft is in the air or off the ground.

resource [ríːsɔːrs] n. (pl.) 지략, 기략; 자원, 재원; 자산; v. 자원을 제공하다
Someone's resources are the qualities and skills that they have and can use for dealing with problems.

ingenious [indʒíːnjəs] a. 기발한; 재간이 많은, 독창적인 (ingenuity n. 기발함)
Ingenuity is skill at working out how to achieve things or skill at inventing new things.

glance [glæns] v. 흘낏 보다; 대충 훑어보다; n. 흘낏 봄
If you glance at something or someone, you look at them very quickly and then look away again immediately.

squeeze [skwiːz] v. 꼭 껴안다; 꼭 쥐다, 짜다; 비집고 들어가다; n. 꼭 껴안기; 꼭 쥐기
If you squeeze something, you press it firmly, usually with your hands.

appreciative [əpríːʃətiv] a. 고마워하는; 감탄하는, 감상을 즐기는 (appreciatively ad. 고마워하며)
If someone behaves appreciatively, it shows that they are grateful.

insist [insíst] v. 고집하다, 주장하다, 우기다
If you insist that something is the case, you say so very firmly and refuse to say otherwise, even though other people do not believe you.

17

1. What did Commander Burnside decide to do with Buzz?

   A. Have him start a new Space Ranger Corps

   B. Put him in jail as a punishment

   C. Try to fight Zurg again

   D. Design a new kind of ship

2. Why did Buzz not want Zap Patrol members on his team?

   A. He decided not to be a Space Ranger anymore.

   B. He did not trust the Zap Patrol.

   C. He wanted the Junior Patrol members instead.

   D. He needed more time to recover from the battle.

3. What was the new elite group responsible for doing?

A. Keeping the galaxy safe

B. Figuring out how to get off the planet

C. Mining other planets for fuel

D. Training everyone at the base

Check Your Reading Speed
1분에 몇 단어를 읽는지 리딩 속도를 측정해 보세요.

$$\frac{630 \text{ words}}{\text{reading time ( ) sec}} \times 60 = (\quad) \text{ WPM}$$

Build Your Vocabulary

command [kəmǽnd] v. 지휘하다; 명령하다; n. 명령; 지휘; 사령부 (commander n. 사령관)
A commander is an officer in charge of a military operation or organization.

* **stern** [stəːrn] a. 엄중한, 근엄한; 심각한 (sternly ad. 엄격하게)
If you say something sternly, you do so in a very serious and strict way.

attention [əténʃən] n. 차려 (자세); 주의; 관심; 배려
When people stand to attention or stand at attention, they stand straight with their feet together and their arms at their sides.

pace [peis] v. 서성거리다; (일의) 속도를 유지하다; n. 속도; 걸음
If you pace a small area, you keep walking up and down it, because you are anxious or impatient.

ranger [réindʒər] n. 경비 대원; 기습 공격대원
A ranger is an armed guard who patrols a region.

dressing-down [drèsiŋ-dáun] n. 비난, 질책
If someone gives you a dressing-down, they speak angrily to you because you have done something bad or foolish.

abscond [æbskánd] v. 무단이탈하다, 종적을 감추다; 도주하다
If someone absconds from somewhere such as a prison, they escape from it or leave it without permission.

‡ **property** [prápərti] n. 재산, 소유물; (사물의) 속성
Someone's property is all the things that belong to them or something that belongs to them.

* **experimental** [ikspèrəméntl] a. 실험의; 실험적인
Something that is experimental is new or uses new ideas or methods, and might be modified later if it is unsuccessful.

LIGHTYEAR

spacecraft [spéiskræft] n. 우주선
A spacecraft is a rocket or other vehicle that can travel in space.

defy [difái] v. 반항하다, 저항하다; ~하기가 (거의) 불가능하다
If you defy someone or something that is trying to make you behave in a particular way, you refuse to obey them and behave in that way.

hang one's head idiom 낙심하다, 기가 죽다, 부끄러워 고개를 숙이다
When a person hangs their head, they are feeling dejected or ashamed.

conduct [kándʌkt] n. 행동; 수행, 처리; v. 지휘하다; 특정 활동을 하다; (열이나 전기를) 전도하다
Someone's conduct is the way they behave in particular situations.

unbecoming [ʌnbikémiŋ] a. 부적합한; 어울리지 않는
If you describe a person's behavior or remarks as unbecoming, you mean that they are shocking and unsuitable for that person.

colony [káləni] n. 거주지; (동·식물의) 군집; 식민지
You can refer to a place where a particular group of people lives as a particular kind of colony.

annihilate [ənáiəlèit] v. 전멸시키다; 완패시키다, 완파하다 (annihilation n. 전멸)
Annihilation refers to total destruction.

gesture [dʒéstʃər] v. (손·머리 등으로) 가리키다; 몸짓을 하다; n. 몸짓; (감정·의도의) 표시
If you gesture, you use movements of your hands or head in order to tell someone something or draw their attention to something.

activate [ǽktəvèit] v. 작동시키다; 활성화시키다 (deactivate v. 정지시키다)
If someone deactivates an explosive device or an alarm, they make it harmless or impossible to operate.

corps [kɔːr] n. (특수한 임무를 띤) 부대; 군단; (특정한 활동을 하는) 단체, 집단
A Corps is a part of the army which has special duties.

division [divíʒən] n. (조직의) 부; 분할; 분열
In a large organization, a division is a group of departments whose work is done in the same place or is connected with similar tasks.

patrol [pətróul] n. 순찰대; 순찰; v. 순찰을 돌다
A patrol is a group of soldiers or vehicles that are moving around an area in order to make sure that there is no trouble there.

to one's liking idiom 취향에 맞는, 기호에 맞는
If something is to your liking, it suits your interests, tastes, or wishes.

security [sikjúərəti] n. 보안, 경비; (미래를 위한) 보장; 안도감, 안심
Security refers to all the measures that are taken to protect a place, or to ensure that only people with permission enter it or leave it.

salute [səlú:t] v. 경례를 하다; 경의를 표하다, 절하다; n. 거수 경례; 인사
If you salute someone, you greet them or show your respect with a formal sign.

fade [feid] v. 서서히 사라지다; (색깔이) 바래다, 희미해지다
If someone's smile fades, they slowly stop smiling.

decline [dikláin] v. 거절하다, 사양하다; 감소하다; n. 감소, 하락
If you decline something or decline to do something, you politely refuse to accept it or do it.

launch [lɔːnʃ] n. 발사; 시작; 개시; v. 던지다; 발사하다; 맹렬히 덤비다
A launch refers to the action of sending a rocket, missile, or satellite into the air or into space.

bay [bei] n. 구역, 구간; 만(灣)
A bay is a partly enclosed area, inside or outside a building, that is used for a particular purpose.

reveal [riví:l] v. (보이지 않던 것을) 드러내 보이다; (비밀 등을) 밝히다
If you reveal something that has been out of sight, you uncover it so that people can see it.

outfit [áutfit] v. (복장·장비를) 갖추어 주다; n. 한 벌의 옷, 복장; 장비
To outfit someone or something means to provide them with equipment for a particular purpose.

state-of-the-art [stèit-əv-ði-á:rt] a. 최첨단의, 최신식의
If you describe something as state-of-the-art, you mean that it is the best available because it has been made using the most modern techniques and technology.

galaxy [gǽləksi] n. 은하계; 은하수
A galaxy is an extremely large group of stars and planets that extends over many billions of light years.

sworn [swɔːrn] a. 공공연한; 맹세한, 선서한 (sworn enemy n. 원수, 숙적)
If two people or two groups of people are sworn enemies, they dislike each other very much.

galactic [gəlǽktik] a. 은하계의, 성운의; 거대한, 막대한
Galactic means relating to galaxies, which are large groups of stars and planets that extend over billions of light years.

* **alliance** [əláiəns] n. 동맹, 연합; 협력, 제휴
An alliance is a group of countries or political parties that are formally united and working together because they have similar aims.

복습 **investigate** [invéstəgèit] v. 조사하다, 살피다; 연구하다
To investigate is to examine, study, or inquire into systematically.

‡ **arm** [a:rm] v. 무장하다; 폭발하게 하다; n. 무기, 화기; 팔 (armed a. 무장한, 무기를 가진)
Someone who is armed is carrying a weapon, usually a gun.

‡ **complain** [kəmpléin] v. 불평하다, 항의하다
If you complain about a situation, you say that you are not satisfied with it.

‡ **attitude** [ǽtitjù:d] n. (정신적인) 태도, 사고방식; 자세; 반항적인 태도
Your attitude to something is the way that you think and feel about it, especially when this shows in the way you behave.

vest [vest] n. 조끼; v. (권리를) 주다, 부여하다
A vest is a sleeveless piece of clothing with buttons which people usually wear over a shirt.

* **weird** [wiərd] a. 기이한, 기묘한; 기괴한, 섬뜩한
If you describe something or someone as weird, you mean that they are strange.

* **reassure** [ri:əʃúər] v. 안심시키다
If you reassure someone, you say or do things to make them stop worrying about something.

* **statue** [stǽʧu:] n. 조각상
A statue is a large sculpture of a person or an animal, made of stone or metal.

복습 **puff** [pʌf] v. 부풀리다; (연기·김을) 내뿜다; 숨을 헐떡거리다; n. 부푼 것
If you puff out your cheeks or your chest, you fill them with air so that they look bigger.

복습 **chest** [ʧest] n. 가슴, 흉부; 상자, 궤
Your chest is the top part of the front of your body where your ribs, lungs, and heart are.

복습 **strap** [stræp] v. 끈으로 묶다; 붕대를 감다; n. 끈, 줄, 띠
If you strap something somewhere, you fasten it there with a piece of cloth or other material.

* **takeoff** [téikɔ̀:f] n. 이륙, 도약; 제거, 분리
Takeoff is the beginning of a flight, when an aircraft leaves the ground.

^{복습} **compartment** [kəmpáːrtmənt] n. 칸; 객실
A compartment is one of the separate parts of an object that is used for keeping things in.

^{복습} **console** [kánsoul] n. 제어반, 계기반; v. 위로하다, 위안을 주다
A console is a panel with a number of switches or knobs that is used to operate a machine.

^{복습} **munition** [mjuːníʃən] n. 군사 물품, 군수품
Munitions refer to materials used in war, such as weapons.

sustenance [sʌ́stənəns] n. (음식·물 등) 생명을 유지해 주는 것, 자양물
Sustenance is food or drink which a person, animal, or plant needs to remain alive and healthy.

^{복습} **concern** [kənsə́ːrn] v. 걱정스럽게 하다; 관련되다; n. 우려, 걱정; 관심사 (concerned a. 걱정하는)
If you are concerned about something, it worries you.

^{복습} **nod** [nad] v. (고개를) 끄덕이다, 까딱하다; n. (고개를) 끄덕임
If you nod, you move your head downward and upward to show that you are answering 'yes' to a question, or to show agreement, understanding, or approval.

^{복습} **insert** [insə́ːrt] v. 끼우다, 넣다; n. 부속품; 삽입 광고
If you insert an object into something, you put the object inside it.

^{복습} **internal** [intə́ːrnl] a. 내부의; 내면적인; 국내의
Internal is used to describe things that exist or happen inside a particular person, object, or place.

^{복습} **navigate** [nǽvəgèit] v. 조종하다; 길을 찾다; 항해하다 (navigator n. 자동 조종기)
A navigator is a person or device for assisting a pilot to navigate an aircraft.

^{복습} **initiate** [iníʃièit] v. 개시되게 하다, 착수시키다; 가입시키다; n. 가입자
If you initiate something, you start it or cause it to happen.

flare [flɛər] v. 확 타오르다; 버럭 화를 내다; n. 확 타오르는 불길; 신호탄
If a fire flares, the flames suddenly become larger.

^{복습} **sequence** [síːkwəns] n. 순서, 차례; (일련의) 연속적인 사건들
A particular sequence is a particular order in which things happen or are arranged.

^{복습} **declare** [diklɛ́ər] v. 분명히 말하다; 선언하다, 공표하다
If you declare that something is true, you say that it is true in a firm, deliberate way.

^{복습} **infinity** [infínəti] n. 아득히 먼 곳; 무한성
Infinity is a point that is further away than any other point and can never be reached.

^{복습} **tap** [tæp] v. (가볍게) 톡톡 두드리다; n. (가볍게) 두드리기
If you tap something, you hit it with a quick light blow or a series of quick light blows.

수고하셨습니다!

드디어 끝까지 다 읽으셨군요! 축하드립니다! 여러분은 이 책을 통해 총 25,157개의 단어를 읽으셨고, 1,000개 이상의 어휘와 표현들을 공부하셨습니다. 이 책에 나온 어휘는 다른 원서를 읽을 때도 빈번히 만날 수 있는 필수 어휘들입니다. 이 책을 읽었던 경험은 비슷한 수준의 다른 원서들을 읽을 때 큰 도움이 될 것입니다.

원서는 한 번 다 읽은 후에도 다양한 방식으로 영어 실력을 끌어올리는 데 활용할 수 있습니다. 일단 다 읽은 원서를 어떻게 활용할 수 있을지, 학습자의 주요 유형별로 알아보도록 하겠습니다.

리딩(Reading) 실력을 확실히 다지길 원한다면, 반복해서 읽어 보세요!

리딩 실력을 탄탄하게 다지길 원한다면, 같은 원서를 2~3번 반복해서 읽을 것을 권합니다. 같은 책을 여러 번 읽으면 지루할 것 같지만, 꼭 그렇지도 않습니다. 반복해서 읽을 때 처음과 주안점을 다르게 두면, 전혀 다른 느낌으로 재미있게 읽을 수 있습니다.

처음 원서를 읽을 때는 생소한 단어들과 스토리로 인해 읽고 이해하기가 매우 힘듭니다. 전체 맥락을 잡고 읽어도 약간 버거운 느낌이지요. 하지만 반복해서 읽기 시작하면 달라집니다. 내용은 일단 파악해 둔 상황이기 때문에 문장 구조나 어휘의 활용에 더 집중하게 되고, 조금 더 깊이 있게 읽을 수 있게 됩니다. 좋은 표현과 문장을 수집하고 메모할 만한 여유도 생기게 되지요. 어휘도 많이 익숙해졌기 때문에 리딩 속도도 탄력이 붙습니다. 처음 읽을 때는 '내용'에서 재미를 느꼈다면, 반복해서 읽을 때는 '영어'에서 재미를 느끼게 되는 것입니다.

따라서 리딩 실력을 더욱 확고하게 다지고자 한다면, 같은 책을 2~3회 정도 반복해서 읽을 것을 권해 드립니다.

리스닝(Listening) 실력을 늘리고 싶다면, 귀를 통해서 읽어 보세요!

많은 영어 학습자들이 '리스닝이 안 돼서 문제'라고 한탄합니다. 그리고 리스닝 실력을 늘리는 방법으로, 무슨 뜻인지 몰라도 반복해 듣는 '무작정 듣기'를 선택합니다. 하지만 뜻도 모르면서 무작정 듣는 것은 엄청난 인내력이 필요합니다. 그래서 대부분 며칠 시도하다가 포기해 버리고 말지요.

모르는 내용을 무작정 듣는 것보다는 어느 정도 알고 있는 내용을 반복해서 듣는 것이 더 효과적인 듣기 방법입니다. 그리고 이런 방식의 듣기에 활용할 수 있는 가장 좋은 교재가 오디오북입니다.

따라서 리스닝 실력을 향상시키길 원한다면, 이 책에서 제공하는 오디오북을 이용해서 듣는 연습을 해 보세요. 오디오북의 활용법은 간단합니다. 그냥 MP3를 플레이어에 넣고 자투리 시간에 틈틈이 들으면 됩니다. 혹은 책상에 앉아 눈으로는 책을 보면서 귀로는 그 내용을 따라 읽는 것도 좋습니다. 보통 오디오북은 분당 150~180단어로 재생되는데, 재생 속도가 조절되는 MP3를 이용하면 더 빠른 속도로 재생이 가능하고, 이에 맞춰 빠른 속도로 듣는 연습을 할 수도 있습니다.

중요한 것은 내용을 따라가면서, 내용에 푹 빠져서 반복해 들어야 한다는 것입니다. 눈으로 책을 읽는 것이 아니라 '귀를 통해' 책을 읽는 것이지요. 이렇게 연습을 반복해서, 눈으로 읽지 않은 책도 '귀를 통해' 읽을 수 있을 정도가 되면, 리스닝으로 고생하는 일은 거의 사라질 것입니다.

 왼쪽의 QR코드를 스마트폰으로 인식하면 오디오북 MP3와 한국어 번역 파일을 다운로드할 수 있는 링크로 연결됩니다. 더불어 롱테일북스 홈페이지(www.longtailbooks.co.kr)에서도 오디오북과 한국어 번역 파일을 다운로드받을 수 있습니다.

스피킹(Speaking)이 고민이라면, 소리 내어 읽기를 해 보세요!

스피킹 역시 많은 학습자들이 고민하는 부분입니다. 스피킹이 고민이라면, 원서를 큰 소리로 읽는 낭독 훈련(Voice Reading)을 해 보세요!
'소리 내서 읽는 것이 말하기에 정말로 도움이 될까?'라고 의아한 생각이 들 수도 있습니다. 하지만, 인간의 두뇌 입장에서 봤을 때, 성대 구조를 활용해서 '발화'한다는 점에서는 소리 내서 읽기와 말하기는 큰 차이가 없다고 합니다. 소리 내서 읽는 것은 '타인의 생각'을 전달하고, 직접 말하는 것은 '자신의 생각'을 전달한다는 차이가 있을 뿐, 머릿속에서 문장을 처리하고 조음 기관(혀와 성대 등)을 움직여 의미를 만든다는 점에서 같은 과정인 것이지요. 따라서 소리 내서 읽는 연습을 꾸준히 하는 것은 스피킹 연습에 큰 도움이 됩니다.

소리 내어 읽기를 하는 방법도 간단합니다. 일단 오디오북을 들으면서 성우의 목소리를 최대한 따라 하며 같이 읽어 보세요. 발음뿐 아니라, 억양, 어조, 느낌까지 완벽히 따라 한다고 생각하면서 소리 내어 읽습니다. 따라 읽는 것이 조금 익숙해지면, 옆의 누군가에게 이 책을 읽어 준다는 생각으로 소리 내서 계속 읽어 나갑니다. 한 번 눈과 귀로 읽었던 책이라 보다 수월하게 진행할 수 있고, 자연스럽게 어휘와 표현을 복습하는 효과도 거두게 됩니다. 또 이렇게 소리 내어 읽는 것을 녹음해서 들어 보면 스스로에게 좋은 피드백이 됩니다.

라이팅(Writing)까지 욕심이 난다면, 요약하는 연습을 해 보세요!

최근엔 라이팅에도 욕심을 내는 학습자들이 많이 있습니다. 원서를 라이팅 연습에 직접적으로 활용하기에는 한계가 있지만, 역시 적절히 활용하면 유용한 자료가 될 수 있습니다.
특히 책을 읽고 그 내용을 요약하는 연습은 큰 도움이 됩니다. 요약 훈련의 방식도 간단합니다. 원서를 읽고 그날 읽은 분량만큼 혹은 책을 다 읽고 난 후에 전체 내용을 기반으로, 책 내용을 요약하고 나의 느낌을 영어로 적어 보는 것입니다. 이때 그 책에 나왔던 단어와 표현을 최대한 활용해서 요약하는 것이 중요합니다.

영어 표현력은 결국 얼마나 다양한 어휘로 많은 표현을 해 보았느냐가 좌우하게 됩니다. 이런 면에서 내가 읽은 책을, 그 책에 나온 문장과 어휘로 다시 표현해 보는 것은 가장 효율적인 방식입니다. 책에 나온 어휘와 표현을 단순히 읽고 무슨 말인지 아는 정도가 아니라, 실제로 직접 활용해서 쓸 수 있을 만큼 확실하게 익히게 되는 것이지요. 여기에 첨삭까지 받을 수 있는 방법이 있다면 금상첨화입니다.

또한 이런 '표현하기' 연습은 스피킹 훈련에도 그대로 적용할 수 있습니다. 책을 읽고 그 내용을 3분 안에 다른 사람에게 영어로 말하는 연습을 하는 것이지요. 순발력과 표현력을 기르는 좋은 훈련이 됩니다.

'스피드 리딩 카페'에서 함께 원서를 읽어 보세요!

이렇게 원서 읽기를 활용한 영어 공부에 관심이 있으시다면, 국내 최대 영어원서 읽기 동호회 스피드 리딩 카페(http://cafe.naver.com/readingtc)로 와 보세요. 이미 수만 명의 회원들이 모여서 '북클럽'을 통해 함께 원서를 읽고 있습니다.

단순히 함께 원서를 읽는 것뿐만 아니라, 위에서 언급한 다양한 방식으로 원서를 활용하여 영어 실력을 향상시키고 있는, 말뿐이 아닌 '실질적인 효과'를 보고 있는 회원들이 엄청나게 많이 있습니다. 여러분도 스피드 리딩 카페를 방문해 보신다면 많은 자극과 도움을 받으실 수 있을 것입니다.

원서 읽기 습관을 길러 보자!

일상에서 영어를 한마디도 쓰지 않는 비영어권 국가에서 살고 있는 우리에게 영어에 가장 쉽고, 편하고, 저렴하게 노출되는 방법은, 바로 '영어원서 읽기'입니다. 언제 어디서든 원서를 붙잡고 읽기만 하면 곧바로 영어를 접하는 환경이 만들어지기 때문이지요. 하루에 20분씩만 꾸준히 읽는다면, 1년에 무려 120시간 동안 영어에 노출될 수 있습니다.

영어원서를 꾸준히 읽어 보세요. '원서 읽기 습관'을 만들어 보세요! 이렇게 영어를 접하는 시간이 늘어나면, 영어 실력도 당연히 향상될 수밖에 없습니다.

아래 표에는 영어 수준별 추천 원서들이 있습니다. 하지만 이것은 절대적인 기준이 아니며, 학습자의 영어 수준과 관심 분야에 따라 달라질 수 있습니다. 이 책은 Reading Level 3에 해당합니다. 이 책의 완독 경험을 기준으로 삼아 적절한 책을 골라 꾸준히 읽어 보세요.

영어 수준별 추천 원서 목록

리딩 레벨	영어 수준	원서 목록
Level 1	초·중학생	The Zack Files 시리즈, Magic Tree House 시리즈, Junie B. Jones 시리즈, Horrid Henry 시리즈, 로알드 달 단편들 (The Giraffe and the Pelly and Me, Esio Trot, The Enormous Crocodile, The Magic Finger, Fantastic Mr. Fox)
Level 2	고등학생	Andrew Clements 시리즈 (Frindle, School Story 등), Spiderwick Chronicle 시리즈, 쉬운 뉴베리 수상작들 (Sarah Plain and Tall, The Hundred Dresses 등), 짧고 간단한 자기계발서 (Who Moved My Cheese?, The Present 등)
Level 3	특목고 학생 대학생	로알드 달 장편들 (Charlie and the Chocolate Factory, Matilda 등), Wayside School 시리즈, 중간 수준의 뉴베리 수상작들 (Number the Stars, Charlotte's Web 등), A Series of Unfortunate Events 시리즈
Level 4	대학생 상위권	Harry Potter 시리즈 중 1~3권, Percy Jackson 시리즈, The Chronicles of Narnia 시리즈, The Alchemist, 어려운 수준의 뉴베리 수상작들 (Holes, The Giver 등)
Level 5	대학원생 이상 전문직 종사자들	Harry Potter 시리즈 중 4~7권, Shopaholic 시리즈, His Dark Materials 시리즈, The Devil Wears Prada, The Curious Incident of the Dog in the Night-Time, Tuesdays With Morrie 등등 (참고 자료: Renaissance Learning, Readingtown USA, Slyvan Learning Center)

'영화로 읽는 영어원서'로 원서 읽기 습관을 만들어 보세요!

『버즈 라이트이어』를 재미있게 읽은 독자라면 「영화로 읽는 영어원서」 시리즈를 꾸준히 읽어 보시길 추천해 드립니다! 「영화로 읽는 영어원서」 시리즈는 유명 영화를 기반으로 한 소설판 영어원서로 보다 쉽고 부담 없이 원서 읽기를 시작할 수 있도록 도와주고, 오디오북을 기본적으로 포함해 원서의 활용 범위를 넓힌 책입니다.

『하이스쿨 뮤지컬』, 『업』, 『라푼젤』, 『겨울왕국』, 『메리다와 마법의 숲』, 『몬스터 주식회사』, 『몬스터 대학교』, 『인사이드 아웃』, 『주토피아』 등 출간하는 책들마다 독자들의 큰 사랑을 받으며 어학 분야의 베스트셀러를 기록했고, 학원과 학교들에서도 꾸준히 교재로 채택되는 등 영어 학습자들에게도 좋은 반응을 얻고 있습니다. (서초·강남 등지 명문 중고교 방과 후 보충 교재 채택, 전국 영어 학원 정·부교재 채택, 김해 분성 초등학교 영어원서 읽기 대회 교재 채택 등등)

ANSWER KEY

Chapters 1 & 2

1. D But to Buzz Lightyear, she was the kind of friend only time could bring. The two of them had entered the academy and trained together as cadets.

2. A "Speaking of which, you forgot to take the rookie with you." "Ugh. Commander Hawthorne, you know how I feel about rookies," Buzz said, hacking through more vines. "They don't help. They just overcomplicate things. I'm better off doing the job myself."

3. A Buzz sprinted forward and sliced through the vine trapping the rookie's leg. Without missing a beat, he grabbed the kid's outstretched hand to keep him from being carried off by the bug.

4. C If there was one thing Buzz trusted even less than rookies, it was autopilots. He confidently took hold of the control wheel on the console.

5. C "It's bad, Buzz." Alisha emerged from the wreckage of the engine room, covered in soot, holding a shattered fuel cell.

Chapters 3 & 4

1. C "Buzz Lightyear mission log: Star Date three-nine-oh-two. After a full year of being marooned, our specialized crew and robotic assistants have put this planet's vast resources to incredible use. Finally, our first hyperspeed test flight is a go."

2. A An explosion ripped through the hull! Alarms wailed. "Failure in engine one," said IVAN. "Fuel cell unstable." "IVAN, status!" Buzz yelled. "Trajectory error: plus four degrees."

3. B "What is this?" Buzz asked, an unsettling feeling growing in his chest. "How long was I gone?" Díaz paused before answering. "Four years, two months, and three days."

4. B "Oh, I got engaged!" Alisha revealed. "Wow! That's—that's great!" Buzz said, feeling a mixture of happiness and surprise.

5. C He sighed and swiped his own card, plodding heavily into his quarters. He glanced down and noticed an unopened Star Command box on the floor. On top was a note: You're welcome! Alisha. He knelt to open it, removing the cardboard packaging to reveal a small mechanical mouse and an adorable robotic cat.

Chapters 5 & 6

1. D Then a young girl bounded into the frame of the hologram projection. She was wearing a homemade Space Ranger suit. "Hi, Grandma!" she exclaimed. Alisha hugged the child. "Hey, sweetheart. I'm leaving a message for my friend Buzz."

2. C "Oh . . . uh, did no one tell you?" Commander Burnside fidgeted nervously. "We're shutting down the program."

3. A Sox softly came up beside his Space Ranger companion. "I've got some good news, Buzz. I figured out the fuel problem."

4. D "Okay, here goes," Buzz said, lifting the handle of the fuel cell. The liquid inside turned into a multicolored crystal that refracted rainbows of light. Buzz could already see that this fuel crystal was different from the others.

5. B "Allow me," Sox said. He climbed onto the console and the tip of his tail opened to reveal a flash drive. He plugged his tail into the port. "Beep boop beep boop beep boop," Sox said as he overrode the override.

Chapters 7 & 8

1. A Every inch of the ship rattled as the velocity increased. Normally, at this point, a huge explosion would rip through the engines, shattering Buzz's hopes of success. But things were different this time. The gauge kept climbing.

2. B "Right." Izzy nodded. "The Zurg ship showed up about a week ago."

3. D "We've figured out the Zurg ship powers the robots on the ground," Izzy said.

4. B "Not trained?" Buzz exclaimed, his deepest fear coming true. There was no mistaking the frightened and slightly bewildered face of the lanky soldier who had removed his helmet. A rookie, if Buzz had ever seen one. "What do you mean you're not trained?"

5. A Buzz grunted. Mustering superhuman strength, he crunched up again and tore the remaining bolt from the bot's shoulder plate. The wiring sizzled and popped as the arm came loose, firing its laser ray wildly, now that it was disconnected from its main controls. Buzz tumbled down once he was free from the robot's grasp.

Chapters 9 & 10

1. D Buzz closed the rover door. "So . . . if you could just point me in the direction of another ship . . ." "Oh, they have some old ships at the abandoned storage depot," Mo said. "Great," Buzz replied.

2. A "Oh, there they are!" Mo spotted them on the dolly. He went to grab the keys, but accidentally knocked them off the cart, causing them to hit the floor and trigger the truck's alarm outside. Flashing lights and the honking horn reverberated around the depot. "Shhh, quiet!" Buzz warned as Mo fumbled with the key fob. Mo finally turned off the alarm, but it was too late. The bugs were already stirring from their sleep.

3. C "Everyone grab a weapon!" Buzz ordered, tossing the team blasters from the ammo cart. "Boy, I'd love to," Darby said. "But my parole—"

4. C Then he gasped. "Wait—the timer! They don't know about the timer!" Panicked, Buzz looked out the hatch door to where Izzy, Mo, and Darby were only halfway toward the depot exit—in full view!

5. B Izzy and Darby tried to roll Mo toward the exit, but it was blocked by a legion of bugs. With a yelp, they turned around and started pushing him toward the Armadillo. The army of bugs followed.

Chapters 11 & 12

1. D "Huh," Buzz said. Despite his earlier frustration, he couldn't help feeling a tiny bit proud of Izzy for figuring a way out of their predicament. "Now that's thinking like a Hawthorne," he told her. "Let's go get that part and get out of here . . . before that thing finds us again."

2. B As Mo pocketed the pen, his elbow hit a large red button on a wall. "Security measures activated," a robotic voice announced. Warning lights flashed, and before the group could react, the door to the control room sealed shut.

3. D Then Izzy's hand clasped around Buzz's wrist, abruptly halting his descent. He looked up in disbelief. The team had formed a chain, one hand to another, giving Izzy just enough length to reach down and catch him. "We got you," she said.

4. A The robot's foot lowered . . . and passed right over them. The bot marched on, leaving the team untouched, heading straight for the Space Ranger. "What?" Buzz whispered, backing away. He looked at his team, then back at the advancing robot. And his eyes grew wide with a cold rush of clarity. "It's after me . . . ," Buzz said, realizing.

5. C Buzz kicked open the side door, and he and Izzy sprinted across the rocky terrain to where the fuel cell lay. The robot that had been tailing them bore down, heading for it as well. Buzz aimed his wrist blaster. "Grab the crystal!" he yelled to Izzy.

Chapters 13 & 14

1. D "I want the same thing you want, Buzz." Zurg took a step closer. "I want to help you. I want you to finish the mission."

2. D Buzz furrowed his brow. Was it fair to erase all those people down there so that his crew might have the chance to go home? Was it fair to erase Izzy?

3. B Sox padded up to her. "I've completely lost Buzz," he said sadly. "He's too far away to track."

4. C "We need to protect our escape ship," Izzy directed, taking control like a real Space Ranger, feeling the strength of her grandma coursing through her. "If the robots get to it, we'll never get out alive. So nothing comes through that door."

5. C Over on the bridge, Buzz tried to make sense of the futuristic command console. Unlike the plasma engine from before, none of it looked familiar. "I don't know any of this technology," he said, frustrated. For the first time in his life, he wished he had an autopilot to tell him what to do. "Computer, is there an autopilot?" he asked hopefully.

Chapters 15 & 16

1. B In the observatory, Izzy desperately searched for escape options. "How do we get over there?" Sox scanned the room. "Through the air lock." Izzy looked to where Sox indicated and felt her chest seize up in panic. The cat wanted her to walk through a door leading into space! "Through there?" she exclaimed. "There's nothing out there!"

2. B Then something inexplicable happened. A figure materialized out of thin air in the middle of the bridge. Buzz watched in disbelief as Izzy became visible, leaving stealth mode, with Sox on her shoulder, and they were right next to his fallen wrist blaster. She had made it across—and they had one shot. "Now!" Buzz gasped. Knowing exactly what to do, Izzy snatched up the wrist blaster and threw it just as Buzz stretched out his hand. It was the perfect throw and catch.

3. A "Not today, Zurg!" Buzz exclaimed. With that, Buzz fired his laser and blasted the crystal.

4. C But all that was in the past now. Buzz had a new mission. He aimed himself toward the Armadillo and engaged his jet pack, shooting forward on an intercept course to save his friends.

5. D Mo's eyes brightened with a sudden realization. "The pen! I've got the pen!" He popped the pen out of his suit and wielded it like a sword. He leaned over and pried open the cover, allowing Darby to pull on the air brake with force and fury.

Chapter 17

1. A "But I have other plans for you," Burnside told Buzz. Burnside gestured to the deactivated robots on the ground. "We want you to start a new version of the Space Ranger Corps: Universe Protection Division. You're going to be a Space Ranger again, Buzz. You can hand-select your team from the very best of the Zap Patrol and train them to your liking."

2. C Buzz smiled as he took in the news. To be a Space Ranger again, out among the stars. It felt like coming home. But his smile quickly faded. "Well, that's very kind of you, sir," he said. "But . . . I'm afraid I'm going to have to decline." Everyone looked at Buzz in shock. "I already have my team," Buzz said, turning to look at Izzy, Darby, Mo, and Sox.

3. A The doors of the launch bay opened, revealing a team of Space Rangers outfitted in new, state-of-the-art suits. As members of the Universe Protection Division of Space Ranger Corps, this elite group protected the galaxy from any sworn enemies of the Galactic Alliance.

버즈 라이트이어(LIGHTYEAR)

초판 발행   2022년 12월 12일

지은이   Meredith Rusu
책임편집   강지희
편집   박새미 명채린
콘텐츠제작및감수   명채린
번역   강지희
디자인   박새롬 이혜련
마케팅   김보미 정경훈

기획   김승규
펴낸이   이수영
펴낸곳   롱테일북스
출판등록   제2015-000191호
주소   04033 서울특별시 마포구 양화로 113, 3층(서교동, 순흥빌딩)
홈페이지   www.longtailbooks.co.kr
전자메일   help@ltinc.net

ISBN 979-11-91343-45-8 14740